HOMEWARD

*Map of Boston (Shaded) Showing the Residences of the
Boston Reentry Study Respondents One Week After Release from Prison*

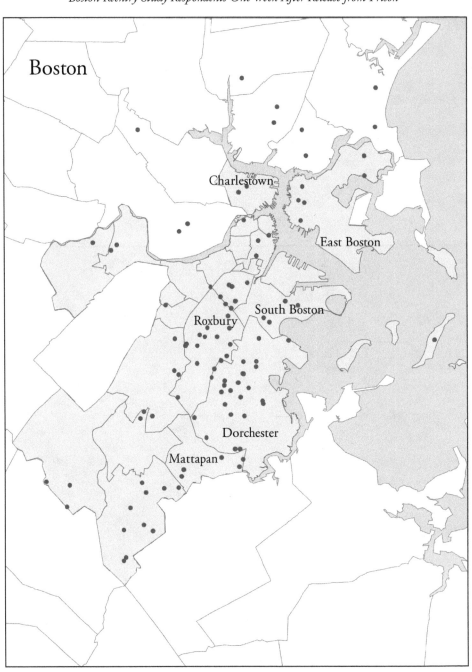

Homeward

....

LIFE IN THE YEAR AFTER PRISON

Bruce Western

Russell Sage Foundation   **NEW YORK**

LIBRARY OF CONGRESS
CATALOGING-IN-PUBLICATION DATA

Names: Western, Bruce, 1964- author.
Title: Homeward : life in the year after prison / Bruce Western.
Description: New York : Russell Sage Foundation, [2018] | Includes bibliographical references and index.
Identifiers: LCCN 2017045104 (print) | LCCN 2017052282 (ebook) | ISBN 9781610448710 (ebook) | ISBN 9780871549556 (pbk. : alk. paper)
Subjects: LCSH: Ex-convicts—United States—Social conditions. |Prisoners—Deinstitutionalization—United States. | Imprisonment—United States.
Classification: LCC HV9275 (ebook) | LCC HV9275 .W424 2018 (print) | DDC 364.80973—dc23
LC record available at https://lccn.loc.gov/2017045104

Text design by Linda Secondari.

RUSSELL SAGE FOUNDATION
112 East 64th Street
New York, NY 10065

CONTENTS

....

LIST OF ILLUSTRATIONS

.................,...........

ABOUT THE AUTHOR

....

Bruce Western is Daniel and Florence Guggenheim Professor of Criminal Justice Policy and professor of sociology at Harvard University and co-director of the Justice Lab at Columbia University.

Whan Jim was released from state prison by the Massachusetts Department of Correction, he was sent straight to the county jail at Nashua Street in Boston. He had been convicted of sex crimes involving children and would now await trial on new charges. He wore orange scrubs when I met him. Orange was for protective custody— people locked in isolation for their own safety. Jim was different from most of the people I interviewed. He was white, in his fifties, estranged from his family. He'd been itinerant, wandering around the country and homeless for long periods.

Most of the people I spoke to in prison were African American or Latino men in their twenties and thirties, like Hector, Sam, and Juney. They were close to their families, and many lived with their mother after they got out. Around half found jobs in that first year. A year after prison release, two-thirds of the 122 men and women interviewed for the Boston Reentry Study had stayed out of jail.

Jim never got out. He went straight to Nashua Street.

I liked many of the people I had come to know through the reentry study, but I never looked forward to meeting with Jim. I liked the African American neighborhoods of Dorchester and Mattapan and the Irish enclaves of South Boston and Charlestown. I didn't like Nashua Street. The gray clouds that shrouded Boston for weeks at a time seemed to hang pretty low on those days. Jim would talk about his beefs with the staff. He'd ask us to send him books and the *Spare Change News,* the local paper distributed by the homeless in Boston. I felt that we weren't learning anything about life after prison by talking to him. The interviews revealed nothing about the origins of Jim's pedophilia. He was a pariah in the jail, and his family had cut him off.

All these things were running through my head during one interview as we sat in the small attorney's meeting room on the fourth floor of the jail. In the middle of the interview, I was stopped by a thought: if we weren't here getting Jim's story down, no one would. His voice, like the voices of millions of others, would be lost in the din of America's vast prison population.

This book tells the stories of the men and women I met through the Boston Reentry Study (BRS), a series of interviews my research team and I conducted with people leaving prison for neighborhoods around Boston. We were trying to understand what happens when people return to a community, and the challenges faced by them and their families. How did they look for work and housing? How did they manage their addictions or mental illness, and why did some return to incarceration? As we sought answers to questions like these, we tried more than anything to bear witness to the lives of those held captive in America's experiment with mass incarceration. This book is one effort to get people's stories down.

Many researchers have studied the contours and effects of American incarceration. The sociologist David Garland provided a sweeping account of social and economic insecurity after the postwar golden age that produced tectonic shifts in crime control and astonishing incarceration rates in the United States. Loïc Wacquant produced a macrosociology of the new penal regime, contained within a history of American race relations and compared to crime policy in Europe. Building on this work, I tried to spell out the connections between incarceration, poverty, and racial inequality in *Punishment and Inequality in America*. Electoral implications were weighed by Chris Uggen and Jeff Manza. Devah Pager examined employer responses to job-seekers with prison records. Becky Pettit's research illuminated corners of the population made invisible by incarceration, and Sara Wakefield and Chris Wildeman examined how children fared when their parents were sent to prison. Research by these scholars was just the tip of a much larger iceberg. A 2014 panel of the National Academy of Sciences (NAS) chaired by Jeremy Travis reported on the entire research program.[1]

The research on U.S. incarceration is what we hope for in the social sciences—pluralistic in method, scientifically rigorous, and relevant to pressing social problems. After social research helped frame mass incarceration as a problem of inequality and injustice, policymakers began to explore ways to reduce incarceration and its pernicious effects.

Despite the success of the sociological research, I worried that my own work—statistical analysis of large data sets—filtered out a harsh and complex reality. I was gaining a sense of this reality from my teaching. I had taught at New Jersey State Prison when I was at Princeton and then in medium security at MCI Norfolk when I moved to Harvard. The men in my classes had led complicated lives. They'd grown up poor and had been on both sides of serious violence. Some were serving life sentences and would die in state custody. They also brought sharp and energetic minds to class. The lives of these men were somehow missing from my research.

A clue to solving this problem was offered by Jeremy Travis, who had conducted research on what is called "prisoner reentry"—the term used by policymakers and researchers for the transition from incarceration back to communities. Travis's book *But They All Come Back,* published in 2005, reviewed what we knew about the challenges of leaving incarceration. The topic of prisoner reentry, he said, takes the perspective of those who pass through the system. This perspective raises a new kind of public policy question: what are our obligations to those who are punished?

I also use the process of reentry to learn about the perspective of those who are incarcerated. In this book, I report on the journeys of a group of men and women who left the Massachusetts state prison system in 2012 and 2013 and returned to neighborhoods around Boston. Many returned home to live with their families. Some had no home to return to and spent much of the year in Boston's shelters and transitional housing. All the people I interviewed, however, were trying to find a place in society after incarceration. If they were not yet home after release from prison, they were at least trying to go homeward.

Several papers published by the reentry study research team analyzed the survey data we collected. These were mostly statistical studies of outcomes like recidivism, housing, and employment. This book aims to capture more of the lives of the people we interviewed. In taking this approach, I hope not only to meet Travis's challenge to be curious about those who are incarcerated, their families, and their neighborhoods, but also to provide a window on the larger phenomenon of mass incarceration.

While conducting research for this book, I made several visits to Addis Ababa for a project studying justice institutions in Ethiopia. At dinner one evening with a few Ethiopian researchers, one of them, Mulagetta, told me about a colleague at his research institute, a German anthropologist. One day the anthropologist was in a remote area driving through a small village.

His car fatally struck a small child who had strayed onto the road. The girl's parents ran outside to see what had happened, and a crowd quickly formed around the anthropologist.

He asked that the police be called but was told that there were no police there. The village dealt with matters like this by itself. The anthropologist was told that he could go, but that they would send for him in a few days. Later that week a message came that he must return, and he was told to return alone. He went to Mulagetta and asked what he should do. "You have to go back to the village," said Mulagetta. So he returned. When he arrived, he was escorted to a meeting with the elders. They told him to pay 2,500 Birr (about $125) to the family of the dead child. Next, he was ordered to buy a goat for the family. He purchased the goat, which was immediately slaughtered. The father of the dead child was called to the front of the meeting. The anthropologist, standing at the front of the room, was told to hold out his hand. He held out his hand and his wrist was bound to the wrist of the child's father with the entrails of the goat. The village elders announced that the anthropologist was now a member of the dead girl's family. And that was that. He was free to go.

The anthropologist returned to Addis, very upset. He felt that he hadn't properly compensated the family, nor had he been punished. Mulagetta said, "You have to understand, for the rest of your life, you are now part of that man's family. You have all the obligations of a family member. You have to visit from time to time. If they are going through problems that you might help with, you should help them just as a member of their own family would."

Western ideas about punishment and retribution were radically absent in this case of customary justice. Like the Ethiopian story, the problem of reentry raises the question of when punishment ends. When and how are debts extinguished? These questions are as ethical as they are empirical. I have tried to maintain an ethical perspective throughout the book. To guide politics or policy, the ethics of punishment must confront the real lives of those who are incarcerated. By testing our values against the conditions of poverty, racial inequality, and violence that surround mass incarceration, I hope that we might imagine a better path to justice.

A few notes on the text: All names are pseudonyms. Direct quotes are from audio-recorded interviews or field notes taken at the time of an interview. Quotes have been lightly edited for grammar and verbal tics.

ACKNOWLEDGMENTS

....

I thank the men and women of the Boston Reentry Study and their families and friends for generously sharing their time and life experience with me. This book is an attempt to honor their contribution to the research.

Rhiana Kohl, leader of the Research Unit at the Massachusetts Department of Correction, was an invaluable partner in this project, opening the doors of the many prisons we visited and sharing with us the time and expertise of her staff. I am very grateful, too, for the cooperation and assistance of the Department of Correction.

My co-investigator, Anthony Braga, has been an experienced and supportive ally. Deeply knowledgeable about Boston and its criminal justice agencies, Anthony brought an equanimity to the research process that eased crises large and small.

However much this research has illuminated the path followed by men and women newly released from prison is due to the work of Catherine Sirois. As project manager, Cathy was brilliant, diligent, and patient, and she reminded us always of the ethical imperatives of the study. Her relentless follow-up with the respondents and her management of the research were models of scientific rigor. I turned to Cathy many times for help, both while we were in the field and afterwards as we were analyzing data and writing up. My thinking about the book was shaped by our long-running conversation, conducted over years. Cathy coauthored chapter 2 and commented in detail on the manuscript. I could not have completed my part of the research without her.

The reentry study was unique in sustaining a very high response rate. Credit goes to Cathy and also to Jackie Davis, the other full-time researcher. Jackie was a superb interviewer, good-humored, inhumanly reliable, and unfailingly attuned to the many details of research design. Jackie was the mainstay of the fieldwork.

After Cathy and Jackie went on to graduate school, I was lucky to be working with Jennifer Arzu, who managed the project as we consolidated and cleaned the data. Quiet, tireless, and committed to the project's larger goals, Jennifer's contribution has been indispensable.

Monica Bell, Caroline Burke, Kelley Fong, David Hureau, Abena Mackall, Tracey Shollenberger (now Lloyd), and Jessica Simes made up the student research team, and they did a marvelous job in the field and provided a lively intellectual influence for the research. Jessica also created the map that begins this book. I am also grateful for the research assistance of Kendra Bradner, who conducted interviews, and Kathleen Culhane, LeShae Henderson, Rosa Otieno, and Caroline Walters, who constructed many of the timelines analyzed in chapter 4.

The manuscript benefited greatly from many thoughtful reactions to earlier drafts. Mary Pattillo, Pat Sharkey, and Chris Wildeman provided incisive and constructive reviews for Russell Sage. Jen Silva wrote generous and encouraging comments on an early draft at a time when the writing felt entirely experimental. Chris Muller, Natalie Smith, Laura Tach, John McCormick, Jo McKendry, Marie Gottschalk, Ron Corbett, Vinny Schiraldi, Peter Bearman, and Martha Minow also provided invaluable advice. I talked often about the ideas in this book with my colleagues Matt Desmond, Devah Pager, and Rob Sampson. Matt provided a brilliant review of the entire manuscript. I'm grateful for their inspiration and support. The Justice and Inequality Reading Group at Harvard read a number of drafts of chapters and papers and were always constructive. I'm grateful, too, for the support of the Department of Sociology and the John F. Kennedy School of Government at Harvard. Suzanne Nichols at the Russell Sage Foundation has been a persistent supporter of the project.

Parts of the text were adapted from earlier publications. Chapter 2 draws from the paper "Study Retention as Bias Reduction in a Hard-to-Reach Population," coauthored with Anthony Braga, David Hureau, and Catherine Sirois and published in the *Proceedings of the National Academy of Sciences* (2016). Chapter 3 draws on the paper "Stress and Hardship After Prison," coauthored with Anthony Braga, Jackie Davis, and Cathy Sirois and published in the *American Journal of Sociology* (2014). Parts of chapter 4 were adapted from "The Rehabilitation Paradox," published online by *The New Yorker* (2016). Chapter 5 draws on the paper "Lifetimes of Violence in a Sample of Released Prisoners," published in *RSF: The Russell Sage Foundation Journal of the Social Sciences* (2015).

The Boston Reentry Study was supported by grants from the National Institutes of Health (5R21HD073761-02), the National Science Foundation (SES-1259013, SES-1424089, and SES-1627693), the Russell Sage Foundation (83-14-15), and the Ford Foundation (0160-1516) and by a fellowship from the Radcliffe Institute for Advanced Study.

A year before we went into the field, my father passed away. John Western was a distinguished sociologist and a kind and gentle man. When he and my mother, Tasnee, were visiting a few years earlier, he came to a seminar I was teaching on "The Sociology of Crime and Punishment." We were at MCI Norfolk, and it was the only time we'd ever been in class together. This book is dedicated to his memory.

CHAPTER 1

....

Introduction

In the early 1970s, the United States embarked on a strange new experiment in public policy. After using incarceration sparingly, like in other Western democracies, the U.S. justice system began to send people convicted of crimes to prison in vast numbers. Beginning in 1972, the prison population charted a steady increase that was to continue for the next four decades. By the early 2000s, the United States led the world in incarceration and the U.S. incarceration rate stood at five times its historic average. The people who were sent to prison were mostly African American and Latino, male, and overwhelmingly poor. Incarceration rates got so high by the 2000s that well over half of black male high school dropouts in their thirties had been to prison. The sociologist David Garland called this "mass incarceration." The lawyer Michelle Alexander focused on the racial inequality and called it "the new Jim Crow."[1]

Life changed in poor communities. Black and brown men with little schooling were getting locked up for felonies and doing, on average, two years of prison time, though often very much longer. Going to prison became commonplace for a whole generation.

Researchers studied this new reality. Academic papers picked apart the demography of the prison population and tried to calculate the effects of incarceration on crime, employment, health, mortality, and families. Researchers drew on criminology, theories of labor markets, epidemiology, and family demography to make sense of the new world of mass incarceration. The research showed that the vast American penal system only modestly reduced crime but was associated with a variety of negative effects. Mass incarceration was tearing up families, stoking unemployment, and harming children whose parents had been incarcerated. All these effects were concentrated in poor communities of color. At an annual cost of $80 billion, the nation was spending more on prisons and jails than on the main antipoverty programs—food stamps ($74 billion) and the Earned Income Tax Credit (EITC) ($69 billion).[2]

Despite an impressive research literature, scholars often had to rely on data that were not designed to study the problem of incarceration. Most quantitative studies analyzed big national data sets that were usually used to calculate unemployment or poverty for the whole U.S. population. People who had been in prison were often overlooked by big data collections because they did not live in conventional households or work in traditional ways. They lived in homeless shelters or doubled up with family. They worked off the books or made money illegally by dealing drugs or through other crime, so surveys and the tax system did not accurately record their income. Their family lives were often tangled, living perhaps with the mother of one child, in close contact with another, but estranged from a third by a court's restraining order. The big data sets did not record these complicated family relationships.

The shortcomings of data reflected shortcomings of theory. Researchers collected data in a certain way—from households, the Internal Revenue Service (IRS), or the welfare office—because they had theories of how social life was organized. Researchers assumed, through their choice of data, that people lived in households and worked for employers who paid taxes. If they were not working, they applied for unemployment benefits. Such theory assumed that people who went to prison were better off, healthier, and more socially stable than they really were. In reality, incarceration draws disproportionately from the homeless, the mentally ill, and the drug-addicted. For example, a leading theory claims that a prison record causes unemployment because employers are concerned that a job applicant with a prison record might be unreliable or cause trouble on the job. But what does such a theory tell us about the many people who have been to prison and never really applied for a proper job? What about those who are coping with mental illness, or whose homelessness has crowded out any time or motivation to look for work? In these such cases, the leading theory cannot tell us much about the employment of people who were incarcerated. Even worse, the life complications that leave the incarcerated below the radar of our big data collections also harm their well-being. Not only were the theories and data collections often incomplete, they were also likely to misread the effects of incarceration.

Limitations of theory and data led to two major problems with the research. First, the characteristics of the prison population were largely reduced to the markers of age, race, and education. Age, race, and education are easily measured, and incarceration strikingly follows their contours. The incarceration rate is less than 1 percent of the general population, but fifty times higher for twenty- to forty-year-old African American males who have no education beyond high school. However, age, race, and education are often associated with a bleaker reality that includes trauma in childhood, learning problems at school, poor health, and mental illness. The use of these easily measured variables unwittingly sanitized the disadvantages of those who were sent to prison. The accompanying theories often overlooked hazards of biography, health, and ability, and the truly grim conditions of American poverty were papered over.

Second, research on the social world of incarceration said little about crime. The basic reality that people who were imprisoned had been convicted of crimes did not enter the analysis. In part, the absence of crime in these analyses reflected deficiencies of measurement. Crime and criminal involvement were often unmeasured—or at least were not measured well—in the surveys and administrative records used for research. Even more important, the division of labor among different research specialties meant that researchers from the field of family demography or those engaged in labor market studies, for example, took little notice of the criminal involvement of people coming out of prison. Crime—and violence, specifically—are important parts of the world in which incarceration operates. To omit violence from the analysis was to misunderstand the social inequality on which mass incarceration rests.

The social reality of incarceration, embedded in conditions of violence and severe material hardship, has raised not just empirical questions for social science understanding. There are also urgent ethical questions about what is just and fair where suffering is widespread and often encompasses a lifetime. Mass incarceration answered this question one way: harsh punishment could somehow bring justice to poor communities that struggled not only with crime but also with a corporeal hardship that inscribed the pains of poverty on people's minds and bodies in the form of addiction, mental illness, and disability.

As this book examines the social reality of incarceration, the ethical questions will loom just as large as the empirical. So much of the ethical talk about incarceration, in law and philosophy, is naive about the empirical reality in which it is administered. Nothing is gained in public policy or scientific understanding by abstracting away from a complex social reality that is soaked in moral ambiguity.

To develop a detailed understanding of the aftermath of incarceration, a team of researchers at Harvard University began the Boston Reentry Study in April 2012. Five times in the course of a year, we interviewed 122 men and women who were leaving Massachusetts state prisons and returning to neighborhoods in Boston: the first time a week before prison release; then again two weeks later in the community; and then at two, six, and twelve months after release. We visited sixteen of the seventeen facilities operated by the Massachusetts Department of Correction (DOC), including two secure psychiatric units. The interviews ranged widely. To capture the complexity and insecurity of life for men and women just released from prison, we asked about housing, family, employment, health, drug use, crime, and social background. Outside of prison, we interviewed people on the streets and in private households, treatment facilities, psychiatric wards, and homeless shelters. We tried to measure the complicated webs of family relationships that shifted unevenly after prison. We heard and followed vivid reports of relapse to drug addiction and recurrence of mental illness as respondents drifted off medication. Family members spoke with us about their experience of the incarceration of a loved one and gave us their own life histories. We obtained police and court records on all the respondents in the sample.

More than anything else, we tried to keep track of people. The urgent problems many people experience after prison release—homelessness, mental illness, drug addiction, crime—often make them less willing or able to participate in research studies. Big surveys often failed to interview men and women who were likely to go prison and then missed their first days and weeks after prison release when life was most unsettled. The Boston Reentry Study worked hard to trace the monthly progress of people who lived on the streets and were infirm in mind and body. Prior research with the big surveys provided demographic and social insight but failed to capture the texture of life during the transition from prison to community, particularly in the first days and months, and particularly for the most disadvantaged.

It is in describing this transition that I hope the reentry study makes a contribution.

Release from a Massachusetts prison to a Boston neighborhood resembles the transition from incarceration to community in many urban areas, particularly in the Northeast of the United States. Massachusetts prisoners tend to be incarcerated for somewhat longer than the national average because the state imprisons only felony defendants sentenced to at least two and a half years. In most other states, those sentenced to one year or more are imprisoned. Similar to the national pattern, people released from Massachusetts prisons return mostly to poor and minority neighborhoods.[3] In some ways, Massachusetts is a best-case scenario for prison releasees. The state economy has been strong. Some government benefits are more widely available to releasees in Massachusetts than in other states. Nearly all respondents in the reentry study could see a doctor, their health care paid for by Medicaid, the federal program for low-income people. Most were enrolled in food stamps in the first two months after prison release. Former prisoners are broadly eligible for food stamps in the Northeast, but restrictions are common in Southern and Western states for those with prior drug convictions.[4]

People who have been incarcerated face a harsh type of poverty. The men and women we interviewed were mostly African American and Latino (62 and 23 out of 122), with a median age of thirty-two and an average of ten and a half years of schooling. The sample included 107 men and 15 women. In these respects, our respondents looked like the people who leave U.S. prisons every day. But beyond age, race, and education, two-thirds of our sample reported histories of drug addiction and mental illness. Many had been homeless before they went to prison. Exposure to serious violence and other trauma in childhood was common. Chronic unemployment was widespread, and many had cycled in and out of incarceration through much of their adult lives.

A lot of research on the aftermath of incarceration views the prison as the cause of certain effects on family life, economic status, and so on. My interest is different. By observing the transition from prison to community, I hope to understand a process. This is a study of social integration where fortunes are shaped by race and poverty, and personal agency is tested by the frailty of mind and body. The process tells us something about the prisons from which people have originated and the families and neighborhoods to which they return. In the era of mass incarceration, social integration also teaches us about the nature of freedom as men and women released from prison struggle to regain it.

Tracing the many paths from prison to community required special methods. A description of study methods is often consigned to an appendix for the most dedicated readers. What we learn from data, however, is inseparable from how we collect it. Thus, the book begins in chapter 2 by describing how we recruited people into the study and how we followed them for a year after their release. Working with what survey researchers call a "hard-to-reach population," we completed 94 percent of the scheduled interviews, a higher rate of study participation than obtained by earlier studies of samples newly released from prison. Nearly complete participation ensured we spoke to those facing the greatest struggles with homelessness, addiction, and crime. Conducting research with vulnerable people creates as many ethical challenges as scientific ones. Chapter 2 discusses how we thought about the issues of obtaining consent, paying interview incentives to people who desperately needed money, and keeping data confidential.

Chapter 3 examines the first weeks and months after release, as revealed in our interviews. The period immediately after prison release was a time of unique stress for the people we spoke to. The tempo of life in free society was disorienting in those first weeks, and respondents often experienced anxiety, fear, and depression as they confronted the everyday challenges of public transport, new technologies, and the many small tasks involved in finding a place in society. Many were able to return to families and networks of social support. But we saw social isolation, loneliness, and anxiety among the older men and women coming out of prison. Social isolation in the first week after prison release was associated with high rates of unemployment, greater housing insecurity, and detachment from family. The period immediately after prison release also revealed the character of poverty for people embroiled in the criminal justice system. Their incomes were extremely low, most of the financial support they received came from government programs, and families were the leading supplier of housing.

People who go to prison have slipped through the holes of the American safety net. Many struggle with a human frailty where adversities of mental illness, untreated addiction, and physical disability all come together under conditions of poverty. In chapter 4, I describe the depression, post-traumatic stress, and anxiety that were common among the people we spoke to. A few suffered from the psychotic conditions of schizophrenia and bipolar disorder. Alcoholism and crack and heroin use were also widespread. For people mostly in their thirties and forties, poverty combined with a lifetime of drug use also took a physical toll, yielding high levels of chronic pain and infectious disease. For this mostly male population who did not consistently live with their families in stable households, there were few government programs. Prisons, though intended for punishment, had become the backstop for the American welfare state.

The environments inhabited by the men and women of the Boston Reentry Study after they were released from prison were not just meager and insecure, but also violent (chapter 5). They described violence that was highly contextual, emerging in the chaotic and unsupervised homes of their childhood. Violence was so common in the lives of our respondents, and attached so tightly to the conditions of poverty in which they lived, that it amounted to another type of hardship—alongside food insecurity, housing instability, and poor health—that afflicts the poorest Americans. Living in the harsh conditions of American poverty, the reentry study respondents circulated through the roles of victim, witness, and perpetrator of violence, muddying the question of who should be punished and for what. Human frailty, combined with histories of trauma and victimization, complicates the moral status of those who are sent to prison. In contrast to the stereotypes of tough criminals preying upon weak citizens, the reentry study sample was a group of sometimes troubled people, often surrounded by violence, struggling to keep mind and body together under conditions of acute material hardship.

As we see in chapter 6, this social reality often made earning an income after incarceration an insurmountable challenge. A small number of white, older men got steady, well-paying union jobs in the construction industry. Their experience illustrates the restorative powers, not of work by itself, but of *skilled* work that opens a door to working-class life beyond poverty. For many others, family members provided meals, clothing, and most of the housing that we observed. Receipt of government benefits, usually through food stamps or Supplemental Security Income (SSI), was also common. By the end of the first year after incarceration, over half the sample reported some form of employment, but the work they did was typically informal, often cash jobs offered by friends or family.

A key finding of the research is the crucial role of family support in the year after prison (chapter 7). Facing high rates of unemployment, the men and women of the reentry study relied heavily on their kin, particularly for a place to stay. Most research on the family lives of those released from prison has focused on partners and children. In our own study, we found that the main supporters were older women—mothers, grandmothers, aunts, and sisters. These women, most in their fifties and sixties, had struggled for economic and social stability in their own lives, but they took in their younger relatives, and often their children too. It is hard to make sense of the support that older women provide to their younger kin who are just out of prison in any terms other than love.

Policymakers concerned about the transition from prison to community tend to focus on the problem of recidivism. Recidivism is usually viewed as a behavioral problem—a continuation of criminal conduct or a failure of rehabilitative transformation. Choice, motivation, and agency lie at the heart of this behavioral perspective. Chapter 8 finds that for the reentry study respondents these powers of decision-making and self-discipline battled hard with human frailty, demography, and the criminal justice system itself. Reincarceration was most common for those who struggled with drug addiction: among the thirty-eight respondents who returned to custody, relapse to addiction was the single biggest predictor of reincarceration. Next most likely to be reincarcerated were people released from prison to the supervision of a parole or probation officer, even though they were less involved in crime upon their release. Community supervision alone appears to make reincarceration more likely. Finally, we also found higher rates of reincarceration among younger respondents, whose youthful peers were more likely to be involved with the authorities.

Most research on the effects of incarceration focuses on the experience of men, but the experience of women is so distinct that I provide a separate discussion in chapter 9. Most people who go to prison have known great vulnerability through trauma, victimization, mental illness, and drug addiction. The biographies of the women we interviewed were regularly the most troubled. They reported the most serious mental health problems and lifetimes of victimization that began in childhood. But these women also retained strong connections to their children and families. Women's incarceration presented the deepest moral ambiguities and underscored the segregative character of incarceration—having one's connection to family and community severed as a mode of punishment.

Massachusetts has a low incarceration rate by national standards, and the African American population in the state's prisons is small compared to the big jailers in the Southern and Western states (chapter 10). Still, there is great racial disparity in incarceration in Massachusetts, and black incarceration is distinctly different from white. Boston's history of racial conflict hung heavily over the field site, especially for the older respondents—black and white—who had grown up through the tumult of the city's school desegregation in the 1970s and 1980s. The older men and women in the study had lived through the imposition of a racial divide that separated the city's black neighborhoods to the south—in Roxbury, Dorchester, and Mattapan—from the white enclaves in the north, in South Boston, East Boston, and Charlestown. The white men and women we spoke to were older, with long histories of drug addiction, mental illness, and homelessness. The black respondents were mostly younger, with little schooling or work history. Race differentiated two types of poverty. The skid row poverty that afflicted older whites was marked by homelessness, mental illness, and addiction, reflecting deficits of support for serious and lifelong health problems. Younger African American and Latino respondents struggled with school and work. They were involved in drug dealing and gun violence concentrated in the poor minority neighborhoods of Boston's inner city. Their poverty was rooted in deficits of economic opportunity, stemming from the failures of the school system and a labor market that offered few jobs to young men without high school diplomas. The incarceration we observed was racialized, but less by overt discrimination in the criminal justice system than woven into the structure of institutions and urban geography. Racial inequality embedded in the history of a city and the structure of its economy makes the challenge of racial justice no less urgent but more difficult to resolve.

Through all the different phases of prison release, we witnessed racial inequality, deep poverty, layers of trauma, and human frailty. This is the setting in which America's unique experiment with harsh punishment has come to operate. Although the experiment emerged from a moral analysis that drew a bright line between guilty offenders and the innocent victims on whom they preyed, that reality is hard to find when the social contexts of incarceration are closely examined. Instead, we find failures of social policy and support stacked upon communities that live with daily violence on the streets and at home. The moral analysis, like some of the academic research, imports assumptions from middle-class life, in which a basic level of order and security prevails. In reality, in the social spaces in which incarceration operates, life is chaotic, most residents are poor, and victims and offenders are frequently one and the same. In these social spaces, large doses of punishment do little to promote the social solidarity on which a robust public safety is built, and the problem of criminal justice becomes fundamentally a problem of social justice. How can families and communities that, through their deep social and economic marginality, have enjoyed something less than full membership in American society be drawn into the social compact?

Thus, in chapter 11, we confront the ethics of mass incarceration and look at how we might move forward in politics and public policy. The challenge is twofold: to find a socially integrative response to violence under harsh conditions of poverty and racial inequality, and to find justice. Here, justice means a level of fairness that acknowledges not only the harms suffered through crime but also the harms to those who, through poverty and racial minority, have historically been denied the full extent of their humanity by mass incarceration.

CHAPTER 2

Learning About Life After Prison

People just released from incarceration are what survey researchers call a hard-to-reach population. They can be difficult to locate and interview, and they are more likely to drop out of panel studies that follow research subjects over time. Formerly incarcerated people are missed by conventional surveys because they are insecurely housed, homeless, or otherwise living outside of conventional households. Involvement in crime, outstanding warrants, reincarceration, relapse to addiction, and mental illness also make formerly incarcerated men and women unwilling or elusive research subjects. Many studies of life after incarceration have relied on data from large national social surveys, specialized reentry surveys of parolees, and court administrative data linked to unemployment insurance and other records. Even with administrative data, we can learn about the transition from prison to community only from individuals' contact with the unemployment insurance system or other government agencies.

The difficulties of keeping track of formerly incarcerated respondents can be seen from the dropout rates in earlier reentry surveys. Listing eight earlier studies along with the Boston Reentry Study, table 2.1 shows the percentage of respondents retained over a one-month to twenty-four-month follow-up period. Most studies retained 50 to 70 percent of their samples. The BRS, by comparison, retained more than 90 percent of the sample one year after prison release.

Survey nonresponse and study attrition can bias studies of former prisoners and other highly marginal groups. The vulnerabilities that make people miss interviews or hesitant to participate in research studies also contribute to their economic and social insecurity. When the reasons for

Table 2.1 *Retention Rates of Longitudinal Studies of Released Prisoners*

	YEARS	SITE	SAMPLE SIZE	FOLLOW-UP (MONTHS)	RETAINED AT EXIT
1. First Month Out	1999	New York	88	1	56.0%
2. Returning Home Maryland	2001–2003	Baltimore	324	6	32.1
3. Returning Home Illinois	2002–2003	Chicago	400	16	49.5
4. Returning Home Ohio	2002–2003	Cleveland	424	12	69.0
5. Returning Home Texas	2004–2005	Houston	676	8–10	55.9
6. Serious and Violent Offender Reentry Initiative (SVORI)	2004–2007	Fourteen states	2,391	15	68.5
7. Michigan Reentry Study	2007–2009	Southeast Michigan	22	24	86.4
8. Newark Smartphone Project	2012–2013	Newark	152	3	70.0
9. Boston Reentry Study	2012–2014	Boston	122	12	91.0

Sources: (1) Nelson, Dees, and Allen 1999; (2) Visher et al. 2004; (3) Kachnowski 2005; (4) Visher and Courtney 2007; (5) La Vigne, Shollenberger, and Debus 2009; (6) Lattimore and Steffey 2009; (7) Harding et al. 2014; (8) Sugie 2014; (9) Western et al. 2015.

Note: First Month Out interviewed prison and jail releasees. Returning Home and the Michigan Reentry Study interviewed former prisoners. SVORI interviewed former adult prisoners and juveniles. The Newark Smartphone Project interviewed parolees.

dropping out of a study are related to the outcomes being studied, the research design is statistically biased. In reentry research, the well-being of released prisoners is overestimated and correlations between preexisting disadvantages like mental illness and postrelease outcomes like homelessness are underestimated.[1] Those who are least likely to participate are exactly those whom we most want to interview. The most vulnerable and hardest-to-interview respondents face the greatest obstacles to social integration.

In planning the reentry study, I worried a lot about the low response rates in earlier research. This is one source of the invisible inequality associated with incarceration—an extreme disadvantage that evades our efforts at data collection.[2] More than this, previous data collections, particularly national social surveys, were not designed to observe the process of prison release or the conditions of material hardship facing men and women after prison. A flexible survey instrument was needed that could keep up with the fluid and complex social lives of a sample of people who moved frequently, divided their time between different addresses, had intricate and changeable family relationships, and worked sporadically, on and off the books.

The Boston Reentry Study was originally hatched with my colleague Anthony Braga as we rode the bus back from MCI Norfolk, where we had been teaching a class of Harvard students and incarcerated students. Anthony had a deep knowledge of Boston as a field site and had collaborated for many years with the Boston Police Department. I told him about my ideas for a reentry study, the inflexibility of standard survey instruments, and the nonresponse rates in earlier research. With his local knowledge, Anthony was confident we could achieve a very high rate of study participation. Next, Anthony and I approached Rhiana Kohl, who headed the research division of the Department of Correction. Rhiana, too, was interested. She had worked on the Urban Institute's Returning Home survey in Massachusetts and hoped to use some of our survey questions to validate the DOC's records. The study would also be a good research experience for her staff, who would help coordinate our interviews with the prisons and join us on baseline interviews inside. With Rhiana on board, we cleared the first and highest hurdle to doing research in prison—gaining the support of the Department of Correction.

We began our work by meeting with a few small groups of incarcerated men. We experimented with survey questions that had been used in other studies, tried out a few questions of our own, and asked our focus groups what questions they thought were important. Once our surveys were drafted, we next moved into a pretest with a group of ten men and women. We administered a draft of each wave of the survey to the pretest sample and also talked to them about question wording and the relevance of the topics we were exploring. Several of the pretest respondents became important collaborators in the design of the study.

In addition to Rhiana, Anthony, and myself, our research team consisted of two staff researchers, Cathy Sirois and Jackie Davis, a group of Harvard graduate and undergraduate students, and Rhiana's team at the Department of Correction. Cathy and Jackie were recent college graduates, and they proved to be gifted and tenacious interviewers. Cathy had been in prison before, having gone into MCI Norfolk for a semester with her undergraduate sociology class. Jackie was a political science major and was going inside a prison for the first time as a researcher for the study. Apart from Anthony, one of the graduate students, and myself, all of the interviewers were women in their twenties and thirties. All were white, except for two of the graduate students who were African American and one who was Asian American. Although race and class differences created social distance between respondents and interviewers, the gap closed over time as the interviewers developed rapport. The respondents seemed to me to be inclined to make a positive impression on the interviewers, and sometimes minimized their involvement in crime or their economic hardship. We were able to check their self-reported crimes against arrest and court records Supplementary interviews with family and friends also helped to validate the respondents' interviews.

In the design of the study, the baseline interview was conducted about one week before respondents were released from prison, and follow-up interviews were conducted at one week after release, then at two months, six months, and twelve months after release. We interviewed frequently after prison release because research had shown that the first weeks and months are a volatile time for those returning to the community. We aimed to get a very fine-grained picture of where respondents lived, how they made ends meet, and how they interacted with family after years of penal confinement. If a respondent returned to incarceration, the DOC research unit helped us schedule a reincarceration interview, sometimes in a Massachusetts prison, but often in a county jail.

With study attrition looming as one of the biggest challenges for the research, we devised four strategies to keep respondents engaged and in contact between interviews.

1. Interview incentives. The respondents were paid $50 for each interview. Cash payments of this size have been found to increase participation among low-income respondents and parolees.[3] Because the initial interview in prison was scheduled so close to release, we paid respondents at the first community interview two weeks later. At the first meeting after prison release, each respondent received $100 in cash, $50 for the prison interview two weeks earlier and $50 for the first community interview. One hundred dollars was a significant payment for people with little income, particularly for the one-fifth of the sample who had less than $100 in their commissary account when they were released. When asked at the one-week interview why they were participating in the study, one-quarter of the sample cited the interview payment. The interview incentive appeared to be less crucial to study retention over time. By the twelve-month interview, only about 10 percent of respondents said that they were participating in the study for the money.

We also wanted the interviews to be positive experiences. We tried to present a nonjudgmental and informal tone that allowed for unscripted probes, digressions, and curiosity about the respondent's life and welfare. Interviews often ended with conversations that turned up new topics or revisited old ones in greater depth. We met respondents over cups of coffee and meals, which we paid for, and often gave them rides to a train or bus afterwards. Interviews lasted for about an hour and a half. The longest exchanges ran about three hours. Our conduct in these meetings did not fully erase the formality or power differentials that also accompanied appointments with probation and parole officers, but respondents did say that our approach contrasted with officials' and that the attitude of the interviewers gave them another reason to participate. After a year of interviews, one-third of the sample said that they stayed in the study because they were committed to finishing it or because they liked the interviewer. Another fifth said that it was helpful to share their experiences. Nearly half of the sample hoped that their participation would help others or have an impact on criminal justice policy.[4] Indeed, as the research continued we felt a growing sense of accountability to the respondents' aspirations for the research.

2. *Phone check-ins and letters.* Incentives surely added to the study's response rate, but much of the work of staying in contact consisted of regular phone check-ins. Between the baseline, one-week, two-month, and six-month interviews, interviewers phoned respondents every few weeks, then checked in each month between the six-month and twelve-month waves. Interviewers used these check-ins to update the respondents' residential information and to maintain contact and rapport. When phone contact was lost, we emailed or wrote letters to the respondents, often using address information provided by family members and friends. Over the course of the study, we made over 2,500 phone calls (two-thirds of them successful) to locate or check in with respondents.

3. *Secondary contacts and interviews.* We asked respondents at the first interview for a list of family members or friends who could help us stay in contact with them after prison release.[5] At each interview, we updated the list of secondary contacts, adding new names or new phone numbers. The best secondary contacts had stable contact information themselves, were supportive of the respondent, and over time had come to trust us and understand our work. Mothers and other older women whose phone numbers rarely changed were particularly important for retaining respondents in the

study. They supported their children and other younger relatives just out of prison, often in moments of crisis when participation in the study was overshadowed by homelessness or a new arrest. Our calls to mothers and grandmothers about the whereabouts and well-being of their sons, daughters, and grandchildren also helped reduce suspicion and enlisted close family members as allies in our study retention effort.

4. *Justice agencies and community contacts.* When all retention strategies were exhausted, we reached out to local justice agencies and community contacts to help reestablish contact with respondents who had gone missing from the study. Each week the DOC research division updated us on any new violations or returns to custody among those in our sample. We met with Boston Police Department, parole, and probation officials to seek their help with study retention, and all of them occasionally helped us locate respondents. Respondents had earlier consented to these requests for help, and generally, we just asked for a phone number or a last known address.[6]

To find those who were not on parole or probation, we sometimes tried to reestablish contact through community workers operating in neighborhoods where respondents were living. Gang outreach workers, called streetworkers, drawn from local communities, could sometimes provide us with phone numbers or addresses for younger respondents who were involved in gangs and other street groups. More often, however, streetworkers "knew someone who knew someone" and connected the research team to an exgirlfriend or a former youth worker who could arrange contact with a missing respondent. When respondents dropped out of the study, community contacts could sometimes explain why. For example, we learned that one subject had developed extreme paranoia about being set up following a shooting in his area in between survey waves and was reluctant to meet or talk with anyone but a small group of trusted friends.

With our basic research design in place, we began pretest interviews in April 2012, and then started interviews with the research sample in May 2012. We recruited respondents through March of the following year. Our final twelve-month interview was held in December 2014, bringing our total field period to three years. We completed 569 interviews with formerly incarcerated respondents with a response rate of 94 percent over the five interview waves and 91 percent at the final exit interview. We conducted another eighty-one supplementary interviews with friends and family.

Table 2.2 *Demographic and Incarceration Characteristics of BRS Respondents and State Prison Releases to Boston, 2012–2013*

	BRS SAMPLE	OTHER DOC RELEASES	TOTAL
Demographic characteristics			
Female	12.3%	12.2%	12.2%
Under age thirty	31.2	28.0	28.8
Ages thirty to thirty-nine	27.9	34.2	32.5
Ages forty and older	41.0	37.8	38.6
Non-Hispanic white/other	30.3	28.9	29.3
Non-Hispanic black	50.8	45.8	47.2
Hispanic	18.9	25.3	23.6
Incarceration characteristics			
Minimum security	44.3	33.3	36.2
Medium security	41.8	55.4	51.7
Maximum security	13.9	11.3	12.0
Incarcerated less than one year	21.3	23.2	22.7
Incarcerated one to three years	46.7	47.3	47.2
Incarcerated three to ten years	29.5	27.1	27.7
Incarcerated ten or more years	2.5	2.4	2.4
Total (N)	122	336	458

Source: Author's calculations from BRS data.

The study was buffeted by a series of events that roiled the Massachusetts criminal justice system during our long recruitment period. A year before we entered the field, a parolee shot and killed a police officer, much of the parole board was replaced, and parole releases were rare as we were recruiting respondents to the study. In 2012, the year we went into the field, a crime lab was found to have tampered with evidence in thousands of cases, resulting in the court-ordered release of many prisoners at short notice, before we had any chance to recruit them to the study. Early releases mounted further that same year when new drug sentencing laws went into effect. Despite these events, the reentry study captured one-quarter of all releases to Boston communities in the study period, and the sample closely resembled the population of all prison releases to the Boston area (table 2.2).

Eligible respondents had to be in the custody of the Massachusetts Department of Correction, housed in one of the DOC's eighteen prisons, and within a few weeks of their release to the Boston area. The DOC research team worked with program officers in each prison to schedule interviews for people who wanted to participate. (Program officers, in contrast to correctional officers, administer prison programs. One officer was usually responsible for reentry, and one in particular was often assigned as our contact with each prison.) At the beginning of the study, we met with a large group of program officers to explain the project and ask for help in recruiting respondents. We asked them to give every eligible prisoner an information sheet that described the study. Prisoners who wanted to participate would tell the program officer, who would then help us arrange an interview. This procedure often worked just as we hoped, and many of the officers took an interest in the research. They knew our respondents well, but only through the lens of incarceration, and had little knowledge of prisoners' lives outside the prison.

Realities on the ground, however, sometimes overtook our carefully planned design. Although program officers were to distribute information sheets, we heard that news of the study rapidly spread through several of the prisons, fueled perhaps by word of the $50 interview payment. Some prisoners volunteered for the study even without seeing the information sheet. Others arrived at our interviews with little information about us or the project. Some facilities, at least from our perspective, became hotbeds of research, while others provided only a few respondents. In the latter cases, the program officers had little time for the work of subject recruitment and scheduling interviews.

The prison interviews amounted to one-fifth of our total data collection but were critical for the entire study. The prison interview provided our first contact with each respondent, and it was here that we started to make plans for staying in touch over the coming year. Research over a one-year recruitment period was a constant work in progress. University researchers working in an institution where everyday interactions were governed by rules and commands could produce a culture clash, followed by apologies and discussions within our team about how we could better comply. We had to adhere to the prison dress code (no jeans, sneakers, tight clothing, jewelry, or hair clips, among other restrictions), and we could bring in only certain kinds of study materials (no retractable pens, ring binders, or audio recorders). We violated the dress code several times, though these and other mistakes became less common as we developed our routines (and wardrobes) and prison staff became familiar with us.

At prison, staff would escort us usually to a classroom, an attorney's visiting room, or an office. The first interview was conducted with a Harvard researcher and an interviewer from the DOC research unit. Like the Harvard interviewers, the DOC researchers were mostly young white men and women in their twenties and thirties. We provided assurances of confidentiality, but we learned later in the greater privacy of the community interviews that many respondents were uncomfortable being interviewed by DOC staff, even those who were researchers from outside the prison. Still, the DOC staff were well informed about prison programs and services, and their local knowledge was often useful in interviews. Several had a strong interest in social research and were able to project the curious and nonjudgmental posture that we tried to cultivate in all our meetings.

The prison was a focal point for our research, but most of the interviews took place in Boston neighborhoods. Each member of the research team took the lead with a number of respondents whom they had to call regularly. When a respondent changed phone numbers or moved to a different address, the lead researcher would follow up with a secondary contact. Over time, respondents would call in to our field phones to chat or share news between interviews. We also received calls from them in times of crisis—after being thrown out of housing, for example, or coming down off a bender. During these calls, we put respondents in touch with a local reentry program and often just stayed on the phone to talk.

Because interviews were conducted in pairs, each researcher came to know a lot about some respondents but also saw a wide cross-section of the sample. The full-time researchers, Cathy and Jackie, together attended nearly 500 interviews. I conducted around 150 interviews over the three-year field period, kept close tabs on fifteen respondents, and got to know many others quite well.

As the research team got rolling, we were going into the prisons each week and marveling at the small miracle of the first community interview. Respondents in their blue-and-green tunics, sometimes in shackles or behind Plexiglas, said they would meet us in two weeks' time on the outside. Dozens of times we then saw a new person revealed when the prison uniform had been swapped for street clothes, and the prison classroom replaced by the local pizzeria.

Study retention quickly became our top priority. Although a few of the respondents told us that they dropped out because they no longer wanted to be part of the study, most of the no-shows and hard-to-reach respondents

Table 2.3 *Contact Insecurity Among Respondents as Measured by Changes in Phone Contact, Residence, or Criminal Justice Status at Four Contact Points After Prison Release*

	RELEASE TO ONE WEEK	ONE WEEK TO TWO MONTHS	TWO MONTHS TO SIX MONTHS	SIX MONTHS TO TWELVE MONTHS
No phone (excluding the incarcerated)	5.0%	6.7%	4.5%	17.3%
Changed phone	56.8	44.8	42.4	52.3
Unstable or unknown residence	39.3	38.5	44.3	53.3
Changed residence	40.2	34.7	49.1	57.9
New charge or arraignment	0.0	5.7	9.8	27.9
Entered prison or jail	0.8	0.8	7.4	13.9

Source: Author's calculations from BRS data.

Note: N = 122. "Unstable residence" includes staying in multiple residences, treatment programs, transitional housing, shelters, or correctional facilities and being homeless or living on the street. Data on new charges and prison or jail stays are drawn from administrative records and thus are complete for the whole sample.

were overcome by the many dramas that marked the transition from prison to community. Respondents lost their phones, moved, or were sent back to jail. Table 2.3 illustrates what we call "contact insecurity": the unstable points of contact with respondents that were closely associated with late interviews and study attrition. Around half the respondents changed phones between interviews, and a similar proportion changed their address. By the end of the study, nearly one-third had been arrested and charged again (and would often go missing around this time) and one-quarter had been returned to incarceration. Faced with these challenges, we applied our retention strategies continuously and concurrently throughout the day-to-day operations of the study.

Contact insecurity was closely linked to insecurity in daily life. Omar, a Puerto Rican man in his midforties, changed his phone number seventeen times over the course of the study. He had been a heavy drug user ever since he suffered a traumatic brain injury in a car accident as a teenager and was using heroin regularly by the time we interviewed him. Omar often lost his phone and found it hard to remember the dates of medical appointments and study interviews. Still, he was eager to participate, and on days when he was clearheaded and had a working phone, he would call to check in.

Omar lived at several addresses and was periodically homeless for the first three months after incarceration. He rekindled a relationship with a former girlfriend, Jessie, who was just out of prison herself. Jessie had been a heavy drug user but was in better health after her release, and she helped Omar attend appointments, including survey interviews. She stayed with him on the streets and moved with him to a friend's apartment four months after his release. When Omar's cell phone was out of service, we would often call Jessie and she would hand her phone to him so that we could check in.

Omar was sentenced to community supervision after release, but he never reported to his probation officer because of his drug use. Just before his six-month interview, he received a warrant for not reporting. Omar had mentioned his trouble with probation during his interviews and phone calls with us, but we received further information from the DOC. He entered a residential drug treatment program after being told that his warrant would be dropped if he completed it. When we called the program, a staff member told us he was no longer there. During this period when Omar's legal status was compromised and he was no longer living with Jessie, we struggled to reach him to schedule the twelve-month interview.

At times when both Omar and Jessie were out of contact with us over the course of the year, we would call Omar's sister Lena, an older woman in her late fifties. Lena was sixteen years old when the family moved from Puerto Rico to Boston, and she was more comfortable talking with the Spanish-speakers on the research team. Lena had lived for about fifteen years in an apartment in public housing. She was the most stable person in Omar's life, and he used her apartment as his mailing address. Lena would get new contact information from him when he stopped by for meals. After Omar left the treatment program, we contacted Lena, who gave us his new phone number. Two days later, we conducted Omar's twelve-month interview. The interview took place two and a half months late, but we learned a lot about his housing, drug use, and probation late in the year after incarceration.

Between the six-month and twelve-month interviews, we completed five phone check-ins with Omar, failed to reach him on eighteen call attempts, and spoke to his sister or girlfriend five times. Throughout this period we also received information on his legal and residential status from local criminal justice agencies. His case points to the value of numerous redundant strategies to retain vulnerable study participants and the high risk of nonresponse from people who are struggling with housing insecurity, drug relapse, mental illness, and criminal involvement.

Working with respondents like Omar who could be erratic and had histories of violence, I worried about the safety of our researchers, most of whom were young women interviewing older men. However, by interviewing in pairs, using field phones rather than personal phones, and confining contact with the subjects to the terms of the research protocol, not only was the quality of our data collection improved but we were able to keep staff safe. In the hundreds of interviews we conducted, respondents occasionally propositioned the interviewers and at times made them feel uncomfortable. When this happened, we swapped interview assignments and sent men to accompany women on interviews. (It should also be noted that we also received declarations of love and respect that were heartfelt and did not make us feel uncomfortable.) Perhaps most striking, over a three-year field period conducting thousands of face-to-face meetings and phone contacts, overwhelmingly in Boston's highest-crime neighborhoods, we encountered no serious threat to any of the researchers. Exposure to crime is partly a matter of chance, but the study design was devised with the safety of respondents and interviewers in mind.

Research on the very poor and other hard-to-reach populations often asks whether the effort required to interview the most marginal respondents is worth it.[7] The reentry study suggests two answers. First, while retaining the most elusive respondents does require significant effort, developing a culture within the research project that promotes rapport and connectedness with respondents can improve retention at little extra financial cost. Second, the effort to sustain 100 percent retention very likely improves the quality of the interviews that are completed. Interviews conducted in a climate of trust with an interviewer whom a respondent has come to know through numerous interactions are likely to produce survey responses that are more forthcoming and complete, particularly in sensitive areas.

Conducting ethical research with people who had been incarcerated presented complex and sometimes insoluble challenges. The overriding goal of ethical research is to protect those who participate from any harm. Norms and regulations have proliferated to ensure that subjects participate voluntarily, that protections for privacy are in place, and that research instruments do not cause injury or distress. Like all university research with human subjects, the Boston Reentry Study had to pass an ethics review by Harvard's institutional review board (IRB). The incarcerated, like children and pregnant women, are a protected class of research subjects. Research with incarcerated respondents requires stringent review because they are so vulnerable. IRBs are in a difficult position with this kind of research. Prison studies are rare, and review boards often have few if any members who have been in a prison, much less conducted prison research. It took us months to work through many questions of research design and data security with the IRB. When board members raised concerns about consent, we redrafted our forms, making them longer and perhaps more impenetrable for a population with a low reading level. Agreements were drafted on data use, warnings and disclaimers were attached to our interview scripts, and protocols were developed to help keep prison staff at arm's length from the research. I doubt that much of the paperwork made our subjects safer, but research in prison is a serious business, and the Harvard IRB did its part in discharging its obligation of strict scrutiny.

The IRB is just a starting point for meeting the challenges of ethical research in and around prisons. Three aspects of prison research raise deep ethical questions that perhaps can never be fully resolved. The first issue is consent. The prison itself is, at best, an ethical paradox. Can anyone in shackles or solitary confinement, or who is heavily medicated, freely give their consent to anything, let alone a university research study? To provide consent is to assert a level of power and control over one's body and actions that prisons are precisely designed to restrict. At times during an interview, both in prison and out, we would check in with respondents. "Are you doing okay? Is it okay to keep going?" These brief check-ins acknowledged that we too were uncertain about consent under conditions of incarceration and its aftermath. Monitoring the consent of our research subjects in this conversational way did as much, I think, to respect their agency as the many forms we asked them to sign. That said, we also struggled through interviews with respondents who were medicated, mentally disabled, or confused about the purpose of the interview. With very vulnerable respondents like Omar or another respondent, Aman, who was schizophrenic, we would also be in contact with the protective adults in their lives (mothers and girlfriends) who knew and approved of the interviews. Consent under these conditions was less a decision by the research subject than a relationship, incrementally explored by researcher, subject, and the subject's trusted supporters.

Closely related to the issue of consent is the issue of incentives. Some prison systems have rules against incentive payments for research studies on the argument that money is coercive in the intense authority structure of incarceration and the researcher would be benefiting from the prisoner's extreme vulnerability. Prison work programs pay only a few dollars a day, so an interview incentive of $50 is hard to turn down. Indeed, we had only a few refusals. But research subjects outside of prison are routinely paid, and it seems perverse to withhold payment from research subjects because they are more vulnerable.

Once out in the community, we found ourselves regularly handing over cash payments to poor people addicted to drugs and alcohol. Like the issue of consent, incentive payments presented ethical complexities because the agency and capabilities of respondents were often limited. If I believe that research first requires consent, and that research subjects have the capacity to grant it, it seems inconsistent and paternalistic to withhold payment because I think the payment would be harmful to them. Philosophical consistency provided little reassurance, however, when we talked to addicts who anxiously awaited receiving the $50 at the end of the interview. The problem is that poor men and women diseased by addiction do lack full control over their actions, but they usually have no supporter or advocate who can join the discussion of consent. The social conditions of our research setting were unethical, and this made ethical research difficult.

The third ethical challenge was related to respondents' privacy. We worked closely with the DOC and the Boston police, but they also wielded great power over the men and women we interviewed. Our main tool for protecting respondents from authorities was confidentiality. We endeavored to conduct all interviews in private. Names and other identifying information were encrypted and stored in locked offices at Harvard. Frustratingly at times for the DOC research team, who had worked hard on the study, data could not be shared. We obtained from the National Institutes of Health (NIH) a "Certificate of Confidentiality" that offered some protection in case the data were ever subpoenaed.[8] Measures we took to ensure confidentiality helped to protect the respondents from the prison authorities and the police. We never spoke with DOC research staff about respondents, and we avoided situations that might bring respondents into contact with criminal justice personnel. Despite the protections, some prison staff wanted to eavesdrop on our interviews. DOC research staff would look up respondents on the prison information system, and a parole officer once directed a respondent to call us after he had fallen out of contact. I have tried to set firmer boundaries with correctional agencies in subsequent studies. One agency wanted parole officers informed of respondents' study participation. I disagreed, and the study collapsed. In another study, we insisted on interviewing respondents alone, without correctional staff, and the agency readily agreed.

Confidentiality helps protect people whose vulnerability resides in the criminal databases that list their names and birthdates. Criminal stigma is a special kind of vulnerability that reflexively invites fear, distrust, and moral revulsion. Under the conditions of mass incarceration, such stigma is built on a politics of dehumanization that makes people who are incarcerated something less than full members of the human community. For these politics, criminality is characteristic not of certain kinds of conduct but of certain kinds of people, and harsh punishment becomes the default response to crime.

I have tried to suspend the reflex of moral judgment by painting a rich portrait of people who have been incarcerated. A humanizing social analysis answers a politics of dehumanization and improves our understanding of people who are stigmatized by imprisonment. What does a humanizing social analysis do? First, it places people in social context, acknowledging the importance of biography, family, neighborhood, and history. Understanding action in its social context is the fundamental insight of sociology. Second, in reducing people neither to their criminal acts nor to their suffering, a humanizing social analysis aims to reveal its subjects' creativity and their loving relationships. Creativity and love are the foundations of human agency and the means by which we recognize something of ourselves in others.

For social scientists, there is a tension between respecting the private details of the lives of vulnerable people and portraying their full humanity to dispel antipathy and ignorance. The humanity of the men and women we talked to was rooted in their specific life histories, the neighborhoods they lived in, their jobs, and their families and friends. Ethnographers have struggled mightily with this conflict.[9] I have little to add to these debates, except to say that rich and detailed analysis as much as confidentiality can serve an ethical vision of science. In very poor or socially marginal research sites, much of scientific practice consists of bearing witness, trying to hear voices subdued by poverty, discrimination, violence, and the many other troubles that follow. Much like study retention where a missing observation, out of nearly six hundred interviews, would barely increase statistical bias or uncertainty, efforts to show in detail the human brilliance of those who have been incarcerated is to register voices rarely heard in science or policy. This was an opportunity not to be missed.

CHAPTER 3

Transitions

Jerry called the day he got out of prison. He had just been released that afternoon, taken in handcuffs to a reentry center on Boston's South Shore. He was told that the center could help him find a job and get treatment, but he only stayed a few minutes to get directions to the train. A white man in his fifties, Jerry returned to his neighborhood in South Boston to meet his father. He looked for the old man at the station and then tried calling him, feeding quarters into a pay phone. Unable to reach him, he went to a coffee shop to regroup. "I was at a Dunkin Donuts and threw an ice coffee into the trash and turned around and saw him," he said. Jerry had been locked up for nineteen years. "I was just standing there. I felt like a convict, holding my little bag. I felt like I escaped."

He spent a few hours with his father, but then had to move on. A bed at a shelter had been arranged for him before his release. Late that night Jerry called me from the shelter. He'd gotten a cell phone a few hours earlier, but he was anxious because he wasn't sure how long the battery would last. Would it last longer than an hour? What if he used it a lot? He spent his first night out of prison in a dormitory with fifty other men, worried that his phone would get stolen.

Freedom after prison is not a status granted by release, but something attained gradually. Becoming free first requires adjusting to the everyday tasks and interactions of free society and leaving behind the habits of the institution. If men and women leaving incarceration can manage the first days and weeks after release, they then must confront the larger challenge of establishing themselves in a community. More than just living in a place, community membership involves attachment to a social compact made up of ties to family, a place to live, and a basic level of living. Becoming free is a process of social integration.

The first weeks out of prison were often bewildering and awkward for the men and women of the reentry study. Feelings of stress, nervousness, and loneliness were overwhelming. We heard about anxiety in crowds, discomfort with the pace of life, and clumsiness with small tasks like shopping and riding public transport.[1] Adjusting to free society under conditions of material hardship, without income or stable housing, produced a stress of transition. The stress of transition was intensified by drug addiction and mental illness but relieved by family support. Older men, like Jerry, whose family was exhausted by his lifelong addiction and mental disorder, were the most vulnerable. For people like him, the stress of transition could have long-lasting effects that disrupted community return.

Many people we interviewed had been preparing for release for months. Most had attended workshops in prison on social programs and employment. Some planned to enroll in public assistance, see doctors, or pick up clothing from the state transitional assistance center. Others were incredulous at lectures on preparing résumés when they hadn't worked in years and had little idea about where to apply for jobs. Those who were not being taken in by family or friends met with prison program officers to find a place in a shelter or sober house. Several of the veterans were sent to the large shelter run by Veterans Affairs in downtown Boston. Many were signed up in prison for MassHealth, the Massachusetts Medicaid program. Amid all the planning and activities that culminated in release, some were locked in disciplinary segregation for twenty-three hours a day; they would go from solitary confinement straight to the street.

The departure from prison began with transportation. Just over one-third of the sample were picked up from prison by family members, often parents or siblings. One-quarter were met by a friend or partner, and another quarter took "state transport," a Department of Correction van, to a train station or regional reentry center. The remaining few either walked by themselves from the prison gates to a train station or were picked up by a caseworker. Younger people were more likely to be collected by family or friends. Older people were transported from prison by the state. Being transported from prison by the state was a vivid sign of the social isolation straight after incarceration that we found to be linked to poor social integration six months later.[2]

Back in society, people spoke to us first about the whirl of public life. We talked to Jerry a week after his call from the shelter. He said that his greatest difficulty after prison was "dealing with the mental stimulus." He described the shock of release:

> It's very overwhelming. You have to understand the situation I was in where for the last nineteen years nothing changed, the view, for the most part, the people, the routine, everything was the same. Suddenly there's sights, sounds, options, everything all at once. Bam. There's no transition.

Normal activities—finding an address, riding the bus—were difficult for Jerry. The sheer challenge of ordinary life was itself a source of anxiety. Jerry went on:

> I was very ill prepared for what I had to deal with. For example, I went to my father's house. [He] gave me directions. I only had to walk from here to there. It was kind of convoluted. And when I got there, I was so happy I had tears in my eyes. I felt like at any moment, if I stepped off the known path, I'd be in, like, nowhere's land. I'd just be completely lost. It sounds so pathetic for a fifty-one-year-old man. But there it is. That's what happens. You know, you're locked up a long time and then suddenly you're not.

Panic, depression, loneliness, and the unfamiliarity of free society were all elements of the stress of transition that accompanied the first weeks after incarceration. Jerry met up with his father on his first day out, but he spent many of the following days and weeks by himself. At 7:30 a.m., his shelter would turn out its residents for the day. Jerry would go to a public library in the mornings and use the computers. He would also pass hours in downtown Boston, watching workers from the office buildings around the shelter walk by. I once saw Jerry sitting alone on a park bench while I was interviewing another respondent downtown. He sat in Government Center for an hour by himself around midday, looking out on the square. He said of his people-watching, "I fall in love with everybody, and no one falls in love with me." He put the point more bluntly in another conversation: "I'm fifty-one years old, and I haven't been laid in nineteen years. That's a frustration."

I asked, "Are you talking to anyone?"

"No, and what would I say? Do you want to come back to the shelter?"

He also talked about the pressure he felt as he adjusted to freedom and his new place in society. "My head is in a guillotine, and the clock is ticking," he would say.

> My situation is so lame. I live in a shelter. I have to be back at eleven. I don't
> have a job. I don't have a car. Suddenly being out. And being out of the game
> for so long. And then suddenly having all this freedom. The shock of how
> much the world has changed. You know, it's amazing I can even get out of
> bed. I'm finally coming around to me again. I forgot who I was in there.
> You've gotta leave all that behind you. Like I said. I'm walking down the
> street, [people] bumping into me. In jail you've got to check yourself. Hey,
> where's my apology. Otherwise, I'm a punk.

The jostling and bumping of crowds were difficult for men and women whose movements had been regimented and directed for years. Like Jerry, AJ had trouble in crowds in the first months out of prison. A thin white man with glasses, AJ had a mild and thoughtful appearance that contrasted with the tattoos on his arms announcing his support for white power. AJ had an explosive temper, and he'd suffered since childhood from a learning disability and anxiety attacks. The anxiety attacks became more serious with more incarceration. As AJ described it, "It got worse being in prison most of the time and growin' up on the street always fightin'. I even did a lot of hole time [solitary confinement] over the years, you know. My mind ain't right from that. I'm always on my toes." In his most recent incarceration, AJ had spent thirteen months out of two years in prison in solitary confinement. He'd been taking medication for panic attacks while he was in prison, but he was released without a prescription. A week before he was released, AJ told us that he wanted to "try and be a citizen out there, try to get the help I need."

AJ's program officer in prison was scouting housing options just before he was released. He was expecting to spend some time at the shelter on Long Island, a small colony for Boston's homeless population connected to the mainland by a bridge that stretched across Quincy Bay.[3] The DOC van took AJ to Long Island one Friday morning, but he stayed for only a few hours. He quickly decided to leave because the shelter was "just shady shit" and filled with "young punks." He went to stay with his sister, Kate, in Cambridge, a long train ride away across the city.

Getting home wasn't easy. The ticket machines were hard to operate. "I kind of had a hard time. I ain't know how to . . . stupid damn machines, with the cards and all that. I wanted to smash it." He kept his frustration under control, however, and by late that afternoon he'd made it back home to Cambridge.

Kate and AJ were Irish twins, born eleven months apart. They had looked out for each other since they were children. "I promised my mom I would always take care of him," said Kate. "That's her firstborn." She took her brother in on his first day out of prison, and he stayed with her through his first year. They went out that first night with a few of Kate's girlfriends to celebrate his return. AJ did his drinking on an empty stomach. "They were feeding me champagne, [but] I couldn't eat that day. Anxiety was kicking in." Despite that, "I did pretty good that night. It's been a long time. I walked. I wasn't stumbling."

Crowds worried AJ, and the nightclubs were challenging:

> The day I got out I went to the clubs that night. So it was like I had my back against the wall all night. I had a good time, but at the same time it was wicked bad. . . . It's just being around too many people, like, I start to, like, I feel like everybody's just, I don't know. I get wicked anxiety attacks being around and then people bumpin' into me. Then I get aggravated real quick, so it's like . . .

Although anxiety in crowds was common after release, most people we interviewed regained their confidence after a few weeks. Six months after getting out, however, AJ still spoke of his difficulties with the transition from prison and the enclosed and busy places of free society: "Things ain't going too quick [in prison]. I'm not surrounded with too many people. I could always lock it in if I want. Stay in my cell. . . . Things wasn't hard you know? It was just easy." Worried about crowds and saddled with a potent temper, he spent much of his time locked in his room in his sister's apartment. AJ talked to us a lot in the first few months about the difficulties he faced, but he emphasized that he preferred freedom to prison, saying, "I take this out here any day."

Stress at the moment of prison release could be counteracted by family support and motivation. Peter was an older black man, in his late forties, with salt-and-pepper hair and an elegant bearing. He arrived early for our interview a week after his release. Waiting on the street, he was hesitant to face the crowd inside the diner in Mattapan. We began the interview by asking Peter what the best part of being out was for him.

"Breathing fresh air," he said.

"What's the most challenging thing?"

"Being around a bunch of people. Just being in public areas."

Five years before we first met Peter, he was just out of prison on an earlier sentence in a history of incarceration that had consumed most of his adult life. He was out for two years, before going back in for another three. His previous release, he said, was a rehearsal for his current reentry. "When I was incarcerated that last trip, I pretty much knew what I had to do," he said.

Although he got anxious in crowds, Peter began his latest release with a flurry of activity. He came home on a Friday, and that morning he bought clothes and got a haircut. He spent time with his sister that first day and stayed over at her house. Five other people were living in his sister's house, including her fiancé, one adult son, and two younger children. Peter worried that he was a burden on what was already a crowded family home. He could have stayed with his father, but his father drank. His brother also stayed there, and he was dealing drugs. "Being at my father's wasn't a healthy situation. My sister's is the safest place for me," he said.

Peter spent his first weekend home with his nine-year-old son. They talked, did some shopping, and went to the movies. On his first Monday after getting out, he reported to probation in the morning, then visited his father in the afternoon. On Tuesday he enrolled in food stamps, then met with his older son later in the day. He went to the welfare office again on Wednesday, then visited his younger son's school to introduce himself to the boy's teachers. Thursday was mental health counseling. By the end of his first week out, Peter had spent time with two of his three children, enrolled in food stamps, obtained a mass transit card, made an appointment for counseling, checked in with several shelters, and visited a career center. The following week he would begin his job search.

After decades of incarceration, Peter seemed tired of street life and was motivated to be a larger presence in his children's lives. He said he wanted to see his kids get older. "They're happy I'm home. But they're all waiting to see [if I'll go back to prison], because this happened before. So I don't want to let myself down, as well as them. I feel this pressure, but it's good pressure. It's a form of motivation."

Nearly fifty years old and experienced with prison and prison release, Peter also endured the stress of transition. He walked from place to place and avoided the bus. He disliked crowds. But he was methodical and determined to be successful in his community return. Day by day in his first week back, he assembled many of the pieces that would allow him to find work, independent housing, and a measure of reconciliation with his children.

Family support helped men who were healthy in mind and body absorb the stress of transition. Sam was twenty-eight when he was released after serving a three-year sentence on gun charges. A black man with a close-knit family and two children, Sam was met on the day of his release by his two younger brothers and his sister. They drove him to his mother's place in Mattapan, where he would live for the year after prison. The family then went to lunch at his stepfather's small Jamaican diner in Dorchester.

Sam spent his first week back with his family. On his first day home he got a haircut and went shopping with his brother. He spoke to friends and relatives on the phone, but seemed to avoid those who were still involved in street life. "I just remember how nobody was there when I was locked up," he said. "I ain't messing with you all." On his second day out Sam went out with his brother to buy some gold teeth—a $400 gift. "When you're away for so long, you miss out," Sam said. "He treated me to something nice." He also visited the Registry of Motor Vehicles that day to get his driver's license reinstated.

The third day was a Saturday, and Sam took his five-year old son, Little Sam, to basketball practice. The two of them hung out in the afternoon and played video games. Sam spent that night with Little Sam, who lived with his mother. She and Sam had remained in contact and were on good terms. Sam would meet someone else later that year, but he and Little Sam's mother shared the bond of raising their child.

When the new week started, Sam began the same round of errands followed by most of the men and women we interviewed. He applied for food stamps and shopped for socks and underwear. His sister made him a doctor's appointment for the following week. Between errands, he spent time at his stepfather's diner, hung out with his brothers at his mother's place, and stayed over another evening with Little Sam and the boy's mother.

Sam was welcomed home by his family, but he also had to adjust to the pace and pattern of life in society. Like Peter, he often preferred to walk rather than get a ride or take the bus. At one week out of prison he told us:

> I got no problem walking sometimes. It's good to clear your mind. Walking clears your thoughts, or organizes thoughts that you have. It's hard. It's hard coming back. And you kinda get down at times because you know how you was before. And starting over from the bottom and having to work your way

up, it's kind of like . . . you know, so sometimes I get down. But sometimes it's good for me to clear my mind, clear my thoughts, and kind of give myself that restart.

The stress of transition was often paralyzing for our respondents and depleted their energy for the dozens of tasks that accompanied the first weeks after prison release. For Jerry and AJ, the chasm between prison and community was particularly deep. Jerry had been incarcerated for nearly two decades, and simple technologies like cell phones were unfamiliar. AJ, who had spent a long time in solitary confinement, suffered anxiety attacks in crowds and spent days locked in his room. Peter too was discomfited by crowds, but he returned to his community with the support of his sister and an intense motivation to do well for his children. Sam was surrounded by family immediately after his release, but he too had to adjust to life after prison and sometimes sought solitude in walking.

We heard reports of anxiety in about 40 percent of our interviews with respondents in the first week after their release. They were distressed by public transport and crowded public places like stores and nightclubs. Many respondents stayed off trains and buses for the first few months to avoid being jostled by strangers. Many in the reentry sample acquired cell phones in the first few days after release, but the technology often felt strange, particularly after lengthy prison sentences. In Boston, electronic cards are used to enter the train stations. Some respondents found the cards difficult to use, causing nervousness and embarrassment. Besides the challenges of technology and social interaction, respondents told us that they felt lonely, isolated, and anxious about encountering associates still involved in crime.

The first weeks out were filled with small errands and appointments. Some fulfill basic needs—applying for food stamps, getting a state identification card, seeing a doctor. Those with chronic illness or a history of addiction looked for counselors, treatment programs, and specialists.

Two-thirds of the sample were required to meet probation or parole officers, a necessity to avoid reincarceration. At their initial meetings, community corrections officers went over the conditions of release. Parole and probation supervision usually involved restrictions on drug and alcohol use and required random drug tests. Parolees and probationers also had to pay supervision fees—$65 each month for probation and $85 for parole. Some respondents chafed at these initial meetings and resented the fees imposed at a time when they had no income. Probation and parole officers could monitor the conditions of release, but they had few ways to help with the pressing needs of employment, housing, or family reconciliation. For Sam, probation involved a subway ride downtown for a ten-minute meeting every two weeks and a $65 payment each month. "I just feel sometimes that it's a waste," he said. A few others, however—like Peter, whose motivation was sky high and who had been on community supervision many times— saw probation as a helpful reminder to stay on track.

Other appointments were less necessary but helped to scrape off the residue of the institution. Writing about incarceration in the 1940s, Donald Clemmer described the many small behavioral adaptations to incarceration as "prisonization."[4] Clemmer found that the intense authority structure of the prison forced small changes in behavior and attitude that poorly fit the free flow of human interaction outside the prison.[5] Several of those we interviewed wanted to "wash off" or "remove" the prison from themselves. Shopping, going to cookouts, and spending time with family, girlfriends, and boyfriends all assisted in their deprisonization. Getting new clothes and haircuts erased the uniformity of incarceration, and the time spent with family and partners began to renew their relationships and celebrated return.

We often heard about welcome-home parties in the first week or so of getting out. These get-togethers affirmed bonds of kinship, signaled moral inclusion, and eased the challenge of what the criminologist John Irwin described as "reentering the world as a stranger."[6] The welcome-home event was typically organized by mothers and siblings, and extended family and friends would attend. The gatherings celebrated the return of the formerly incarcerated family member and gave notice that incarceration had ended. Family more than friends were at the center of these events, particularly if friends were still involved in crime. The welcome-home party offered a forum where those leaving incarceration could make a public commitment to loved ones to stay out of trouble and where family members could express their support.

Just as the stress of transition was greatest for those with drug problems and mental illness, rituals of return were also less common among those who were more vulnerable. Nearly two-thirds of those with no history of mental illness or drug addiction reported some kind of welcome-home event in their first week after prison release. By contrast, only one in six of those with mental illness or drug addiction received a welcome-home party. Older releases in their late forties and fifties often left prison by state transport and entered shelters or transitional housing programs, not family homes. Curfews and other restrictions in these settings limited their opportunities for social gatherings. Only about 20 percent of older respondents were given a welcome-home party, compared to nearly 60 percent of younger respondents.[7] Older men and women also reported more loneliness and social isolation in the first weeks out.

Beyond the first weeks of transition lies the task of community membership. To be part of a community is to enjoy the intimate bonds of family, to have a place to live and a means of subsistence. These elements of community attachment draw individuals into the relationships of kin, citizen, and worker. Those who are estranged from family, homeless, and poor have little access to mainstream opportunities. Studying how community membership is regained after release broadens the definition of "success" after incarceration. Policy researchers and policymakers often reduce "success" to the avoidance of a new arrest. The focus on recidivism highlights the burden that reentry might impose on the rest of us. Instead of emphasizing recidivism, I view a successful transition from prison as the attainment of a basic level of well-being consistent with community membership. This view of success after incarceration captures something of what Irwin called the "dignity, fulfillment, [and] achievement of life goals."[8]

Research on the reintegrative role of family after incarceration has focused on relationships with partners and children. Stable marriages have been found to divert young men from careers in crime. A good marriage gives a young man a stake in normal life and draws him out of the social network of peers who together can get involved in crime. Incarceration, on the other hand, is destabilizing and likely to lead to divorce or separation. Release from prison itself can be a shock, interrupting what has been a respite from a shared addiction or domestic violence. Children too are harmed by a parent's incarceration. They are more likely to act out, have trouble at school, and become homeless after a parent is locked up.[9]

The large body of research on incarceration and families has been only loosely connected to the integrative role of families that we observed in Boston. Family life is complicated in the social space occupied by mass incarceration. Fathers often live separately from their children. Men and women entangled in the justice system may have children with different partners. Prison itself disrupts the orderly sequence of life stages from school to work to marriage and parenthood. Family support in contexts like these frequently came not from romantic partners, but from older women— mothers, grandmothers, sisters, and aunts. The support that we saw in the reentry study was foundational. In the immediate period of transition, older women offered the recently released family member a place to stay and helped him or her make ends meet.[10]

Nearly all of the younger men we interviewed, like AJ and Sam, who were in their late twenties and early thirties, were living with family members and receiving money from relatives in the first few months after release. AJ had expected to stay with his sister, Kate, for just a few days but wound up staying with her and her son for the entire year. "He was only supposed to stay with me for the weekend. But he never left," Kate laughed. AJ could have gone to stay with his mother outside Boston, but Kate worried that he would get in trouble. "There's no work," she said, "and there's a lot of punks out there." Even in Boston, AJ was unemployed for most of his first six months out, but he contributed his monthly $200 in food stamps to the household budget and Kate helped him out financially in return. "Whenever I need something, she'll give me money here and there," said AJ. Besides financial support, AJ and Kate shared the companionship of family life. "We hang out," said Kate, listing their shared activities. "He plays pranks on me all the time. There was the bucket on the door thing. . . . No wait, we did that to him. We go Sundays to a softball game. I don't play. He plays, I watch." Kate also gave AJ space to "lock it in," as he did in prison. "He always locks himself in his bedroom," Kate told us. "He calls it his cell."

Sam lived with his mother, stepfather, and younger brothers immediately after he was released. Like AJ, Sam struggled to find work, and his mother and siblings helped him out, providing him with a few hundred dollars each month. Sam's incarceration had been devastating for his mother. "It broke my heart completely," she told us. Eagerly welcoming him back to her house when he was released, she bought him food and clothing in his first months back.

Peter struggled more with his family relationships after release. He worried that he added to the load on his sister's household. After a couple of months, his relationship with his sister had become strained and the two rarely talked. "I don't agree with how she's raising her kids," Peter said. He had three children of his own and seemed most concerned about his youngest son, but he also saw his eight-year-old daughter and her mother. Peter told us that he stayed with his sister mostly because that put him in a better position to support his children. His daughter and his son both came to stay with him on weekends. Family visits would have been impossible at a shelter.

Jerry was a few years older than Peter, and his children were grown. He received no financial help from his family, but he was in regular contact with his elderly father, his brother and sister, and his two sons. He joined the family get-together at Thanksgiving a few months after he got out, and a few months later he went out with his sister and a few of her friends. "I celebrated my first birthday as a free man in almost twenty years. Nice band. The place was jumping," he said. In the absence of financial help from his family, all of Jerry's material support was publicly provided, by the shelter where he stayed and through public assistance.

The connections between Sam, AJ, Peter, and Jerry and their families were broadly reflected in the reentry sample as a whole. About two-thirds of respondents received money or housing from family in the first week after release. As they gained greater independence, overall family support (housing and money) declined to just over 50 percent six months later.

Housing and financial assistance from family members was most common for women and young men and for those who were not dealing with the challenges of drug addiction and mental illness. The respondents who were most isolated from family in the period of transition tended to have histories of drug addiction and mental illness, or were in their late forties and fifties. Around 85 percent of those under thirty received housing or income support from their family in the first six months after prison, but only 40 percent of those age forty-five or older received family support. Around 70 percent of those with no history of mental illness or addiction received family support, compared to only 50 percent of those reporting a dual diagnosis of substance abuse and mental illness.

The role of older women was critical in the provision of support. About 80 percent of respondents who reported staying with family in the first six months out of prison were staying with a female relative, and around half of these were mothers. Just 10 percent stayed with a partner, and 2 percent stayed with their father. Family members, rather than partners, were also key sources of financial support. At one week out of prison, 55 respondents out of 122 received money from family, but only 11 received money from a partner. Six months later, respondents were twice as likely to get money from a family member as from a partner.

Stable housing was also basic to social integration for the men and women returning to Boston from prison. Only a few studies have examined homelessness and housing insecurity immediately after incarceration. Data from New York and Philadelphia shows that, in the late 1990s, 4 to 11 percent of those released from prison stayed in homeless shelters in the two years after incarceration. In Massachusetts, around 10 percent were found to go directly from prison to shelters in the late 1990s. Research on incarceration and housing insecurity has mostly studied shelter use, but a more complete account would also include enrolling in residential treatment programs, occupying single-room housing, and doubling up with relatives.[11]

Housing stability and family support were closely connected. We saw that Sam and AJ lived in private households with family members throughout their first months after incarceration. Sam's mother had steady work with a large health care organization, and she had lived in her apartment for five years when Sam came home. Her economic stability allowed her to provide a home to Sam and his younger brothers, who were in their twenties. As work took Sam out of his mother's neighborhood later in the year, he began to spend more time at his girlfriend's place.

AJ also lived with a family member, his sister, but her housing was less reliable. When AJ first moved in with Kate, she had a Section 8 housing voucher for low-income renters. Kate was less financially secure than Sam's mother. She was younger, had not completed high school, and had moved around more before AJ was released. A few years earlier, she had been homeless herself, living for two years in the city's shelters. When he moved in, AJ's name was not on the lease, and they were forced to find a new place two months later. They rented another apartment nearby, and the landlord let AJ live with Kate and her son for the remainder of his first year out.

Peter also lived with his family throughout his first year after getting out of prison, though his housing seemed less settled than was the case for the younger men. During the year, he talked often about moving to a shelter or perhaps moving from his sister's place to his father's. Speaking about his sister's household, Peter said, "Her house is like a shelter." Occasionally, to relieve the crowding, he did stay with his father, and he sometimes stayed with his daughter's mother.

Jerry lived in a homeless shelter throughout his transition from prison to the community. The shelter was a stable residence but provided little privacy or safety. He had to leave his dormitory early each morning and spend his days outside until the early evenings, when he was allowed to return. He told us that he would have liked to apply for public housing, but he was excluded because he had been convicted of a sex offense.

Insecure housing in the sample as a whole can be described with a measure of temporary or marginal housing that includes shelters for the homeless, like the shelter where Jerry lived; sober houses and residential programs; rooming houses, which usually charge rent on a weekly basis; and hotels and motels.[12] Insecure housing also includes staying at multiple residences, being homeless and living on the streets, and returning to a correctional facility. In all these cases, respondents either had highly insecure housing or lived in a group quarters outside of a traditional household.

Measuring residential insecurity in this way reveals that half the reentry sample were in marginal or temporary housing at some point in the six months after prison release. As with isolation from family, housing insecurity was most common among those who were older and those dogged by a history of addiction or mental illness. Nearly 70 percent of older respondents—those age forty-five and older—were unstably housed in the first week after incarceration compared to just 16 percent of those under age thirty. Although housing would improve for the older segment of the sample over the next six months, over half would remain in temporary or marginal housing. Respondents with a history of mental illness and addiction reported similar levels of marginal housing. Underlining the persistent disadvantage of older respondents and those reporting mental illness and addiction, over 40 percent of both groups were in marginal or temporary housing at each interview through six months after release.

Although the survey data indicated severe housing instability, the quantitative indicators probably overestimate the permanence and independence of housing. Only a few respondents lived independently within six months of leaving prison. Living in a private household with family was safer and more private, but relatives themselves were often either insecurely housed or made so by the arrival of a family member newly released from prison.

As the sisters of AJ and Peter found out, taking in a family member after prison release can add to an already crowded household and sometimes violate a lease, risking eviction. In spite of the relative stability of living with family compared to shelters and other temporary housing, around 20 percent of respondents who were staying with family a week after release lived at a new address two months later.

Finding a regular income was the leading concern of the respondents in the first two months after prison.[13] For a population of largely prime-age men, employment was a major source of income in the first months after prison release. Employment also helped build pride, social status, and a daily routine. Formidable obstacles, however, stood in the way of finding work after incarceration: a criminal record, a poor work history, no high school diploma, poor health—all set the stage for low wages and unemployment. In this context, welfare programs provided the other main source of income.[14]

Before entering the labor market, men and women just out of prison returned to society with savings from prison canteen accounts. Money sent by family or earned from prison jobs was paid into an account that they had used for phone calls or to buy food and toiletries. The account was paid out at prison release. Half the reentry study respondents left prison with $330 or less. Those who had served longer sentences or been employed in a work-release job had more savings, sometimes as much as several thousand dollars. Those with a dual diagnosis of mental illness and addiction, who usually had been given fewer work assignments and received less family support, had less than $200 in their canteen account at prison release.

AJ had spent most of his sentence in solitary confinement and was released from prison with just $50. His anxiety in crowds made both searching for work and being employed difficult. But after a few months he had picked up several small jobs doing home improvements with a neighborhood friend. Work was sporadic at first, but after a few months he made $300 to $400 a week from doing home improvements or painting houses. Each week AJ would keep $100 for himself and give the rest to Kate to help cover the rent. He also contributed $200 in food stamps he received each month for the first six months after his release.

Sam looked for work more intensively than AJ and was frustrated by his unemployment. Two months out of prison, Sam had asked friends and relatives about work, had searched online for jobs, and had cold-called employers. He had applied for "fifteen or twenty" jobs when we spoke two months after his release from prison. The slow economy, he felt, was hindering his job search. "It's kind of hard to be seen or heard when there's hundreds of people who are in front of you, trying to do the same." We asked what type of work he was interested in. "It's nothing specific," he said, "if they're hiring, or even if they're not hiring." He picked up a few small jobs painting apartments, but Sam would not get a steady job until six months after his release. In the meantime, he was enrolled in food stamps and his mother and his younger brothers gave him a few hundred dollars each month.

Peter too was impatient with unemployment in the first months out. But using a referral from a reentry organization, he found work two months after his release through a jobs program for the homeless and formerly incarcerated, doing building maintenance and operating machines. The program initially paid less than minimum wage, but Peter became a respected worker in the shop, he told us, and after a few months he was asked to teach classes. He made just under $1,000 a month. Unfortunately, the program was temporary and could offer no more than six months of employment. Peter supplemented his earnings with food stamps and occasional cash gifts from his daughter's mother. "She supports me a hundred percent," he said. Earning just around the poverty line, he lived simply and spent most of his spare income on his children. "I don't have to buy clothes and I don't go out," he explained. Six months after his release, he told us he was focused on being a stable presence in the lives of his children and had resisted drug dealing and other illegal work in the transitional period after incarceration.

Jerry was continuously unemployed in the year after his incarceration. He worried a lot about his finances in the first few months after his release. "Money is just going in one direction," he would say. He applied for jobs and went to a job fair, but his criminal record and mental health kept him from finding work. Returning one day from a job fair, he reported happily that, though he failed to find work, "at least I didn't kill anyone." A few months after his release, a psychiatric evaluation allowed him to apply for disability payments through the Supplemental Security Income program. "I was diagnosed with intermittent explosive temper disorder, which is just short for saying I'm Portuguese."[15] He was also diagnosed with post-traumatic stress disorder (PTSD). Once he was on SSI, Jerry's income totaled $760 each month—$740 from disability and another $20 from food stamps.

Unemployment was widespread among our respondents after prison release, but their employment rates increased slowly through the year. In the sample as a whole, the employment rate climbed from 18 to 43 percent from one week to two months after release. Employment remained around that level over the next few months. Although the employment rate more than doubled in the first two months, they rarely found steady full-time work. Most respondents initially worked in day labor or at temporary jobs, often doing construction, home improvement, or snow removal in the winter. The few who worked in full-time jobs either were continuing the work-release job they held in prison or had used family connections to find stable employment.

As for the other indicators, social integration through the labor market was weakest among older respondents and those with a history of addiction and mental illness. At two months after release, over half of those under age thirty reported having at least some work, but only one-quarter of those forty-five or older were employed. Employment for those who were neither drug addicted nor mentally ill exceeded 60 percent, compared to 26 percent for those with a dual diagnosis.

While employment varied across these markers of human frailty, public assistance was uniformly high. Income from government benefits was much more common than employment in the first six months after incarceration. By the end of the first week after release, just over 40 percent of the sample were receiving public benefits. Within two months, the rate of public assistance had climbed to over 70 percent, and it remained at that level over the next few months. Nearly all those we interviewed who received public assistance were enrolled in food stamps. Food stamp eligibility is based on a means test for net household income below the federal poverty line. Among the people we spoke to, the food stamp benefit was typically $200 a month. Food stamps often helped support an entire household, as benefits were given to household heads or transitional housing programs. Public assistance tended to accompany housing insecurity and family isolation, being greatest among older respondents and those with a history of addiction and mental illness.

The first months of transition from prison to community reveal three broad patterns. First, social integration after incarceration requires that those recently released manage the stress of transition. The reentry study respondents reported anxiety, loneliness, and alienation immediately after getting out. Many spoke about shedding the habits and behaviors of the institution. Families helped respondents with deprisonization by celebrating the end of their incarceration and providing companionship as they adjusted to the everyday complexity of free society. Extreme material hardship in the first week after release followed by a period of rapid adjustment marked the first months of prison release as a distinct phase in the process of leaving incarceration.

Second, in the first six months after prison release, most of those we interviewed received poverty-level incomes and relied heavily on government benefits and family support. Six months after prison release, four out of five in the sample had received food stamps or other public benefits. Over half the sample were living with family or receiving financial help. Most family support in the first months was provided by older women—mothers, grandmothers, and sisters. Even as family relationships were often frayed, housing was insecure, and poverty was common, our respondents' social integration increased measurably in the first few months after prison. Elected officials have periodically limited the eligibility for public assistance of people with criminal records. With poverty and economic insecurity so common immediately after prison release, such limits on public assistance impose real hardship.

Third, two groups bucked the trend toward social integration and stood out as unusually isolated. Older respondents, those in their late forties and fifties, were more unstably housed and more disconnected from family than the majority of the sample under age forty-five. Those contending with human frailty in the form of mental illness or drug addiction also experienced greater isolation and material hardship. They received less family support and were more likely to be insecurely housed or living outside of regular households, more reliant on public assistance, and less likely to be employed. Needs were acute for a group that suffered from the correlated adversities of addiction, poor mental health, advanced age, and social isolation, and government assistance emerged as a key source of material maintenance for them.

The transition from prison to community was often accompanied by stress and hardship, but nearly all those we interviewed spoke about the joys and happiness of getting out. At the first meeting with respondents who had been out in the community for a week since their release, we began by asking: "What's the best part about being out?" Some answered by renouncing the prison environment. "Not having to stand up for count." "No DOC." "No toilet next to the bed." "I don't have to worry about fighting."

Figure 3.1 *Word Cloud Showing Responses to the Question Asked at One Week After Prison Release: "What's the Best Part About Being Out?"*

Source: Author's compilation.

But most spoke about the highlights of that first week. "Taking a bath." "Breathing fresh air." "Talking to women." "Nieces and nephews I've never met." "I saw my oldest son." Some caught up on movies they had missed, and many took long walks around the city. AJ struggled with anxiety but spent a blissful early morning on his fifth day out of prison on a lake with a friend from his old neighborhood, fishing and smoking marijuana.

We can summarize the responses by representing them in a word cloud that shows the most common responses in large type (figure 3.1). "Freedom" and "family" were the words used most often to describe the best part during that first week about being out of prison. Incarceration is almost always thought of as a deprivation of liberty. In the view of the formerly incarcerated men and women of Boston, prison release not only restored their liberty but also began to restore their most intimate social connections.

Prisons, for all their varied effects, are important for creating an event that begins a struggle for social belonging: the departure from incarceration. The basic conditions of community membership—ties to family, a place to live, and a means of subsistence—must all be established. Most people exit prison and enter poverty. Housing is insecure, and incomes are supplemented by government programs. In the struggle for community membership, men and women in their twenties and thirties and just out of prison rely on mothers, grandmothers, and sisters to play a caring role—to feed, provide for, and house them. By contrast, the family ties of those in their forties and older have often eroded and the state has become their main source of support. Mental and physical infirmity also present barriers to rejoining community life. These markers of human frailty are embedded deep in the lives of people who go to prison. In the next chapter, I examine the human frailty that marks the conditions of poverty in which the justice system operates and consider its implications for the ethics of punishment.

CHAPTER 4

Human Frailty

American public policy efforts to help the most disadvantaged focus on unmarried mothers and their children. The single men and women who fill the nation's prisons have often slipped through holes in the safety net and at different points in their lives have found themselves on the street, desperate, and quite often alone.[1] More than just poor and out of work, these men and women embody vulnerability, struggling with mental illness, drug addiction, and physical disability. Poor mental and physical health are markers of human frailty that add decisively to the insult of poverty. Human frailty physically marks and stigmatizes the poor and compounds their disadvantage. In the current policy environment, human frailty gives poverty an edge that makes incarceration likely and social integration after prison more challenging. It is human frailty that reveals our prisons not just as crime control institutions but as social policy instruments of last resort. Responsibility for delivering a significant fraction of medical and psychiatric care for the most marginal members of society has somehow fallen on an institution designed for confinement and community separation.

Human frailty in prison is typically not just one problem but the accumulation of many. A close look at the mental and physical health of the reentry study respondents suggests the monumental challenge of treatment, of restoring them to health. The details of human frailty imprinted on individual lives points to the ethical challenges faced not just by our prisons but also by our communities, which, to be deserving of the name, must recognize the humanity of all their members.[2]

Aman was a young man, born in the Caribbean, whose lyrical speech was rich in the tangentiality and derailment that neuropsychiatrists associate with schizophrenia.[3] We first interviewed Aman in Bridgewater State Hospital, a Department of Correction facility for psychiatric patients who were serving criminal sentences or were civilly committed to state custody.

Bridgewater was a troubled place. In 1967, the State Hospital for the Criminally Insane, as it was called, was featured in the documentary film *Titicut Follies,* an exposé of the cruel and brutal conditions in U.S. mental institutions. Intermittently in the news, Bridgewater again made headlines four decades later when an inmate died while strapped to a bed after he assaulted a correctional officer.[4] During our fieldwork, the institution's use of physical restraints and solitary confinement came under scrutiny and the corrections commissioner resigned in response to criticism of the slow pace of reform. Few places face sterner challenges than facilities for psychiatric patients serving criminal sentences. They are closed worlds deprived of much of the inmate society that usually contributes to order and humane treatment in prison.

In 2012, when we first interviewed Aman, he was a few weeks away from release from Bridgewater to the secure psychiatric wards that Massachusetts maintains at a community hospital in Boston. Aman had spent his early childhood in the Caribbean. He told us that he had run races with his father as a young boy and eaten Chinese food when he made the honor roll. In the third grade, he left the Caribbean with his mother for the African American section of Dorchester in inner-city Boston. As best we could piece it together, Aman got involved in street life early, getting in fights in the housing projects of Charlestown. He told us that he was involved in gangs and was stabbed three times during his teenage years. He caught his first case, for marijuana possession, at age fourteen and did three months of juvenile probation. Gang life was a recurring theme throughout our interviews. When asked if he was married, Aman replied that he had been in a "gang marriage," but he refused to elaborate. After his release from prison, he was stopped by police for flashing gang signs. And at his transitional housing shelter, he got into a fight as part of an initiation ritual for a gang he started there.

At age sixteen, Aman was arrested again in another drug case. He returned to his Caribbean home for a year to live with his father in a deal struck with a juvenile court judge. He worked for a while in that year away but was fired over an argument with his boss. He went back to school on his return to Boston, but preferred, he told us, cutting class, getting drunk, getting high with his friends, and talking to girls. "I just like freedom," he said, "freedom for everybody." He stopped going to school in the eleventh grade. Before his arrest on a firearms charge the following year at age twenty, Aman was in the mental health system for Boston's homeless population, although he also sometimes lived with his mother.

The peak period of onset of schizophrenia in males is between the ages of fifteen and twenty-four. Rates of schizophrenia are high among Afro-Caribbeans. Childhood adversity and adolescent marijuana use are also risk factors.[5] Schizophrenia is often treated with antipsychotic drugs that help regulate brain functioning but have the side effects of drowsiness, muscle spasms, and weight gain.

After being charged for the firearms offense, Aman did time in county jails before being sent to Bridgewater pending a competency hearing. Bridgewater was also better equipped to treat his schizophrenia, and it was there, we believe, that he began treatment with antipsychotic drugs. We do not have much information about his county incarceration, but at Bridgewater Aman told us that he kept mostly to himself, talking only to staff and his social worker. While incarcerated there, he was assaulted by one inmate and gave up his canteen money to another "to slap a guy in the yard." Altogether, he was incarcerated for eighteen months—the mandatory minimum sentence for his offense.

After he left Bridgewater, we interviewed Aman in the psychiatric ward of the community hospital. He moved slowly down the corridors when we met him and spoke just above a whisper throughout the interviews. He was taking antipsychotic medication and sometimes seemed sedated. "It's supposed to keep you calm," he said about the drugs, "but I don't want to keep taking it." His mother visited him each morning during his first week at the new hospital. He told us that they would talk about his future and the importance of finishing high school, and that she would braid his hair. Over the next few months, Aman received a new diagnosis, paranoia, which required a change in medication. He got into a fight and was moved to a different floor with older patients. He also told us that he worked briefly in the hospital store in the lobby. In June, after seven months at the hospital, Aman entered transitional housing operated by the state's Department of Mental Health. From the housing shelter, he moved back into his mother's small walk-up apartment in Dorchester to live with her, her boyfriend, and his older cousin.

The final interview with Aman, our first outside of an institutional set-ting, took place at his mother's apartment. In the year after his release from Bridgewater, Aman had no significant employment and lived off public as-sistance and his mother's financial support. He had stopped taking medica-tion, but his slow and circuitous speech was much the same as it had been in the hospital. He talked to his mother each day about his plans and his progress. When we asked Aman about his biggest challenge since release from prison, he said: "Wanting progression in life, wanting things to hap-pen, to be complete, wanting overall respect as a young man . . . who is slow. Respect whoever I'm with. Want that togetherness. Stuff like that. That intimacy, that belonging, you know, like belong to each other."

And what had been most helpful to him in staying out of prison? "I don't know," he replied. "Just wanting more, wanting more out of life, wanting to see flowers blossom. I'm tired of calling them flowers, I just want to say blossom and people know what I'm talking about, or bloom and people know what it really is. And that's anybody." At 8.2 percent, the prevalence of severe mental illness—schizophrenia or bipolar disorder—in the reentry study sample was about four times the rate estimated for the general popu-lation (2.2 percent).[6] For Aman, severe mental illness was complicated by gang involvement, which appeared to have drawn him into violence. He described an adolescence filled with fighting, guns, and institutionalization. The interviews offered little perspective on the onset of schizophrenia, re-vealing only that, at some point in late adolescence, he began to exhibit the vulnerability and social detachment that accompanies mental illness. Com-ing from a family too poor to afford private treatment, he had to contend with the deeply challenged state institutions that lie at the intersection of criminal justice and mental health, sometimes slipping more to one side than the other. Policy solutions are not easy in this area where psychosis may be associated with serious violence. In his final interview, Aman talked to us about his desire for acceptance and social belonging. When we asked why he had participated in the study, he smiled. "I just want friends like yourselves to come by." Here, I think, he described rather plainly the goal of a social policy fully infused with the humanity of those it must serve.

At our first interview in prison, Eddie told us that his biggest challenge would be staying clean and sober. African American, in his midforties, he had been incarcerated for three-quarters of his adult life. Eddie was quali-fied as a master carpenter and had little trouble finding employment, but he had worked only a total of three or four years over the last twenty-five. He had used drugs since he was eleven, first trying marijuana and then alcohol and cocaine at age thirteen. Eddie's mother was an alcoholic, though she had not touched a drink in thirty years when we met her. Alcoholism and its accompanying chaos ran deep on her side of the family. Eddie's own childhood was stormy, roiled by his mother's addiction, his father's violent discipline, schoolyard fights, car accidents, drugs, and alcohol.

Personable and handsome, Eddie had served in the military and enjoyed many of the welfare benefits reserved for veterans. Immediately after prison, he stayed in a homeless shelter, but later moved into an apartment in the Boston suburbs with a Veterans Affairs housing voucher. When veterans move out of a shelter into independent housing, the benefit pays first and last month's rent as well as the security deposit. The VA shows what a more robust social policy regime might look like for single people without children. For the men in the VA shelter, veterans' benefits for housing, income support, health care, and training and education are vastly better than what they would receive as homeless civilians. Even though VA benefits often failed to reverse the years of self-destruction and incarceration common among the reentry study's older respondents with military service, they did afford these men a measure of dignity and enabled, at least for some, the struggle for redemption, if not redemption itself.

Eddie started smoking crack in the 1980s, after hearing lots of talk about the drug while he was in the service. "That's all I heard for three years in the military . . . was crack, crack, crack. And like a fool I tried it. And it does what it does. It destroyed my life." Shortly after using crack the first time, Eddie went on a bender, drinking and smoking for days at a time. Hurtling through his newfound addiction, he decided to rob one of his drug dealers. Fleeing the scene, he ran into the police, who had been called to a domestic disturbance across the street. "If that hadn't happened," he said, "who knows? I mightn't have survived that night." After being incarcerated for that first robbery, Eddie returned to prison a few more times, on each occasion at the apex of sleepless sprees of crack and alcohol.

When we talked to Eddie a week after his release, he had served five years for another robbery. He was released in midwinter during a heavy snowstorm. In Boston, a blizzard is like a long weekend. Everything gets slow and quiet for a couple of days, until the streets are cleared and life resumes. Just out of prison, and with the city in hiatus, Eddie took long walks on his own, sometimes riding the T (the subway), then getting out randomly to wander around. He was unusual among the respondents in that he reported having no close friends, either in prison or on the outside. His mother was his closest confidante, but even she had dropped out of his life for a few years, frustrated by his repeated incarcerations and struggles with addiction. He was clean that first week, he told us, but it was difficult to stay drug-free.

We met again a few weeks later, two months after his release. Eddie had found a temporary job doing food service, working thirty to forty hours each week and making $500. Although the job kept him busy and paid reasonably well, he worried that a coworker might have looked up his prison record. She often turned small talk to prison topics, hinting that she knew his secret. At two months out, Eddie had started using, going out on Friday nights at the end of the working week. He took a strict approach—leaving the shelter with just $200 in cash, "having a few drinks, doing a little coke, and calling it a night." In the past, he told us, he would go out for days on end, whereas now he was maintaining his discipline. "The truth is," he said, "I enjoy it."

Over the next few months we checked in with Eddie by phone. Winter had given way to summer, and he'd been out five months. After cold-calling dozens of building contractors in the area, he had found a steady, well-paying job as a carpenter. He was also feeling optimistic about his housing, having made a plan with a VA case manager to find an apartment in the suburbs far from the street-corner dealing of downtown Boston.

Things had taken a turn for the worse a few months later. At our six-month interview, Eddie's hands were scratched and scabbed, and he had a scrape on the side of his face. He had been in a fight. His biggest challenge now, he said, was trying to stop his "progressive use of drugs and alcohol." No longer working, he had fallen into a daily routine that revolved around his addiction. Up at eleven o'clock in the morning, he would hit the streets by four in the afternoon, then drink and smoke crack until seven the next morning. His largest expense these days was his drug habit, which was costing him hundreds of dollars a night.

Eddie was good-looking and well-spoken. In the afternoon, he would dress up in a white shirt and pressed pants before walking over to the well-heeled parts of the downtown area during happy hour. On the way, he'd steal a parking ticket off a car windshield and then approach office workers who were smoking cigarettes outside the bars. Flashing the ticket, he would explain that his car had been towed and he was $12 short. "People [would] literally throw me $20 bills all day long." It was hard to run the scam sober, so he would begin the night with a pint of whiskey to get his nerve up. "With a good pint in me, it's like I lose any sense of consciousness or awareness, or any sense of shame or embarrassment, and I'm just able to do it." He told us that the scam brought him around $800 a night. How much, we asked, did he spend on drugs? "Every penny," he said.

Eddie was determined not to go back to jail and had turned to the street scam as a safe way to make money. "I'll tell you," he said, "I'm scared to death to go back to jail. I will not steal, rob, I will not do anything illegal." The con was illegal, he quickly acknowledged, but it was not violent, and each night's string of petty frauds seemed to pose little risk of getting caught.

Although the scam may have been safe, doing drugs was not. Homeless crack users who score on the street are necessarily opportunistic. Eddie said that he would get high "all over the city. Bathrooms, restrooms . . . I'll go into a restaurant, nice restaurant, use the bathroom. Smoke. Then leave. Alleyways, doorways, just whatever. You just would never notice, you'd never really think what I was up to." "Around here?" I asked. "Right in the downtown area. There's a couple of people that have places, but then you have to split everything with them. . . . They're very lively [places], very, um, unpredictable."

As Eddie described it to us, the world of crack users was secretive and violent:

> It's definitely insanity, it's definitely insanity, it's just, it's just a bunch of real slime-ball people, man, and I'm definitely setting myself up for some type of incident . . . just being around a lot of violence. Not being involved in it, but seeing a lot of fights, seeing a lot of people getting ripped off. You know, just being there and getting high in the middle of all that, it's not a good scene.

Eddie had been in a fight the night before, sucker-punched at three in the morning by another user who tried to steal his drugs. At the end of these nights, fighting or not, he said that he feels beat up and his muscles ache.

Eddie had been stopped three or four times by police while he was on his slow-motion bender, but had not been arrested. Dealers would keep the crack sealed in plastic in their mouths. After the purchase, the crack would be taken from the dealer's mouth and immediately concealed in the buyer's mouth. If stopped by police, the evidence would be swallowed.

The shelter for homeless veterans had a curfew, but Eddie had worked out a plan to stay out all night. Residents could sign out in the evenings if they were working. Employment was monitored and managed by a caseworker who received the worksheets the veterans signed in the logbooks. By signing a worksheet in the afternoon, Eddie could break curfew that night. When he returned the following morning, he would simply remove the sheet before the logbook was sent over to the caseworker. Shelter residents were also required to undergo periodic drug tests, but these were easy to beat too. Cocaine stays in your system for three days, Eddie explained. Ahead of a doctor's appointment or job interview, you could lay off for a few days and then test clean.

During this time, Eddie shrank from the supportive relationships in his life. He was talking to his mother less and less. She worried that he was getting in trouble when he went missing for days at a time. He continued meeting with a therapist, but their sessions focused on his depression and post-traumatic stress, pointedly neglecting his spiraling drug use.

Six months after getting out of prison, Eddie finally left the shelter and moved into his own place. Our final interview was conducted in his small tidy apartment on the outskirts of Boston. At that point, things were going well, and moving out of the city had provided welcome separation from the drug scene of downtown. Several months later, however, Eddie was arrested again and returned to prison.

Eddie's addiction was sustained by a range of deceptions—from lying to counselors and family to manipulating paperwork, engaging in street cons, and destroying drug evidence when confronted by police. The largest of these deceptions crossed the line into illegality. Although the penal framework does not cause the deceits that often accompany addiction, it does little to mitigate them. A criminal record is hidden from coworkers or a drug test is manipulated. In the grip of addiction, the fear of reincarceration produces, not sobriety, but nonviolent street scams instead of robberies.

Over Eddie's long career as a crack addict, drug laws got tougher and the Massachusetts imprisonment rate doubled. As generous as the VA benefits were, the public assistance he received was dwarfed by the hundreds of thousands of dollars spent on his incarceration.[7] Eddie was undeterred by America's massive experiment in punitive drug policy. He enjoyed smoking crack and drinking, but at some point these habits would swallow him up. There was little deterrence in America's war on drugs, but long prison sentences did provide Eddie with the chance to get clean, often for years at a time. Here again, we see the prison forced into a role for which it is ill suited. In the absence of policies aimed at incorrigible addiction, the poorest addicts are institutionalized and sobriety is imperfectly forced on them, with little preparation for prison release.

Over half of the reentry sample (54 percent) reported a history of problems with drugs or alcohol. This figure is in line with national statistics that show both the great prevalence of addiction in prison and a high rate of intoxication while committing crime.[8] Of the thirty respondents over age forty-five, twenty-three had a history of drug problems. Like Eddie, respondents with drug problems had violent and chaotic childhoods. These men and women were much more likely to have grown up amid alcoholism and drug abuse and to have been exposed to family violence, mental illness, and sexual abuse. Many reflected on wasted lives and the pain and disappointment they had brought to their families. Many, like Eddie, were socially isolated, with few if any friends anchored in the mainstream of social life. Family bonds were often frayed by a lifetime of addiction, but many of their parents to whom we spoke revealed a weary mix of love and resignation. When we asked Eddie's mother why she had agreed to an interview, she told us, "Well, I just thought that there may be something that I could say today that may be of help as far as Eddie goes or maybe someone else. . . . These guys don't know where to turn for help."

The anxiety attacks that AJ suffered after prison had a long history. Anxiety, an explosive temper, and learning problems all started when he was young. AJ had blackouts as a child that were never properly explained. "It's been going on since he was eight years old. He was really out of control as a kid," said his sister Kate.

"They thought I was freakin' nuts. They put me on medication and shit. I ain't need it. I was seeing doctors," explained AJ. He was diagnosed with attention deficit disorder and a learning disability. Kate thought that AJ had been diagnosed with bipolar disorder, but he said that diagnosis was wrong. "I don't know why they told me I had it because I never did," he said.

"'Cause you had your highs and your lows," replied Kate.

"Back then," AJ said, "they just frigging wanted to stick me on so much frigging medication that I stopped taking it. Just made me slow. Frigging like a zombie, so I stopped taking it."

AJ's temper added frenzy to a stormy family home. AJ's father was hotheaded, and once AJ found him in the kitchen kicking Kate as she lay on the ground. AJ grabbed him and threw him across the room, allowing Kate to escape. That was the first time she ran away from home. Kate was AJ's closest sibling, but even she wore one of AJ's scars on her forehead, a permanent mark from the door AJ slammed on her, knocking her unconscious, when they were both kids.

Growing up in the largely white towns just north of the Charles River, AJ first got in serious trouble when he was twelve. He tried to stab a bus driver on the way to school and spent time in juvenile detention at the Department of Youth Services (DYS). His mother had such difficulty controlling AJ that she had previously handed him over to the child welfare system. He was in and out of DYS throughout his teenage years and received most of his schooling while institutionalized. When out in the community, he attended school but was expelled several times. He dropped out in the eighth grade and was one of the few white respondents to neither finish high school nor earn a GED. He started smoking marijuana and drinking around the age of twelve or thirteen. "I remember we used to get the forties [forty-ounce bottles of malt liquor]. Getting frigging drunk out of our asses and frigging start fights and all kinds of stuff," he said. By the time he was fourteen, AJ was running with a street gang in East Cambridge. At sixteen, he was arrested for a stabbing and held in detention for a year, then tried as an adult when he turned seventeen.

AJ has a slim build and wears glasses on his boyish face. Going into adult incarceration at age seventeen, he told us, he looked just fourteen.

> I ain't gonna lie, I think I was scared. . . . I knew it's a bit different in DYS, but then when I got there it's like—so I'm from Cambridge, East Cambridge, so it was a lot of older dudes from East Cambridge and everybody sits together. . . . But I remember when I was seventeen, I went in there. Couple days later, they came and grab me up, 'cause they thought I wasn't seventeen, 'cause I looked so young at the time. . . . So they had to put me in the infirmary, lock me up, figure out [what was] really my birthday, and I was really seventeen.

We asked AJ if he was ever given a hard time because he looked so young. "No, I got a hard time tryin' to buy cigarettes. Damn, I was old enough to freakin' be locked up in an adult jail, but I wasn't old enough to buy cigarettes."

AJ told us that he could explode into violence. His temper had flared in his teenage years and as an adult. It had happened on the street and in prison. In prison, he had spent long periods in solitary confinement for fighting. In maximum security, on his third conviction, AJ beat an inmate so seriously that he was sent to hospital.

In spite of all the trouble caused by his volatility, AJ believed that his mental health was further harmed by incarceration. He spoke to us about drinking and fighting in prison and enduring long periods of solitary confinement. Kate told us that when she visited, AJ was often drunk on home brew, a fermented mix of juice, fruit, and sugar. "He's like McGyver," she said. "He can make anything."

On one visit Kate brought news that their father was in the hospital. He had been in an accident and would not survive. AJ was drunk when Kate told him in the visiting room. The news did not sink in until he returned to his cell. "I didn't want to lock in. I ain't lock in." At that time, he was in a disciplinary unit on twenty-three-hour lockdown. He began to get distressed. "I started to freak out," he said. A nurse allowed him to call the family. He was later allowed to visit his father in the hospital. Wearing a gray prison tunic, shackled at the waist and ankles, he saw his father, unconscious, on life support. The officer who escorted him stood back from the bed to let AJ say good-bye.

When we first met AJ in prison, he was finishing a two-year sentence and had spent a long time in solitary confinement. "This last bid broke me," he said. Kate visited him every other Saturday. She told us that he would sometimes black out on these visits, and several men would be needed to restrain him. Because of AJ's severe anxiety after release from prison, enrolling in Medicaid in order to get health care became critical, but help was slow in coming. About seven weeks out of prison, at one of our phone check-ins, AJ shared some good news: "Did I tell you? I'm on my meds now. I got a doctor. I can go out and be around people."

In fact, AJ calmed his anxiety with a mixture of medications and marijuana. He smoked marijuana several times a day and was an enthusiastic proponent of the drug's healing properties. Besides Kate, AJ spent time with Dan, a close friend from his old neighborhood. Dan gave AJ a little construction work when he first got out, and AJ could get high with his friend on the job. As they worked on a deck or a staircase, AJ would announce, "It's Marley time," and work would continue under a cloud of marijuana. If AJ had to confront crowds on the train or go into town, he would rely on the additional fortification of his medication.

AJ's drug use—legal and illegal—helped him manage a mental health problem aggravated by a long history of incarceration. The use of drugs to cope with mental illness was common across the reentry sample. One indication is given by the close correlation in the survey data between mental illness and drug addiction. Of the 54 respondents who reported a mental health diagnosis, 40 also reported a history of heavy drug or alcohol use. AJ connected his anxiety to his experience of incarceration, and to his most recent period of solitary confinement in particular. We heard similar reports from respondents with diagnoses of anxiety or post-traumatic stress. Altogether, 25 out of 122 respondents said that they had been diagnosed with PTSD, anxiety, or both. Of those with PTSD or anxiety, 79 percent said that they found prison stressful, compared to 47 percent of those with neither anxiety nor PTSD. Although these data cannot distinguish cause and effect, individual cases and the sample as a whole reveal the close connections between anxiety, post-traumatic stress, drug use, and a stressful experience of incarceration.

Carla had a turbulent life. She had wrestled with violence, addiction, mental illness, and disability throughout her life, and in the year after her release from prison she suffered from a number of debilitating physical problems. Her life was not dominated by any one particular challenge, but by the confluence of many.

Carla grew up with seven siblings in a working-class family. Her father was a security guard and her mother cleaned houses. She had a quick temper as a child and got into fights at school and arguments at home with her mother. She was suspended a few times for fighting. "I even beat up the boys," she told us. Carla's mother was a Cape Verdean immigrant and a strict disciplinarian who readily used physical punishment to try to keep her daughter in line. With friction in her childhood home and trouble at school, Carla was a runaway in her teenage years. She first appeared in a juvenile court at age fourteen, charged with possession and assault and battery. Her sister told us that Carla got in a lot of trouble around that time, committing robberies and using drugs. Though Carla expressed her aggravation, her mother was clearly the most significant source of support in her life. She would later take custody of Carla's three children from birth and provide her with a place to stay after prison.

We asked Carla if drug or alcohol addiction had ever been a problem for her. "All the time," she replied. She smoked marijuana and drank in high school, but did not try heroin until her twenties. She described her introduction to the drug: "I was stressed out, depressed. I don't know. Me and my boyfriend broke up, and my cousin introduced me into it. I was in pain, and I didn't want to feel it, and she said try this, and I did, and the pain went away. So every time I had problems, I do it, and it got to where I couldn't deal with my problems, I had to get high."

Carla's unsettled and often violent life continued with her heroin addiction. In the six months before her last incarceration, she was using heroin and cocaine daily, changing addresses frequently, and rooming with her "drug friends." During this time, she was making money by "hustling, selling drugs, and doing dates." A drug charge ultimately sent Carla to MCI Framingham, the Massachusetts women's prison, which she had been to many times.

Many of the problems Carla was having on the outside followed her into Framingham. She often witnessed drug use and got into fights with others incarcerated there. One year out of prison, Carla told us about her last fight. It was "in jail, right before I got out. A girl ran her mouth and I choked her." When we asked her why she stopped fighting, she said that she was "just tired of it," adding, "I'm afraid I'm going to hurt somebody. I get so angry and I black out. I can't control my anger sometimes."

In prison, Carla received treatment for a variety of health problems. She saw a doctor and a dentist, received counseling, and also spent time in a detox program. Hepatitis C, arthritis in her hands, back pain (the result of an assault), and a heart condition were all monitored or medicated while she was in prison. Her biggest test, she told us just before her release, was staying clean and sober. If she could do that, she said, "everything else falls into place."

Over the course of the year after her release from Framingham, Carla reported to us that she did remain largely drug-free. Her first two months after incarceration seemed the brightest. She was attending an addiction recovery program and taking a course on religion at the University of Massachusetts and a GED class. She spoke enthusiastically about her women's literature reading list and seemed to embrace this project in self-improvement in the months immediately after incarceration. Two months after release, Carla told us that she got a "client of the week" award in her recovery program: "Always being on time. No dirty urines. Participates in class. All that. I got a certificate." We also spoke about the possibility of continuing classes after she got her GED. Ultimately, though, she would struggle with the math section of the exam.

As the year went on a variety of physical and mental health problems came to dominate her reentry. At each interview, we asked respondents about their biggest challenges. A week after prison release, Carla responded by talking about staying away from old associates, getting her government benefits, and dealing with her kids. For the rest of her first year out, however, Carla's biggest problems were related to her health and physical disability. Many of the physical problems she first described to us while still in prison appeared to worsen over the course of the year. Her hands became swollen and painful, despite treatment with arthritis medication. Her back pain limited her mobility, and she worried that treatment with painkillers might trigger a relapse to heroin use. Indeed, she told us, she failed one drug test for probation after taking a pain pill from a friend that turned out to be morphine. A year after getting out of prison, Carla was wearing a back brace and moved gingerly around her house. Her disability had prevented her from working, and she was now taking seven different medications.

Chronic pain had dulled her mood, and she was also dealing with diagnoses of depression and bipolar disorder. We had often seen her moods swing from bright and optimistic to tearful and regretful. At least some of this volatility appeared to run in the family. Her sister told us that there was a family history of depression and that other family members had struggled with explosive moods, alcoholism, and heroin use.

A year out from prison, Carla had succeeded in her main goal of staying clean. Her sister said that she had made real changes in her life. Carla's relationship with her mother was argumentative but less volatile. Her GED courses also impressed her sister; they were Carla's only experience with formal education that she could remember. In spite of these successes, things had not fallen into place as Carla had hoped. Physical disability—aggravated in part by decades of heroin use and the life that it produces for a poor and single woman—had worn down Carla's enthusiasm for the project of reentry and self-improvement. She had not worked at all during the year after prison, and at age forty-three, she was significantly supported by her mother, who was also supporting two of her three children.

The correlated adversity of mental illness, drug use, and disability characterized the reentry study sample as a whole. Respondents with a history of addiction and mental illness reported worse physical health, both in prison and over the year after release. Thirty-eight out of forty-two cases of back pain, arthritis, or physical disability were found among respondents with addiction or mental health problems. We found only four cases of chronic pain or disability among those with no mental illness or addiction.

Carla's life history illustrates the great difficulty in separating cause and effect. Heroin seemed to offer some relief from her explosive temper and wide mood swings. Heroin addiction and her ready use of violence, however, exposed her and others to physical risks that contributed to her back problems and hampered her ability to work and move around freely. The limiting effects of physical disability and its relationship to self-destructive drug use and mental illness challenge how we think about the willpower and capacity of people who go to prison. Much of the agency—the will to change—that even our most humane rehabilitative programs ask of people in prison is compromised by precisely the physical and mental difficulties that placed them at risk of incarceration in the first place. The people we ask to make the largest changes in their lives often have the least capacity to do so. This is a profound paradox for even the most progressive visions of imprisonment and correctional policy.

People who go to prison are much more likely to have problems with addiction, mental illness, and physical disability than the general population. Among the reentry study sample, two-thirds had a history of mental illness or addiction, and one-third reported serious back pain, arthritis, or some other disability. These vulnerabilities of mind and body were co-occurring. Addicts are often enduring and attempting to relieve anxiety, post-traumatic stress, or some other mental illness. Drugs and alcohol can provide a refuge from chronic pain. Physical disability is wearing, feeding depression and other emotional problems. Most human frailty is also persistent, sustained over the life course, and rooted in family history.

Poverty researchers often point to the poor schooling and bad work histories of disadvantaged men and women at high risk of incarceration, but their disadvantage often runs much deeper than school failure and unemployment. In many cases, it has a physical reality that limits a person's capacity to think clearly, without pain, and to bring energy to daily affairs. Human frailty is marginalizing, even within marginal communities. Addicts find themselves in the company of other addicts as they buy and use drugs. Those with physical and mental health problems spend disproportionate amounts of time in community health clinics and other institutional settings for low-income people.

The bodily reality of mental illness, addiction, and physical disability is not just a risk factor for crime and incarceration, but also a manifestation of failures of support. Only a fraction of those with mental and physical problems wind up going to prison. Those who do are distinguished by a lack of family assistance and failures of institutional help. In many cases, schools had few tools to deal with serious behavioral or learning problems besides suspension and expulsion. The slide into heroin or crack addiction was noticed by no institution other than the criminal justice system. Chronic pain went untreated for years, and marijuana or heroin provided relief in the absence of medical treatment. Moreover, the incarcerated, as a mostly male population without custody of children, can easily slip through a safety net that focuses limited resources on poor unmarried mothers and their children.

In this context, the prison steps in where the welfare state has failed. The illegal and sometimes violent consequences of untreated addiction and mental illness lead to arrests and incarceration. While incarcerated, some respondents stayed sober and received medical and mental health care. For others, however, prison was stressful and traumatic. AJ, Carla, and Aman all got into fights in prison, and AJ and Carla spent time in solitary confinement. These two different experiences of incarceration—the therapeutic and the chaotically punitive—expose a contradiction in the institution. Prison brings together a large group of frequently very troubled people for the purpose of penal confinement. Yet the institution retains the programs and medical services of the rehabilitative project. The dual functions of punishment and rehabilitation unevenly shape the experience of those who are incarcerated.

The liberal vision of correctional policy emphasizes rehabilitation. Programs in prison might develop skills in social interaction, improve education, and promote sobriety. Reentry programs in the community might provide transitional assistance for housing and employment. Some of these programs have been positively evaluated for their success in reducing rearrest rates or, more rarely, increasing employment. Those who staff these programs often say that interventions are effective only when clients really want to change. Scholars also find successful returns from incarceration among people who understand themselves to be deliberately engaged in a project of life transformation.[9]

Human frailty creates two kinds of challenges for the project of rehabilitation. A desire to change one's life is only imperfectly distributed across the population. Self-destructive motivation and behavior are closely tied to the problem of serious addiction and some kinds of mental illness. Yet public policy should not neglect those who are stubbornly inclined to harm themselves and, as a result, often pose a threat to others. Second, the rehabilitative project often assumes a level of agency and willpower that may be unrealistic, not because people are unwilling, but because they lack the physical and mental capacity to effectively intervene in their own lives. For these people, rehabilitative programs often provide too little too late. Because motivation and human capacity for change can be deeply compromised by physical and mental illness, the positive effects of rehabilitative programs are often small.

The great challenge for public policy is to preserve dignity in the face of human frailty. Dignity rests on our shared capacity for virtue. Affirming people's dignity recognizes that they can be creative and loving in spite of great challenges. When Aman, amid all the distortions of schizophrenia, just wants friends to come by, or Carla, slowly crippled by arthritis, revels in her writing class, they are something much more than their frailty. Their dignity is not extinguished even in the face of great adversity.

What is the significance of dignity for public policy? For the most fundamentally disadvantaged—those whose problems are inscribed on their bodies and minds—stable and independent housing, employment, and a functional family life may be out of reach. We can nevertheless respect human dignity by enabling the effort to struggle for it. We can provide help— with education, sobriety, anger management, parenting, wellness, and so on—even when the outcome is uncertain. Among those who are greatly disadvantaged, the struggle for dignity itself is intrinsically meaningful, both for them as they envision a better future for themselves and for their community, which will have done something more than abandon the poorest among them.

Dignity is also promoted when we provide more and better health care for the many incarcerated people with physical and mental problems. There are excellent programs for managing chronic pain, disease, and addiction for patients who move in and out of institutional settings, who are poor, or who otherwise struggle to comply with treatment. While there are good programs, there are fewer good policies. There is too little public commitment to making up the shortfall in treatment services, ensuring continuity of care from prison to community, and sustaining support in the face of relapse. A policy of providing quality care for men and women who go to prison does not just improve well-being. It also expands individuals' capabilities in a system that—even in its most progressive incarnation—demands great feats of human agency.

CHAPTER 5

Lifetimes of Violence

Violence has followed incarcerated men and women over a lifetime. The people we interviewed came from homes that were frantic and unsafe. They were often abused and witnessed abuse as children and they got in fights in adolescence. As adults—sometimes sick with addiction or mental illness—they committed assaults and robberies. Prison was violent too. Besides the coercion of penal confinement, the climate of incarceration could be edgy, tense with the chance of brutality.

The Boston Reentry Study respondents described a violence that grew out of contexts of poverty. Social life in the low-income neighborhoods and homes in which they lived was often chaotic and conducive to victimization. Poverty eroded the steady influence of parents and neighbors who tried to control disorderly behavior. In places that were unpredictable and short on adult supervision, violence could be positively valued as a source of identity or a useful way of getting things done.

Where conditions of poverty give rise to violence, a person's role in that violence is as much a product of the situation as of individual disposition. People living under these conditions are not neatly divided between victims and offenders. Instead, at different times and in different venues, people come to play the parts of victim, offender, participant, and witness.

The social facts of violence sit uneasily with the individualized culpability decided by the criminal justice system. The violence addressed by the courts and prisons is largely stripped of social context and biography. Tough-on-crime political talk is even more disconnected from reality. Life histories rooted in poverty and rich in experiences of victimization as well as offending defy the moral reckoning that splits the world into victims and perpetrators.[1] Mass incarceration embodies a simplistic choice in a world choked with moral complexity.

Supporters of tough punishment may be morally simplistic, but liberal academic writing can also be naive. Commentary on mass incarceration often presents a sanitized picture that erases the violence in the lives of people who go to prison. Some writers who focus on racial and class disparities in incarceration say little about the violence that is concentrated in the communities with the highest rates of incarceration.[2] Violence, however, is a dominating reality in environments of poverty and racial inequality. Building peace and nonviolence in both public policy and community life is one of the most urgent moral challenges presented by mass incarceration.

Scholars have widely observed the violence of poor places and described how poverty influences social environments in a way that makes violence more likely. Psychologists studying human development have observed that poor households are often chaotic, placing children at risk. Sociologists who focus on poor neighborhoods have found that they often lack the informal social controls that curb crime and delinquency. And anthropologists have found that cultures of violence emerge under conditions of poverty. I consider each of these research areas in turn.

Psychologists have linked violence to poverty by studying child maltreatment in the chaos of poor homes. Chaos is characterized by high levels of ambient stimulation, a low level of routine, and unpredictability in daily activities. Gary Evans and his colleagues pointed to the chaotic life of poor children in statistics on crowding at home and school, residential and school relocation, and maternal partner change.[3] Beyond these widely measured indicators, poor homes tend to be noisier and to have less regular mealtimes and bedtimes for children. Evans concluded that chaos is part of the "environment of child poverty."[4] Chaos puts family relationships under stress and frustrates the consistent supervision of children. Producing stress and unpredictability, chaos interferes with warm interactions between parents and children and among siblings. Harsh and impatient family relationships become more likely.

Sometimes the line from economic hardship to chaos is quite direct. In the absence of steady work, daily life for adults can appear to unfold more by accident than by design. Besides financial insecurity, poverty can also bring addiction and mental illness that goes untreated without adequate health care. Housing insecurity, complex family relationships, and high incarceration rates all add to the circulation of adults and children through poor homes.

Chaos produces violence by inviting victimization. Agents of violence—stressed, impaired, or unrelated adults—are abundant in chaotic homes and neighborhoods. The most vulnerable—often women and children—face great uncertainty and cannot plan for their safety or easily hide from trouble. The stress of chaotic homes, neighborhoods, and schools is associated with child maltreatment and sexual and physical abuse.[5]

While psychologists have examined the home, sociologists focused on violence in poor neighborhoods. Robert Sampson and William Julius Wilson traced the concentration of violent crime in urban areas to an unemployment crisis that deepened in inner-city neighborhoods from the 1960s through the 1980s. Black men with no more than a high school education faced mounting joblessness as manufacturing industries fled from American cities. Such men could no longer support families, and the number of single-mother households increased. With fathers in poor neighborhoods now only loosely tied to their children's households, families were less able to play a strong role in supervising adolescent boys.[6] Traditionally, dense social networks of residents and organizations—businesses, churches, community groups—had also helped regularize and monitor urban neighborhoods. In African American communities where poverty was concentrated, however, these networks had been weakened.

Out of the structural conditions of poverty, Sampson and Wilson also argued that a culture emerged in which "youngsters are more likely to see violence as a way of life in inner-city ghetto neighborhoods."[7] Within cities, contiguous clumps of poor and high-crime neighborhoods where black residents lived not only had to deal with their own internal dynamics but were at additional risk because of violence in adjacent communities. The sociological research concludes that the spatial concentration of unemployment, family disruption, and other social problems fuels violent crime in poor urban areas.[8]

Poverty corrodes the social bonds and routines that help keep neighborhoods safe. Low-income families headed by single mothers are often too shorthanded to provide oversight of adolescent boys needed to curb truancy and delinquency.[9] Thus, murder and robbery rates among youth have been found to be highest in areas with the highest rates of single-parenthood.[10] In poor neighborhoods, sparse webs of street-level networks and organizations fail to head off violent conflict or to assist when trouble occurs. In the absence of poverty, families and neighborhoods are better equipped to informally monitor and limit violence. Without such informal supervision, coercive efforts at social control play a larger role. Schools, police, and prisons try to stem violence in poor communities using the tools of expulsion, arrest, and incarceration. When these formal social control agencies kick into gear, they bring their own kind of violence to the effort to maintain order.

Anthropologists have also linked poverty to violence and given us vivid portrayals of danger in situations of extreme hardship. Some anthropologists have used the term "structural violence" to describe the link between poverty and human suffering.[11] Work in this tradition considered physical and other harms that extend beyond the usual instances of crime. Documenting the everyday brutality of poverty in rural Brazil, for example, Nancy Scheper-Hughes described how food is reserved for adults and withheld from children. Parents interpret persistent hunger in their infants as illness, a perception that transforms hunger from a matter of inadequate nutrition into a problem for magic or modern medicine. Philippe Bourgois and Jeff Schonberg likened an encampment of Bay Area heroin addicts to a "gray zone," "an ethical wasteland" in which "survival imperatives overcome human decency." Beatings, stabbings, and the gruesome injuries of heroin use all add to the toll of homelessness and addiction. Writing about the poor urban residents of Buenos Aires, Javier Auyero, Agustin Burbano de Lara, and Maria Fernanda Berti found that violence has an instrumental quality, whether used to discipline children or to defend oneself and one's property.[12] In all these field settings, the stresses of hunger, addiction, and material insecurity make violence readily imaginable. Once imagined, thoughts of violence are a wellspring for action.

Anthropologists have found that in environments of poverty, violence can be positively valued. The positive valuation of violence takes different forms in different settings. Proficiency with violence may signal status in the pecking order of a street gang, masculinity among adolescent boys, or, more instrumentally, competence in handling the exigencies of daily life. There is no single culture of violence that operates across poor contexts, but under conditions of material hardship, violence can become recognized as a practical way of solving problems and overcoming obstacles.

Several implications follow from the observation that poverty creates situations in which violence is likely to occur. First, conditions of material disadvantage contribute not just to street crime but also to family violence, child neglect, and fighting among youth. Instead of focusing just on the statistics of murder and robbery, for example, research connecting poverty to violence should examine different forms of violence over the life cycle and across institutional domains. Another implication is that poverty produces myriad forms of violence, not chiefly through its influence on individual motivation, but in how it structures social interaction. If poverty is a violent context, poor people will see a great deal of violence in their lives and play a range of roles—as victim, offender, or witness. Instead of focusing just on offending, we should study all the roles that make up a violent episode. Last, poverty produces violence in a variety of venues. Researchers focus on local neighborhoods and family homes, but as the reentry study shows, institutional settings—schools for children, prisons for adults—are important sites of everyday violence in contexts of poverty.

Violence was a common theme in the reentry study interviews. Quantitatively assessed, its prevalence was clear. In childhood, 40 percent of the sample had witnessed someone being killed, nearly half were beaten by their parents, one-third grew up with some other kind of family violence, and 16 percent reported being sexually abused. Nine out of ten of the people we interviewed got in fights throughout adolescence. Half the sample said that they were seriously injured while growing up. Violence continued into adulthood. Three-quarters of our respondents said that they witnessed assaults in prison. In the year after leaving prison, half the sample had witnessed an assault, one-quarter said that they had attacked or threatened someone, and another one-quarter had been attacked or threatened themselves.

To better understand the contexts in which violence occurs, we constructed life histories of the respondents. Producing detailed biographies for the respondents required a complete set of interviews and audiotapes, an interview with a family member, and an official criminal record. We collected complete data and created life histories for 40 of the 122 respondents. For each one, we divided their life into three broad periods: childhood (from birth to age twelve), adolescence (ages thirteen to eighteen), and adulthood (over eighteen years). We then coded the life histories, noting episodes of violence and other important events with family, at school, at work, and so on. Coding life histories in this way, we found that the respondents spoke most frequently about events relating to their family relationships, and then about events in their lives relating to the criminal justice system. Violence was the third most common topic.

When describing their early childhood, respondents often talked about family relationships and violence. They described the supportive adults in their lives, but also the domestic violence they saw and were drawn into. The theme of violence became more prominent in their talk about adolescence, which also included accounts of drug and alcohol use and time spent with peers. Family was again an important topic when the respondents talked about their adulthood, when family life extended to relationships with partners and children. The respondents' accounts of adulthood were also dominated by descriptions of arrest and incarceration, a new topic that reflected passage through the life course.[13]

To take stock of violence in the lives of people who have been incarcerated, we first need a definition. By violence, I mean the application of aggressive physical force. A violent event instills fear or inflicts bodily injury. Violence, in this definition, need not be intentional or unlawful—people can be seriously injured in accidents, an important category of violence. The violence revealed in the interviews, however, usually had a social quality, encompassing how people interacted with each other. We coded seven types of violence discussed in the interviews: suicides, accidents, sexual abuse, domestic violence, murders, assaults, and fighting.[14] In this scheme, fighting is distinguished from assault, which is defined as a predatory type of violence perpetrated by an offender on a weak or unprepared victim. A fight, often growing out of an escalating conflict, is a mutual exchange among participants who are prepared for combat.

People can be connected to violence in a variety of ways. Research mostly examines offenders and, less commonly, victims, but these roles are not always clear-cut. In cases of retaliation or fighting, it is more descriptively accurate to identify participants in violence rather than victims or offenders. In addition to active involvement, people also witness violence, which sometimes instills fear and inflicts psychological trauma.[15] For each violent situation described by our respondents, we coded one of four roles: offender, victim, participant, or witness.

We identified a total of 291 violent situations from the 40 life histories. Breaking down the characteristics of each situation reveals clear patterns that evolve over the life course. In the violent situations they experienced in early childhood (before age 13), respondents were most often victims or witnesses. Childhood violence usually unfolded in the family home, owing to high rates of domestic abuse. (Twenty-two of 40 respondents reported at least one childhood incident of family violence.) Respondents also talked about fighting in early childhood, so they were participants in violence as well as victims and witnesses from an early age. Because family violence and fighting were so common, nearly 80 percent of all reported childhood violence happened in the neighborhood or in the home.

The relationship of the respondents to violence changed in adolescence. They were increasingly involved in fights and assaults as teenagers. Their roles in violence evolved from being witnesses and victims to being participants and offenders. With the predominance of fighting and assaults in adolescence, the school and the neighborhood were the most common sites of adolescent violence.

The pattern of violence reported in adulthood is qualitatively different from that reported in childhood and adolescence. When the respondents talked about violence in adulthood, they mentioned their own offending about 40 percent of the time, more frequently than in earlier life stages. In about one-quarter of all violent situations they reported in adulthood, they had been witnesses; over half involved an assault, and fighting was less common. Strikingly, 16 percent of all reported incidents in adulthood were murders. Sites of violence also changed with adulthood: neighborhood violence remained common, but assaults in prison and in other locations (mostly in neighboring states and cities) also became more frequent.

Despite variation over the life course, the respondents had remained close to serious violence throughout their lives. Data on violent death provide one indication. Twenty-four of the forty life-history respondents reported the violent death of a close friend or family member at some point in their lives. The respondents had also sustained many serious injuries. One respondent told us that he fell from a tier in prison. Another was unable to complete the study because a shooting had left him comatose in a hospital. Altogether, ten of the forty reported that they had been shot or stabbed.

How is poverty linked to the child abuse, fighting, assaults, and murders reported by the respondents? Their life histories suggest that chaos at home and in the local neighborhood, deficits of informal social control, and the cultural context all make poor social contexts likely settings for violence.

Chaos. Patrick was born in the early 1980s and for the first years of his life lived in the Old Colony Housing Projects, one of a cluster of public housing complexes in South Boston. In the early 1980s, "Southie," a stronghold of Boston's Irish American working class, remained one of the few neighborhoods of concentrated white poverty in urban America. Patrick's mother was a heroin addict and gave up custody of her son to her parents when he was five. She died of AIDS when Patrick was seventeen. Patrick's father had left his mother when Patrick was two, but twenty years later his father would reenter his life by helping him find a union job in the construction industry.

Patrick's grandparents were reluctant guardians. His grandmother had raised a family of eight children in the small wooden house on J Street, a few blocks from Old Colony, that was to become his childhood home. His grandfather had a seventh-grade education and for many years struggled to find steady work because of his own criminal history. (He later got a city job after his record was sealed.)

Thirteen people lived in Patrick's house when he was growing up. Much of the energy at home was provided by his uncles, a brawling pair of young men who used drugs and alcohol heavily. "My uncles and my mother were all heroin addicts," he said. "It was like being in the Manson family." One of the uncles, said Patrick, "was extremely tough with his hands. I mean, he enjoyed hurting people. Cutting off ears and stabbings and shootings." The house was the venue for violence, sexual abuse, addiction, and a sprawling kind of family life that Patrick described as "emotionally cold" and "insane." And yet, he added, "it was normal to me." Reflecting on the childhood home, Patrick's aunt recalled, "It was just a crazy house, between my brothers coming in either beat up or having some horrible car accident . . . or someone falling asleep with a cigarette and a mattress going up on fire. It was a very traumatic house to live in."

Patrick's mother was not allowed in the house on J Street. We know that she stayed in contact with her son, however, through his descriptions of his beatings at the hands of his mother's boyfriends from age five through his teenage years.

Things were also chaotic on the street. When Patrick was six, a man tried to grab him, and one of his uncles stabbed the offender in retaliation. At age eight, Patrick saw a neighborhood kid get shot in the head in the housing projects. At age ten, he and his uncle stole a car from the neighboring town of Brookline and drove it triumphantly around the Southie streets. The following year he started drinking and smoking marijuana, and at age thirteen he and his friends invaded and robbed the home of a local drug dealer, a neighborhood boy of fifteen. Patrick was sixteen when he used heroin for the first time, encouraged by a girl who lived nearby. With a spate of suicides in the South Boston schools that year, he tried to hang himself, but was cut down by a woman who discovered the attempt. He dropped out of school shortly afterward. In his aunt's account, Patrick was expelled as a result of the suicide attempt because the school wanted to avoid the expense of mandatory counseling.

Patrick's early life illustrates much of the chaos associated with extreme hardship. Hardship spawns the confluence of multiple disadvantages—in this case, untreated drug addiction, housing insecurity, and unreliable parenting. Under these conditions, life is regularly disrupted by catastrophes small and large and hums with the chronic disturbances of noise and overcrowding.

Institutionalization was also a chaotic force in Patrick's life. "You know, I grew up, my entire life, I've been in and out of institutions, between mental hospitals, DYS [juvenile incarceration], lockups, county jail, state prison, you know Bridgewater [the state psychiatric hospital]. The whole nine yards. I've been to a lot of these places."

Patrick moved into a sober house after he got out of prison, but was asked to leave after missing a curfew. He had been out late one night with his "fucking idiot uncle overdosing on him." Patrick was also high that night, his aunt told us. One of his brothers was using heroin around this time, and Patrick struggled to stay sober over the next few months. He moved in with his aunt for a while, then later lived with his brothers and his father. Reflecting on his addiction, he said, "I really feel totally defeated from this disease. Totally broken as a person."

A few months later, Patrick was at a party with his girlfriend, his stepson, and her family. In Patrick's account, his girlfriend's uncle was drunk and confronted Patrick, calling him a "fucking junkie." His girlfriend punched her uncle in the face and "split his eyes wide open." Patrick fumed. Called a junkie in front of his young stepson, he left the house in a rage. The uncle had left ahead of him, and Patrick confronted him on the street:

> I walked up, and I had a couple words with him, and I ended up doing a fistfight with him. I broke three of his teeth out, took three of his teeth out, I fuckin' broke them. I didn't appreciate him calling me a junkie in front of my son, but when I asked him, "What did you say? Did you just say that?" and he said, "Yeah, what are you gonna do about it?" Then he tried to like

grab me, and I just instinctively started throwing punches and I landed all. Yeah, it was bad. I smashed his face, and my son saw it, and that's what bothered me the most, when he saw it. He was with [his mother], and he started screaming, "Daddy is fighting," and stuff like that. It was fuckin' bad.

His stepson's distress over the fight echoed Patrick's own trauma as a young boy facing family violence.

The childhood homes of nearly all those we interviewed were unstable and often chaotic, regardless of whether they reported violence. Two threads ran through the more violent accounts of domestic chaos: the presence of unrelated men in the childhood home and drug and alcohol use by adults.

Of the forty life-history respondents, only eleven reported that both parents were present in their family home at age fourteen. Adult males, where present, included stepfathers, mother's boyfriends, uncles, and older brothers. Unrelated adult males were often sources of violence in the childhood home. Domestic violence was almost twice as likely in homes where only one parent was present (62 percent) compared to childhood homes with two parents (36 percent).

A Puerto Rican man we interviewed, Hector, grew up with his mother and his siblings, living in many different houses that they shared with at least several of his mother's boyfriends. Hector's partner described the emergence of violence in his unstable home life:

If there is one word I can describe his mom [it's] unstable. I've been with Hector for ten years, and she's lived in like twenty apartments from the time I've been with him.

. . . [Hector's mother] is not a provider, she's dependent on [her boyfriends], so that was a lot. During that time, when he was fourteen years old, she may have been ending her relationship with his [Hector's] sister's father, and she got involved with this guy from the Dominican Republic, and at one point [*sighs*], when [Hector's mother] was with Ana's father, he had control over what, what was, where the boys were, what they were involved in, and so forth. And I know him and Hector bumped heads a lot, a lot, and she had given him power to hit, like discipline them, and that was the beating and stuff.

Hector provided his own account of his abuse: "Basically what I felt was a grown man picking a fight with an eleven-, ten-year-old kid, you know what

I mean. A ten-year-old boy and hitting him like a grown man, hitting that boy like a grown man, you know."

The circulation of men through their childhood home created an ongoing climate of instability and violence for some respondents. Manny, a Cape Verdean man in his forties, grew up with several different men in his house.

> Interviewer: When you were growing up, was anyone in your household ever a victim of a crime?
>
> Manny: Yes.
>
> Interviewer: Who was that?
>
> Manny: My mother.
>
> Interviewer: Was that just one time or more than one time?
>
> Manny: She used to get beat up by her boyfriends.
>
> Interviewer: How old were you when that was going on?
>
> Manny: Between twelve and fourteen, I believe. Could have been earlier, but I probably don't remember earlier ages.
>
> Interviewer: So what would happen after one of the boyfriends would beat her up?
>
> Manny: Well, while it was going on, I would run in there with my Louisville slugger bat that I used to sleep with.
>
> Interviewer: And did you ever get involved?
>
> Manny: Oh, yeah. Definitely. Every single time.
>
> Interviewer: And then what would happen?
>
> Manny: Well, the very last time when I hit one of her boyfriends, they fell down the stairs, with the bat, and then . . . my mother basically hit me and said why did I do that. So I just left the house and went to live with my grandmother for a few years. . . . I was about fourteen, yeah.
>
> Interviewer: And was it multiple boyfriends, or just . . .?
>
> Manny: She had a few. She had a few. She had a few.

Drug addiction could fuel violence either directly—a parent's alcoholic rage—or indirectly by parents made indifferent by the consumption and search for drugs. Half of the forty respondents reported growing up in a home where there were problems with drugs or alcohol, and twelve of these twenty reported incidents of family violence before they were eighteen. Alcoholism and cocaine and heroin use were most commonly reported. Whereas heroin and cocaine were often associated with parental neglect, alcohol uncorked an anger that sobriety had bottled up.

Several respondents described the fretful climate that settled on a family with an alcoholic father or stepfather. Jemarcus, an African American man, never met his father and grew up with his mother, stepfather, and older brother. His stepfather was an alcoholic "who passed away because he drank so much." Life at home, Jemarcus said, was "stressful, stressful. It was hard. It was uncomfortable. Stressful. I was on edge. Scared. Nervous. My mother would always fight because my stepfather would always come home drunk. . . . When he was sober, he was the greatest person in the world. And when he drank, he just didn't get on with her and he took it out on us."

Brian, a white man from the Irish working-class neighborhood of Charlestown, described a similarly tense uncertainty surrounding his father's alcoholic moods:

> Brian: He would come home from work . . . he just come home between 5:30 and 6:00 p.m. every night, he'll be feeling pretty good, then he would continue to drink, and we were never quite sure what type of mood he would be in, whether angry drunk, happy drunk, you know.
>
> Interviewer: And what was he like as an angry drunk?
>
> Brian: He would be disrespectful towards my mother and same way toward us, but with physical consequences. That's why I hated Boston College. He had a Boston College ring, and I used to get it whacked off the head, so I hated Boston College, his college ring.
>
> Interviewer: And what was he like as a happy drunk?
>
> Brian: I mean, he was great and like all happy drunks, you know, laughing and jovial.
>
> Interviewer: Was this going throughout your entire childhood?
>
> Brian: I would say yes, as long as I can remember, yeah. Probably mostly from, as I can remember, from nine on. . . . There was like a regular routine.
>
> Interviewer: Was this every night?
>
> Brian: During the week, when he worked, it was typical, probably three or four nights out of the five, but then he would always drink at home. He was better if he started drinking when he got home from work.

Respondents often spoke about chaos in their home life growing up. Family violence at the hands of men, often unrelated and often under the influence of drugs or alcohol, created a climate of fear and uncertainty. Even though the respondents connected poverty, chaos, and violence to their childhood home, many of the men we interviewed now brought along their own histories of addiction and antisocial behavior as they circulated as adults through the homes of other children. In all our interviews, we never heard much about violence against women or children perpetrated by the respondents themselves. Still, it seems possible that, with histories of chaos and violence in childhood, and living under conditions of severe poverty in adulthood, family violence was sustained over the life course by some, but overlooked in the interviews.

Control. Closely related to the chaos of severe deprivation are deficits of informal social control by supervising adults whose presence in households and neighborhoods helps maintain order. Luis was a Puerto Rican respondent who grew up "very poor" in a housing project in the Bedford-Stuyvesant neighborhood of Brooklyn, New York. He and his four brothers and sisters were raised by his mother, though he sometimes lived with his cousins as well. His mother suffered from depression and was unemployed and on public assistance for much of his childhood. She was a strict disciplinarian who sometimes tried to keep her sons in line by beating them with wire cables. His stepfather, Carlos, also lived with them. He was a regular heroin user who used at home, nodding off on the sofa in those early years in Brooklyn. Luis first became aware of Carlos's heroin addiction when he was around thirteen and the police and an ambulance were called in response to his stepfather's overdose.

Bedford-Stuyvesant in the 1980s, when Luis was growing up, was a poor, high-crime neighborhood. Violence was often close at hand on the streets and in the corridors of the housing project. "I saw people get killed and all that," he said. "Shot, stabbed, growing up in New York, looking out the window, you see everything. Coming out in the hallway, you see people arguing, fighting, things like that. I saw a couple of people get killed growin' up."

Luis talked about his family being robbed several times when he was a boy:

> Luis: My father got robbed out there, we all got robbed in New York. We got broke into the house, broke into the car.
> Interviewer: Who were these people?
> Luis: People in the neighborhood, could been a crackhead, a dopehead, anybody.
> Interviewer: What usually happened after something like that?
> Luis: What happened? Nothing. Shit. We had to start over.

Luis himself started to get into trouble with neighborhood kids as he got older. At fourteen, he moved with his mother and siblings to Boston to separate from Carlos and his heroin habit. (Carlos later got clean and followed them up to Boston, where he started a second life as a devout churchgoer.) Soon after moving to Boston, Luis got arrested and served time with DYS for assaulting a police officer. He was expelled from high school for this arrest. Throughout his teenage years in Boston, from fourteen to eighteen, Luis served "two or three years" in DYS custody before dropping out of school in the eleventh grade. From ages eighteen to thirty-three, he spent about half his life incarcerated for assaults and drug dealing. He had three children during this period, and at the time of our last interview, he was maintaining contact with each of his three sons and their three mothers.

At the baseline interview just before release, Luis told us that during his current ten-month incarceration he had witnessed six to ten assaults among prison inmates and another three to five assaults involving prison staff. His neighborhood, he said, was safer than prison. By the time of our final follow-up interview, Luis had been out of prison for a year, his longest period in free society since childhood.

Luis grew up in a two-parent family, but his stepfather was immobilized by addiction, which his mother had to manage, along with her own depression and her four other children. The Bedford-Stuyvesant housing project was racially segregated and poor, but rich in unemployment and single-parenthood. Street crime was common, and Luis witnessed violence or was victimized by it in childhood. Authority in his life was provided mostly by the formal institutions of the school, the police, the juvenile reformatory, and state prison. These agencies themselves were coercive and maintained order through the threat of further punishment.

Weak informal social controls are indicated by the prevalence of neighborhood violence. The neighborhood was the most common venue for violence across the life course and was the site where half of all reported incidents of violence occurred. The working-class neighborhoods where the respondents grew up were dotted with areas of concentrated poverty, where violence took the form of robberies and assaults, street fighting, and serious accidents. Although respondents often talked about street fights, they mostly talked about witnessing violence, and also about accidents, assaults, murders, and a suicide.

As we started talking with respondents about their adulthood, their accounts of violent situations shifted to prison. When asked about violence in prison, thirty-two out of the forty life-history respondents said that they witnessed violence involving inmates, and eleven out of forty repsondents had seen violence involving a correctional officer. A few respondents also reported on their own involvement in violence, resulting in long spells in solitary confinement. Two respondents talked about violent deaths that occurred while they were incarcerated. In one incident, a respondent's friend was murdered. The other involved an uncle's suicide. "He died years ago," the respondent's mother said. "He was in jail. They said he hung himself. We didn't believe it."

Respondents spoke of prison as a stressful place in which the climate of violence promoted extreme vigilance. When asked at one week after prison release about the adjustment of returning to the community, one respondent said: "Big adjustment? Just trying to [*pause*] . . . just trying to, like, ease back into society, like trying to leave the mentality [of] prison thing alone. Leave it in there."

"What is that mentality?" we asked.

> I don't take shit from nobody, or uh, I just, like, I'm real like edgy, like one little thing, like you bump into me, you don't say, "Excuse me," I wanna freakin' flip out, you know? I wanna punch your head in. Don't disrespect me. Stuff like that, you know, like the way people talk to me, you know. . . . Give me respect, I'll give you respect, you know. Just things, you know, like, I like to learn how to just walk away. . . . That's what I gotta do. I know what I'm capable of, and he has no idea. . . . And he's more like, I guess, innocent, and if I get the best of him, he's gonna rat me out, and then I'm gonna be doing time and that's it, I'm done, you know what I mean? So it's like I gotta stop that [and] just walk away. It's not worth it anymore pretty much. . . . It got worse being in prison most of the time and growing up on the street always fighting.

In the four main venues of violence—the home, the neighborhood, the school, and the prison—methods of organized social control varied, but informal controls were weak everywhere. At home and on neighborhood streets, children often lacked the supervision of adults, and any adults present were themselves often involved in violent conflict. The routines and relationships produced by work, family, and community were scarce. In schools and prisons, the informal constraints on violence were weak. In these settings, the lives of the reentry respondents were organized around the discipline of formal authorities.

Culture. Violence became positively valued in chaotic contexts that lacked the steadying networks of parents and neighborhood residents. In disputes among young men, police were widely discredited and resolution was often found through violence. Nearly all respondents had been involved in fighting in adolescence. As one respondent remarked, "I thought it was normal. . . . Everybody was fighting. It was considered a problem if you didn't fight."

Several spoke about the larger meaning of fighting in daily life. For some, fighting marked one's status in the adolescent pecking order. One respondent reported that he got in three or four fights each month, "'cause you always had to prove yourself to your peers on how tough you are." To do otherwise was, in Boston's street slang, to be a punk. While children were often punished for fighting, some adults saw fighting as a life skill. One male respondent described how he came to be repeatedly suspended for fighting:

See, that's the thing, that's what's weird, because my mother seen me lose a fight, right? So she told my uncle I was a punk. So when she told my uncle I was a punk, he took me to boxing school. So now, I know how to fight, you know what I'm sayin', now I'm just abusing what I know.

A similar sentiment was sounded by another respondent, who described his mother's response to a fight in the first grade:

My mother said, "Did he put his hands on you?" I said, "Yeah." She said, "You whipped that ass?" I said, "Yeah." She said, "All right. I'll go up to the school tomorrow." . . . That's one thing my mother said she wasn't gonna raise, she wasn't gonna raise no wussies. In fact, she actually said, "If I was supposed to have bitches, I would have had two girls." She said, "I ain't a punk and my kids ain't gonna be punks," and that was just, she taught us right from wrong, [not] just be going around being a bully, but if somebody put their hands on you, defend yourself. She said if you started it then that's your ass. [*laughs*]

Another respondent saw adult encouragement of fighting as preparation for prison life. "Sometimes the older people encourage you to do that," he said. "They'll encourage you to fight." We asked him why he thought they did this. "Nobody wants their nephew, or their son, or their cousin, to be a punk, so it's like, you wanna go out there and fight. Go on out there and if you wanna fight, you go out there and fight."

We asked, "Did you have that happen? You know other cousins or uncles that. . .?"

> You see, that can be looked at good and bad, 'cause it kinda helped me later on in life. When I was in jail, there's no guns, there's none of that. There's knives and stuff, but mostly everybody fights so if . . . it kinda like gives you a little bit of, you know, gives you a little leeway. Most kids my age, when they were twenty-two, twenty-one, they wasn't fighting, you know, they was shooting guns and stuff, so when you know how to fight when you go to jail, it's like a different world.

In these interviews, experience with fighting and readiness to fight were described as preparation for life and a source of masculinity.[16] In settings that were chaotic, weakly supervised by adults, and where young men were reluctant to call on police or other authorities to settle disputes, violent confrontation was viewed as a reality to be dealt with. Even as some adults reprimanded and disciplined their children for fighting, others sometimes played a role in socializing children into the value of violence. Though we see evidence of violence as valued, this value emerged in contexts where violence could solve problems—where authorities were seen as ineffective or as adversaries. Where violence can solve problems, it also becomes a status symbol, a marker of mastery over one's world.

In short, the interviews revealed cultures of violence in which physical force was readily contemplated, got things done, and conferred power and status in daily life. These cultures of violence arose from the material conditions of poor communities that were often chaotic and deficient in the informal sources of order provided by parents, neighbors, employers, and community leaders.

Three conclusions can be drawn from the violence revealed in the reentry study interviews. First is the great prevalence of violence. Respondents spoke about their own violent offending, but they also had frequently been witnesses to and victims of violence. Forty percent of the respondents had witnessed a violent death in their childhood. Years of chronic violence in childhood and adolescence, in which they were victimized or witnessed domestic abuse and street crime, were largely beyond their control. Serious violence had disrupted the intimate networks of twenty-four of the forty life-history respondents as friends or family members died violently through accident, suicide, or murder.

Second, respondents played many different roles in the violence that surrounded them. Their offending was clearly revealed in both interviews and criminal records. They had committed robberies, assaults, and one self-reported homicide for which the respondent was convicted. In addition, all forty respondents described their own victimization by violence, often in childhood, and often at the hands of adult guardians in the form of domestic violence or sexual abuse. As victims, the respondents were shot, stabbed, beaten, raped, and molested. But even beyond the familiar roles of victim and offender, nearly all respondents reported witnessing serious violence and all reported fighting in which the roles of victim and offender were difficult to distinguish.

Third, the main sites of violence—the home, the school, the neighborhood, and the prison—reveal the influence of poverty. Home life was commonly unstable, with adult males unrelated to the respondent often living in the house. We heard many reports of untreated drug or alcohol dependence among the adults in the childhood home. Even in the most stable settings, mothers worked long hours, leaving the children unsupervised after school and in the evenings. Interviews revealed less about school environments, but fighting was common there, as were the disciplinary measures of suspension and expulsion. Some respondents changed schools frequently, and more than half dropped out before graduation. School counselors appeared to hardly be present. They were mentioned in just a couple of interviews. Few special measures—except for suspension or juvenile detention—were taken for children with behavioral or learning problems. Respondents' neighborhoods, typically in Boston's poorer, high-crime areas, were also violent places with weak informal protections against street crime and gang rivalries. Street violence appeared to stretch across the life course. It was common among youth, and children were often exposed to violent conflict on the streets between adults. Speaking of the recent past, respondents mentioned prisons more often as sites of violence. We heard many reports of fighting among prisoners, and sometimes correctional officers were involved as well.

In contexts of poverty, violence is not just an isolated episode of disorder. Violence is a type of deprivation that suffuses poor contexts and the lives of people who populate them. As such, violence undermines human welfare. Victimization is accompanied by physical injuries and psychological trauma. Witnessing violence, especially in early childhood, not just intermittently but in a sustained way, affects neural development and causes lasting psychological harm.[17] Violent offending and fighting produce stress and hyper-arousal. More fundamentally, one role in violence is not easily divorced from another. In poor families, schools, neighborhoods, and locked facilities, people do not specialize as either victims, offenders, or witnesses. Instead, one inhabits all these roles in due course.

The connection between poverty and violence reveals a fiction that runs through the politics of crime policy. For politicians, violence is a bright line through the prison population that divides those who deserve mercy and compassion from those who do not. People convicted of drug crimes, for example, are called "nonviolent" drug offenders. "Nonviolent" is a halo that identifies those who have not caused real harm to others. Public opinion polls reliably find more support for greater leniency for nonviolent drug offenders in contrast to "violent" offenders.[18] Many of the reentry study respondents did not have felony convictions for violence, but virtually all had known serious violence in their lives as victims, witnesses, and participants. Trying to divide the prison population into good people and bad, between violent and nonviolent, fundamentally misunderstands the nature of violence in poor family and neighborhood contexts. The division between the violent and the nonviolent is a moral distortion of a complex social environment in which victims, witnesses, participants, and offenders are often one and the same individuals who suffer harm from each part they play in episodes of violence.

The idea that violence emerges under conditions of poverty also diverges from the view of criminal justice authorities. In the criminal justice system, there are only two main parties to violence—a victim and an offender. Offenders, through their intentions and actions, are culpable. The criminal justice system identifies offenders and renders punishment. Social context is introduced in a limited way through defenses against criminal charges or mitigation in sentencing, but even here the legal process abstracts from much of the defendant's biography and social context. The deep social fact that violence attaches to poverty and that roles in violence circulate in poor contexts is hard to reconcile with a system of individualized judgment in sentencing. Even if the individualized justice of the criminal trial were rightly decided in every single case, the collective effect is to heap punishment on the poor who are owed this individualized justice by virtue of their own victimization.

From the sociological perspective taken here, the implications for criminal justice are even more basic. Where violence is contextual and offenders are also likely to be victims and witnesses, justice is not achieved through the punishment of the offender but through the abatement of violent contexts.

Violence triggers our moral sensibilities. Policymakers are reluctant to extend compassion and leniency to those convicted of violence. Liberal academic writers rightly observe that poor families and neighborhoods are not reducible to their high rates of violence. But some go further to claim that resilience flourishes alongside deficits, that serious violence is confined to a small number, and that poverty leads to variation in social outcomes, not collective disadvantage.[19] Policymakers and academics alike get trapped by the stigma of violence. Tough-on-crime policymakers treat perpetrators of violence as stained individuals who must be distinguished from those who have refrained from violence, and they are inclined to severely punish those who have committed violence. Liberal writers can minimize violence as a social problem, concerned that analysis might somehow stigmatize the poor communities whose violent crime rates are highest.

The social reality of violence and its moral implications are hard to square with either perspective. For the people we interviewed, violence was prevalent and grew out of contexts of poverty. Contextual violence more than the violent dispositions of individuals drove the physical harms we found in childhood homes, schools, prisons, and neighborhoods. Emphasizing the contextual character of violence does not deny moral agency to criminal offenders. Instead, it acknowledges that the offender's role is often temporary, that violence has been present in this person's life since early childhood, and that violent offenders have commonly suffered serious victimization. This is the context in which justice must be found.

·····················

CHAPTER 6

Income

The livelihoods of men and women coming out of prison are often tenuous and underwritten by family support and government programs. In the reentry study sample, the median annual income through the first twelve months after incarceration was $6,428, about half of the federal poverty line for individuals living alone. For many, a life of irregular work sometimes combined with illegal income was followed by persistent unemployment after prison. For those who had worked in low-wage jobs before incarceration, opportunities afterward were confined to minimum-wage work. A handful of the Boston men—most of them white and in their forties or older—had access to skilled jobs in the construction trades.

Much of the research on economic life after incarceration has focused on employers' responses to job-seekers with criminal records.[1] Some respondents attributed their employment problems to their criminal records and the reluctance of employers to take a chance on job-seekers just released from prison. But for many of the respondents, a criminal record was just one of many deficits weighing on their search for work. Over half of all the formerly incarcerated people we interviewed had failed to complete high school. Some contended with physical disabilities, addictions, or mental illness. For them, a criminal record may have been an obstacle, but their job opportunities would have been very poor even without the added challenge of incarceration.

For most of our sample, employment was hard to find and easy to lose. By the end of the year after prison release, about half the sample were unemployed, and one-quarter had never worked at all. Under conditions of pervasive joblessness, their strategies for survival often took them outside the labor market. Researchers have overlooked how formerly incarcerated people make ends meet outside the labor market, yet these efforts consume much of the energy of the reentry process.[2] The men and women of the reentry study stitched together support from programs and family members, covering the necessities piecemeal. Although research and policy interest has focused on employment as essential to economic well-being after incarceration, a poverty-level income in a minimum-wage job is often a best-case scenario for this population.

The striking exception among the reentry study interviewees were those who found work in skilled trades. For those few, skilled employment provided a powerful source of social integration. For those who climbed over the hurdles to employment, it was steady, skilled work that provided a path out of poverty. But more than this, regular skilled work was a source of structure and pride, capable of repudiating the stigma of incarceration and making one's livelihood a positive source of identity, not just the basis of material well-being.

Mike was fifty-four years old when he was released from the Massachusetts Alcohol and Substance Abuse Center (MASAC). He had been working closely with a community program before his release, and by the time he left prison he had made plans for his housing, health coverage, and union card. A white man of Portuguese and Irish descent, Mike had grown up in Charlestown. He dropped out of Charlestown High School at age seventeen, in the year of riots and unrest in Boston over school desegregation. He would later get his GED in prison at Walpole, but his main education was as a welder. Mike was an ironworker and union member. Before his release, his prison counselor told us, he had pestered her for months to help him get his union card reinstated. Mike's union membership, which kept him eligible for a union job, would have lapsed if his brother had not paid his dues throughout his incarceration.

Mike had been locked up for most of his adult life—thirty-three out of thirty-six years—for crimes that were often related to his drinking and drug use. He started drinking and smoking marijuana at age sixteen. A little later, he began using PCP and mescaline, and then cocaine in his twenties. He first served time in prison at age eighteen for an armed robbery. His long criminal record consisted mostly of robberies and drug offenses.

When we first interviewed Mike, he was finishing a five-year sentence for his fifth conviction for an armed robbery. At the time of his release, he had little employment history and a long list of mental and physical problems. He suffered from back pain, depression, and bipolar disorder.

Work was a theme that ran through our many conversations with Mike. He traced his most recent prison sentence to a layoff a week before Christmas six years earlier. He had been working for a year since his prior prison term, but after the layoff, he said, unemployment sent him into a funk and he started drinking heavily and using drugs. A few days later, he said, "I did the robbery up on Washington Street."

Because Mike's union membership was paid up when he came out of prison, he could get a job through his local's hiring hall. Boston unions supply skilled construction workers to building sites in the area. By acting as the authorized supplier of skilled labor, the hiring hall averts the obstacle of an employer's criminal background check.

When Mike left prison, he had $165 left from his prison commissary account and $66,000 in debt for accumulated child support arrears. His two daughters were now in their twenties, too old to benefit from child support. But a portion of any wages he earned would be garnished until the debt was repaid. He owed probation $65 a month in supervision fees, he paid $25 a month for his cell phone, and medications cost him about $40 a month. His reentry program initially covered his $480 in rent and also helped cover the costs of a state identification card and work clothes.[3]

A week after release from prison, Mike projected motivation and organization. He had neatly listed a week's worth of appointments on a folded sheet of white paper and had been attending meetings on Relapse Prevention, Positive Thinking, Financial Planning, and "Rexo" (for the reintegration of ex-offenders). On the Friday of his release from MASAC, Mike visited his reentry program to get his housing placement at a sober house in the African American section of Dorchester. The following Monday, his sister drove him to his union hall to pick up his membership card. On Tuesday, he completed his MassHealth enrollment, and on Wednesday he signed up for food stamps, which would pay $200 a month.

Although Mike was an ironworker by training, he had found more consistent employment in the past doing demolition—taking down old buildings to make way for new construction. "I started out welding," he said, but "you're on the iron, you're off the iron. The wind is over eight knots and you're off the iron. So I just transferred my book. Got more steady work. I'm a building wrecker. I burn it. I drop it. I don't erect it."

Mike stayed in close contact with the union in the first few weeks he was out of prison. He was confident that work would come along soon. One week out of prison, Mike told us, "I'm number one to be pulled off the list. All I have to do is to call in [to the union] every day. I'm a union member, I don't have to hunt jobs." The business agent at Mike's local, knowing he was eager to get back to work, found him a few small jobs while he waited for a demolition project to come up. Mike had certification for handling hazardous materials, and his first job, three weeks after getting out of prison, was for one eight-hour day doing environmental cleanup at a building site, for which he was paid $31.80 an hour, almost four times the minimum wage. A few days after that, Mike worked for three days shoring up a crane at a big construction project at MIT. Five weeks after getting out of prison, Mike began his first big demolition job, working for $40 an hour.

When we talked to Mike a few months later, he told us that work had taken on a central place in his life after prison. He had been working consistently over the last three months taking down the Old Colony housing projects in South Boston. The work paid over $5,000 a month for a forty-hour week and also paid a retirement annuity. Mike remained steadily employed for the remainder of the year, working on a half-dozen other demolition jobs. Only once did his pay dip below $5,000 a month, when, midway through the first year out of prison, he lost about a week's wages between projects.

Demolition work is very physical, and Mike suffered from chronic back pain, which he treated with prescription painkillers. Boston's winter was also tough on the construction industry. "There are tit days, but some days are brutal. Like tomorrow morning, they say it's going to be in the low twenties. [And] last week with the winds, [the temperature] was below zero." For all that, Mike said, "I'm into it. I think it would be a grind if I didn't like what I was doing."

Mike reflected on the place of work in his life:

I'm realizing that work is probably the most significant and important key for me to maintaining my focus. . . . I realize now that at this point in my [life], I don't have another bid in me. I'd rather work and bust my ass now. Believe it or not, when you cash a check on Friday, and this may seem a little trivial or juvenile . . . it feels good.

At the end of his first year out of prison, Mike talked about the larger rewards of his job. "Stability, confidence, self-respect, a sense of meaning, and self-gratification. I'm kind of proud of myself that I've maintained work for over a year now," he said.

Over the course of the year, work appeared to transform Mike in many ways. Physically, we saw him change from the look of a man just out of prison, wearing blue jeans and an oversized white T-shirt, into a construction worker wearing the overalls and boots of his trade and carrying a hard hat that signaled his membership in the world of work. A stable union job allowed Mike to live well above poverty. His work contributed to a variety of routines that formed the pillars of a normal life. Besides his job, he moved in with his girlfriend and helped cover a significant share of her rent. He accumulated retirement savings that provided a measure of security for the future. He was also closely involved in the lives of his two siblings.

Still, after a lifetime of incarceration, a year of stable employment on a living wage provides only a good start. Demolition work is physically demanding, especially for a fifty-four-year-old man with a bad back. Even a union job is a thin reed for someone with chronic pain and little work history whose incarceration was rooted in a life of drug and alcohol problems. Perhaps just as important as his job, Mike actively sought out counseling and received regular medical treatment for pain, high blood pressure, and asthma.

A good job going forward may also be too little to repair relationships that have eroded over a lifetime. Even as he spoke about the importance of steady work, Mike also talked about the difficulties of reconciling with his two daughters. He had never been a source of support for them, and in one interview he described himself as having "robbed them of their childhood." He tried for a year to establish regular contact, but by our final interview he reflected that he would probably never be a presence in their lives. For Mike, the restorative powers of work provided material well-being and promoted behavioral change, but could not repair broken relationships with previous partners and his children.

Only eight of the 122 reentry study respondents were union members. Six of these eight were white, all were men, all of them tended to be older, in their forties and fifties. All but one of the union members in the sample worked in the construction industry, and nearly all of them had family connections to construction unions. Union membership conferred significant benefits. Employment rates for union members were between 70 and 85 percent at six and twelve months after incarceration, compared to around 50 percent for nonmembers. Earnings were about four times higher for union members. In his first year after prison, Mike earned about $49,000, nearly five times more than the poverty-level average income of the rest of the reentry study sample. Work and pay were also consistent for union members compared to the work experience of the rest of the sample. Construction work in Boston is seasonal and project-based, but even in the precarious labor market for formerly incarcerated workers, Mike's pay was steady from month to month. In his first year out of prison, as a union construction worker, Mike paid taxes, paid down his child support obligations, and helped support a household with his girlfriend. More than this, steady well-paying work brought him, in his own words, self-respect and a sense of self-gratification.

Besides experiencing violence in his childhood home, Hector, also had trouble at school. He got into fights, used drugs from an early age, and left school without graduating. We first interviewed him in his early thirties, when he was finishing a four-year prison sentence. He had completed a number of programs in prison, earning a certification in "green technologies," completing one college course, and enrolling in a seminar on life skills that provided advice on topics from family relationships to retirement savings. Hector had begun his incarceration in medium security but was transferred to a minimum-security facility that offered a work-release program. Like nearly one-quarter of the reentry study respondents, he was employed in a work-release job. In the final five months of his incarceration, he left prison each day to work as a dishwasher in a local restaurant chain.

Work release offered two concrete benefits. First, respondents who had work-release jobs saved their earnings and left prison with significantly more money than the rest of the prison population. Work-release participants had saved a median of $2,000 at the time they left incarceration, compared to $200 for all other prisoners. Second, work release offered employment continuity, as some continued in their work-release jobs immediately after incarceration. Over 30 percent of work-release respondents held a job at the end of their first week out of incarceration compared to just over 10 percent of the remainder of the sample. Having savings and being employed immediately after prison gave work-release participants a big advantage in the first weeks back in free society. (A third benefit for Hector, we learned six months after his release, was visiting his girlfriend, Naya, when he was signed out from prison.)

When Hector left prison, he had $3,000 in his savings account. His savings helped him meet his initial expenses for food, a cell phone, clothes, and transportation. Right after being released, he moved in with Naya and her family in a working-class, largely black and Latino neighborhood. Just out of prison, he was able to contribute $450 each month toward rent. Unusual among the reentry respondents, Hector never applied for food stamps or other public assistance.

He returned to his work-release job as a dishwasher on the second day after being released from prison. Working about twenty-five hours a week, he earned the minimum wage of $8.50 an hour. This gave Hector a take-home paycheck of around $800 each month, nearly all of which he spent on necessities. Besides rent, he spent $80 each month on his phone bill, about $50 in groceries for the household, and $200 on gas for his car. The job provided no benefits, but Hector could buy health insurance at $30 a month from the state-subsidized plan for low-wage workers. He worked nights, starting his shift at 6:00 p.m. after Naya dropped him off. The restaurant had been only about ten minutes from the prison, but his commute grew to forty-five minutes after he was released.

As minimum-wage work at the bottom of the food service business, Hector's dishwashing job was a step down from his pre-incarceration employment as a cafeteria manager, making $13 an hour. Even though he had earned more before he went to prison, he had always been entrenched in the low-wage labor market. Dishwashing nevertheless provided steady work, and Hector consistently maintained his hours in the first six months back in the community. When we asked him what was the best thing in his life two months after incarceration, he spoke about working and his fiancée Naya. Asked again at six months, he said that the best thing about his life was "that I have an income."

Six months after prison, Hector's life was transformed dramatically. Naya gave birth to his daughter, his first child. The new baby became the focal point of the couple's lives. Although there was a new mouth to feed, the household income included not only Hector's paycheck but also the earnings of Naya's mother (who worked in a law office) and stepfather, a plumber.

A few months after the birth of the baby, and after working at the restaurant for over a year, Hector was able to leave the dishwashing job. Naya's stepfather had found Hector a non-union construction job as a carpenter. Instead of working nights, his new hours ran from 7:00 a.m. to 3:00 p.m., his commute was reduced, and his pay doubled, to about $2,000 a month. The job also included benefits, providing health insurance for Hector's new family.

Apart from the handful of union workers in the reentry sample, who had long-standing ties to organized labor, Hector's employment record was among the very best. Work release had allowed him to work immediately after incarceration, and he held on to his work-release job for over a year. The job was a source of pride and satisfaction and allowed Hector to provide for his family.

Despite his strong employment record, Hector earned poverty-level wages—around $11,000 a year—and work long hours in a job that offered no benefits or opportunities for advancement. Making ends meet would have been impossible without Naya and her family, who provided a stable household in which to live and a network of social support. When economic opportunity finally came, it arrived not through promotion along a well-defined career path, but through family contacts that allowed Hector to move into a skilled occupation.

Young men experienced some of the most serious employment problems after incarceration. Avery was twenty-two years old when he was released from prison after serving three years for gun possession. A tall, soft-spoken African American man, Avery looked hard for work but struggled to get a job in the year after he was released.

Avery grew up in a solidly working-class household and seemed to have had many advantages over other young black men who were sent to prison. He and his younger brother were raised by both of their parents, and for a time he was part of Boston's Metco program, which bused inner-city children to more affluent suburban schools. "My husband and I put an effort into staying together as parents," his mother told us. "My husband always said he didn't want his boys to ever end up in there [prison]. But sometimes you can just give it 100 percent and it doesn't matter where they come from as far as you being the parent."

Avery's father had steady work as a mechanic, and his mother had a government job. However, the markers of working-class respectability conferred relatively few advantages. Avery often got in trouble at school and was suspended "five or ten times" for talking back to his teachers. In seventh grade, he broke another boy's nose in a fight, and his juvenile record shows an arrest for disturbing a school assembly. At the age of twelve, Avery learned that his father was a heroin addict. Over the next couple of years, the family lived through two overdoses and finally an intervention. By eighth grade, Avery was smoking cigarettes and marijuana regularly.

Avery caught his first case at age eighteen and never finished high school. He told us that he was wrongly accused of a shooting and missed half his senior year, sitting in jail on charges that were later dismissed. His school counselor helped him find a couple of jobs through a summer program. He worked for two years before his incarceration in a literacy program for low-income children in elementary school. The summer before going to prison, he also picked up a gardening job through a city youth program. Two years after high school, Avery was living with his mother and making just over the minimum wage of $8.00 an hour. The literacy program and the gardening job represented his total adult work experience by the time he was sent to prison.[4]

Twenty years old at the time of his incarceration, Avery was one of the youngest men in the study to be sentenced to state prison. He began his incarceration taking GED classes and classes on "Criminal Thinking," a project he would continue after his release. A month before he got out, he got word that his father had died of a heart attack. Not allowed to attend the funeral, he would struggle, his mother told us, to find closure throughout the year after release. "That's why he sometimes gets so upset," she said. "It's always about his dad. He has this thing now that he doesn't believe in God anymore. He doesn't understand why he took his father so young."

Coming home from prison, Avery set about completing his GED and finding a job. A local prisoner reentry program provided a voucher to Roxbury Community College for GED classes. Avery completed the classes and took the test, doing well in math and science but narrowly failing the reading section.

Avery also committed himself to his job search. He told us that he was getting advice from his cousin, aunt, and uncle. Still, in his first week out, he felt like he was still trying to settle back into free society. "It's like I'm moving and I don't know where I'm going," he said.

A few months after his prison release, Avery was still hard at work trying to find a job. He cited unemployment as the biggest challenge in his life. The job search was difficult, he said, because of his lack of schooling and his criminal record. "I thought it was my record, but it seems like it's not," he said. "People telling me I got to get my GED. I really don't know why people are not hiring [me]. Maybe it's because of the GED, or maybe some people check my record and they can't hire me because of that. I really don't know the reason." Later he said, "I'm just waiting for someone to call me back and give me a chance."

Most of Avery's job search was focused on retailers that, in the Massachusetts vernacular, were CORI-friendly. Distinguished by their attitude toward the state Criminal Offender Record Information (CORI) system, which was used for background checks, these employers were known by employment programs and probation departments to have a history of hiring people with criminal records. Avery's prisoner reentry program helped him write a résumé and file it with these firms. His probation officer had a list of CORI-friendly employers, which were mostly offering unskilled jobs that paid around minimum wage, usually for customer service work or jobs in the warehouses of large retailers.

In 2010, two years before the reentry study began, Massachusetts passed a law restricting the use of criminal background checks in employment. The law reform was one front on a national campaign to "Ban the Box" that aimed to remove the conviction history question from job applications. Under the new Massachusetts law, employers were no longer allowed to ask job-seekers about prior convictions on a job application. Background checks were deferred until later in the hiring process. Although the law did indeed "ban the box," our interviews suggested that compliance by employers was spotty and that the negative effects of background checks were not overcome by just delaying them. Respondents widely felt that their employment problems were due to their criminal records and hiring had often been going well until their records were disclosed. When we asked unemployed respondents why they were not working, around 20 percent mentioned their criminal record.

One theory of the employment problems of young African American men is that they are holding out for jobs and wages above their level of skill and work experience.[5] In the language of economic theory, their "reservation wages" are too high. This is a difficult theory to test, particularly in the absence of job offers that they might reject. Certainly, Avery seemed eager for any available work, and he was not asking, he told us, for a particular wage. "If they start me off at the minimum, and I work myself up, so be it," he said. How far would he be willing to travel to work? "Anywhere that's close," he replied. "Somewhere I can get on a train. Maybe two buses and a train," he elaborated. "Maybe an hour or two." Average commuting time for Boston-area zip codes is thirty minutes. He also said he was flexible about hours and hoping just for any and all hours he could get. By these measures, Avery seemed eager to work and ready to take any offer.

Six months after his release, Avery still had not found work. He told us that he would apply for around a hundred jobs in a month and typically go to around twenty interviews. He was feeling tired and stressed. "Maybe because I'm just at home on the Internet and do applications all day. And I don't do nothing all day. I stay in the house so I won't get into trouble." By the second half of the year, Avery's unemployment had dulled his motivation and hardened into idleness. His mother said his biggest challenge was "trying to find something to do. It's not good to sit and actually do nothing and play video games all day." She said that Avery grieved for his father and that his idleness made things worse. "Sitting around just gets you into trouble. You know. It just gets you into trouble."

Around nine months after his release from prison, Avery was arrested again. It is difficult to piece together facts, but in his account his state identification card was found at a crime scene after he had dropped it there several days earlier. Police say they saw him fleeing the scene but only caught up with him once he got back to his mother's house. Either way, the arrest was a probation violation, and Avery returned to jail for forty-five days. The charge itself was ultimately dismissed.

By a full year after his release from prison, Avery reported that he had been unemployed in each of the preceding twelve months, despite an intensive job search in which he applied for hundreds of jobs. His mother told us that he had lined up a warehouse job at one point, but had barely started work before he returned to jail on the probation violation. During the year, Avery had been entirely supported by his mother and his girlfriend. He lived mostly with his mother but stayed over with his girlfriend a few nights a week. She lived near the community college where he was taking his GED classes.

Given the many obstacles that Avery faced when he got out of prison, it is hard to pin down exactly why he had such trouble finding work. He had neither a high school diploma nor much work experience outside of the summer programs available to disadvantaged school-leavers. He also had a felony record, and he was depressed and withdrawn following the death of his father while he was incarcerated. By the end of the year, there were also signs that Avery had some continuing involvement in crime, and a short period of incarceration for a probation violation appeared to have interrupted his one employment opportunity. Still, he searched intensively for work, particularly in the first six months after release, and went on dozens of job interviews.

Nearly all of Avery's income and other material support came from his family, but the most important assistance for his job search came from government-supported programs. His state-subsidized reentry program helped him write a résumé, file it with employers, and apply for jobs. The program also covered his educational costs and gave him a bus pass that he used to travel to job interviews. Outside the program, Avery's probation officer gave him a list of employers that he thought was helpful. As other research has found, young black men with criminal records seem to find employment opportunities more often through the formalized channels of programs and probation than through social networks.[6] The social support of family and partners contributes more to their material well-being, providing them with housing and income. Reflecting on Avery's year with his mother after incarceration, she said, "I would rather have him home than prison, because I sleep better."

For Carla, whose drug use, fits of temper, and physical disability consumed her daily energy, some days seemed like a battle for survival. As she fought off the many threats to her physical and emotional well-being, how could Carla stay housed and fed in the year after incarceration?

Before she went to prison, Carla pieced together her income from drug sales, prostitution, and a government disability check for a painful back injury sustained in a fight and aggravated by another brawl while she was in prison. She also worked part-time on and off as a personal care assistant. By age forty-two, Carla estimated, she had worked in a legitimate job for about eighteen months in the twenty-six years since she dropped out of school. Just before she went to prison, Carla was using cocaine and heroin every day and renting a room in a house she shared with five other friends who were also using drugs regularly and heavily. The money she was making at that time "depended on how the day went."

Carla left MCI Framingham on a sunny Thursday morning early in the fall with $116 from her prison canteen account. She checked in with her probation officer that afternoon and then went to her mother's place, where she would live with her twenty-one-year-old daughter (herself recently released from prison) and teenage son. Because of her back injury, Carla had little expectation of working. Nevertheless, she was up at 6:00 a.m. on the Monday after her release for the one-hour walk to the probation program she was required to attend. By Wednesday, she had signed up for programs in Trauma and Addiction, Recovery Education, Women's HIV Education, and Self-Esteem. With no money for transport, Carla walked from place to place in her first weeks out. She applied for state welfare benefits and food stamps at a local community center, where she waited two hours to hand in her paperwork. "There's like a thousand people ahead of you," she said. She walked another hour to a Social Security office to apply for SSI, the federal cash benefit for low-income people with disabilities. To save money, she did community service one day each week instead of paying the $65 a month probation fee.

Small expenses loom very large immediately after incarceration for those who have no income. "I'm walking a lot," Carla said. "I don't have no income. I've been trying to get a bus pass from [a state transitional aid agency]. I've been calling them and calling them." With no food stamps until her second week after incarceration, Carla ate sparingly at home. "I hate to, though," Carla said. "I'm taking from my kids and my mom." She would eat in the morning and then at the end of the day when she returned home. Her girlfriend bought her cigarettes, which cost $8.75 a pack and were her biggest expense in these early weeks.

Things went well for Carla over the next few months. She finished her probation program and was enjoying her GED classes, particularly the class on women's literature. Her back problems kept her from looking for work, but a few months after her release from prison she was receiving $200 a month in food stamps and another $300 from Emergency Aid to the Elderly, Disabled, and Children (EAEDC), a state program that provided interim assistance for up to two months for people who could not work because of disability and were waiting for federal disability benefits to begin. Besides $500 in public assistance, Carla estimated that she received about $100 each month from family and friends.

Each morning, as a condition of her probation, Carla had to report to a community corrections program, which consisted mostly of group meetings focused on anti-addiction therapies and health. But besides these meetings, Carla received help getting her monthly probation fees waived in return for weekly community service. The program also helped Carla enroll in GED classes and paid for the exams (which cost about $100) that she would take at the end of the year. About a month after her release from prison, her case manager at the probation program referred Carla to a community program that served people with serious drug problems. The substance abuse program got Carla a monthly pass for public transport (worth about $70), provided her with money for clothes, and covered her $50 cell-phone bill.

Burdened with physical disability, a long history of heroin use, incarceration, and no real prospects for employment, Carla was able to piece together a livelihood from government programs, significant housing and economic assistance from family and friends, and a patchwork of support from criminal justice agencies and community programs. This complex combination of income streams and in-kind assistance took Carla several months to assemble, and only through great effort. As a high school dropout with a tenth-grade education, Carla navigated complicated bureaucracies, filling out forms and leaving phone messages. As someone with chronic back pain, she walked for miles through Boston's inner-city neighborhoods to visit programs, welfare offices, and health clinics. Upon arrival, she would wait for hours for her name to be called. With her income pieced together in this way, nothing was left to her own discretion, and Carla's spending was governed by how her income was earmarked. Her monthly grocery bill came to $200 because that was what food stamps would cover. When the substance abuse program gave her a clothing allowance, she spent $100 that month on clothes. Her cell-phone bill never exceeded $50 a month because this too was covered by a program. Her largest out-of-pocket expense was the copayment for her medications, which came to around $15 a month. If there was a luxury item in this budget, it was her cigarettes.

When a livelihood is patched together from so many sources, it requires active management, and each of the pieces is periodically at risk of being lost. For former prisoners who will never work, income insecurity takes this form. The state EAEDC benefit paid Carla $300 a month and was subject to periodic reviews of her disability status. Meanwhile, Carla had applied for the federal SSI benefit, which paid about twice as much, but six months after her prison release her SSI application had twice been denied. By the end of the year, she was seeing a lawyer to help her with the application.

Carla's health was also getting worse. Her hands and feet had become swollen, and walking and standing for long periods was painful. "All I do is stay home all day. I can barely walk to the corner. The only reason why I go [to the probation program] is that I'll go to jail if I don't go." Six months after getting out of prison, her rounds around the probation, welfare, and community offices in Roxbury and Dorchester had become physically impossible.

At six months after release, Carla was still collecting the EAEDC benefit and food stamps, for a total of $500 each month in public assistance. She was using her disability benefit to help pay the electricity bill and her phone bill, which was no longer being covered by the community drug program. She had to cover the costs of her monthly bus pass and was continuing to make copayments on her medications. She was also assessed over $1,000 in probation and other court fees, which she worked off with community service. By six months out of prison, most of the cash she had left after expenses was going to cigarettes, about $80 a month.

A year after her release from prison, Carla's health problems were leaving her little room to take classes or search for a job. She moved around her mother's small apartment in pain, wearing a back brace. Although she enjoyed her English classes, she had not yet passed the GED because of a failing math score. She continued to collect the same $500 in public assistance. In the year she was out of prison, Carla never succeeded in receiving federal disability benefits. She sometimes shared her frustrations about the long lines at the welfare office and the long walks from welfare to the probation program, but she also shared her joy at her success in her reentry program and GED classes. By the end of her year out of prison, chronic pain had become her dominating concern. Even the challenges of a poverty-level income and economic insecurity appeared small in the face of significant health problems.

One-quarter of the reentry study sample, like Carla, remained jobless throughout the entire year after leaving prison. Like Carla, many of these respondents also reported high levels of chronic pain related to back injuries or arthritis. Those who never worked were also more likely to report a history of depression or psychotic symptoms, including bipolar disorder and schizophrenia. They also were significantly more likely to have a history of drug addiction.

The most important consequence of persistent joblessness was a very low income. Over the year, Carla averaged around $600 a month in income, $500 from food stamps and the disability program and another $100 each month from family and friends. On average, the continuously unemployed received incomes just over one-third as high as the incomes of those who found at least some work in the year after incarceration. Those who found some work were merely poor, living on an average of $1,440 a month. With an average income of $570 a month, the continuously unemployed lived in extreme poverty. Government programs were indispensable to them. About

85 percent of Carla's income came from food stamps and her disability check, and these covered food, utilities, and other necessities.

Even among formerly incarcerated people as a whole, those in extreme poverty faced severe hardship. Being extremely poor often meant walking from appointment to appointment because public transport was unaffordable. Sometimes meals were missed because buying takeout was too expensive. And days were spent waiting in the offices of criminal justice and social services agencies. Carla was fortunate to live with her mother, but housing was unstable for many of the other continuously unemployed. About half of those who never worked in the year after incarceration were living in shelters, had found transitional housing, or had returned to incarceration. Among those who found at least some work, only one-third lived in unstable housing.

There's a certain cruelty in this situation. Those who live with chronic pain, serious mental illness, and a long history of drug addiction—about one-quarter of the Boston Reentry Study sample—also cannot work and face the deepest poverty as a result. Thus, mental and physical hardship tends to accompany the greatest material hardship after incarceration.

Leaving incarceration is most often a transition from prison to poverty. The income data we collected from the reentry study sample revealed that respondents' median annual income was about half the federal poverty line, a striking level of extreme disadvantage for a sample that consisted overwhelmingly of prime-age men. Low incomes in the general population are concentrated among single mothers and their children. The economic disadvantage we find among people coming out of prison falls far outside the usual boundaries of American poverty.

Only at the very top of the reentry study's income distribution, in the top 10 percent, do we see incomes and labor market experiences that resemble the mainstream of the American economy. Formerly incarcerated men in this high-income category reported making $28,000 a year or more. Those at the top of the income distribution were mostly white men in their forties or older, like Mike, who were working in union jobs in the construction industry. Nearly all were long-standing union members who were able to return to the labor market very quickly after incarceration.

Black and Latino respondents earned $5,000 a year less than white respondents on average. Some black and Latino men, like Hector, found only minimum-wage work and thus remained dependent on family support or public assistance. Hector benefited, however, from being in a work-release program while incarcerated. Work release ensured the continuity of his employment immediately after release, setting him on a different path from Avery, who was continuously unemployed. Most of the earnings gap between white and minority former prisoners was related to the relatively high level of employment for whites. Whereas only 15 percent of whites never found work in the year after incarceration, over one-quarter of blacks and one-third of Latinos were continuously unemployed.

Motivation is often held out as the special ingredient that distinguishes those who do well after release from prison.[7] Among the reentry study sample, motivation was abundant, particularly in the first few months after release. Opportunities for work, however, were distributed unequally, partly because of the racial and social structure of occupations and partly because of family connections.

Most of the men and women we interviewed were motivated to do well. In his first week out of prison, Mike had drawn up a long list of appointments and organizations that could assist his reentry. Hector worked as tirelessly as a dishwasher after incarceration as he did during his time in the work-release program. Avery applied for hundreds of jobs for months before burning out and retreating to his mother's house, where he then spent much of his time playing video games. And Carla embraced her recovery programs and GED classes with joyful enthusiasm. Although each of the respondents approached the tasks of reentry with energy, Mike—at fifty-four years old and with a bad back—had a union card that opened the door to high wages and steady work. Hector's work-release job also placed him at an advantage. Neither Avery nor Carla worked during the year after prison, and whatever work prospects Carla might have had slowly dissolved as she was crippled by arthritis in her back and hands.

The continuously unemployed in the reentry study sample—about the bottom quarter—experienced very deep economic hardship that was often compounded by physical disability and mental illness. Even as employment rates steadily increased for most of those we interviewed, the poorest of them had extremely high and enduring rates of unemployment. They relied almost entirely on public assistance and support from families for cash and housing. Their consumption was shaped largely by the welfare programs for which they qualified. These men and women had often been dealing with lifelong disabilities and addiction, and it is difficult to see how their membership in society could be sustained without a lifetime of state support.

For them, even the most progressive vision of rehabilitation was unlikely to provide much help. Their well-being currently depends crucially on their families. Without family support, there are no clear alternatives to prison and jails for these men and women. In this way, institutions designed for punishment are pressed into service to feed and house those with no real survival strategies in free society.

CHAPTER 7

Family

The main source of support for Boston Reentry Study participants after their release from prison came not from jobs, criminal activity, or government programs, but from families. Families would meet their loved ones at prison on the day of release, drive them home, house them, and support them financially and emotionally. Men (because they were mostly men) who did not receive help from family members were more likely to be on the streets or in shelters. They relied more on government benefits, and often had few friends they could talk to.

For most of our respondents, the term "family support" entailed not a rich reservoir of kin relations, but a mother or sister who was economically more secure. They could offer a bed to a son or brother—and often to other relatives who needed somewhere to stay or someone to keep an eye on the children. Most of these supportive family members—nearly all of them women—were also poor and were doing well only by the standards of a household that struggled financially. Support under these conditions of hardship was enabled by bonds of love. An expansive but not boundless resource, the bonds of love were often marked by weariness and sometimes undone by harsh words and other conflict.

Largely missing from this story are romantic partners and their children. Two-thirds of the reentry study sample had children, and another 10 percent said that they felt like a father figure to children who were not their own. Still, these children's parents who were partners to the men and women of the reentry study were not a great source of support. A year after prison release, only about 10 percent of parents in the sample were living with their partner and children, fewer than the 25 percent who were living with family and the 14 percent who had returned to incarceration.

Shortly after being released from prison, Bobby met with us on the Harvard campus to talk about his first week out. At twenty-four, Bobby was one of the younger respondents in the sample; a high school graduate, he was one of the few whose criminal career consisted almost entirely of drug offenses. Before his current incarceration, he had not served time in prison, though he had spent a few months in juvenile detention on a drug charge.

Bobby had been raised by his mother, Isabel, a petite Puerto Rican woman in her early forties who worked at an administrative job in the local school system. Bobby was the older of Isabel's two boys, and she had spent much of the last decade trying to keep Bobby out of trouble and helping him out when he got arrested. Around age thirteen, Bobby started smoking marijuana and shortly after started staying out late with his middle school friends. When he was fourteen, Isabel got a court-ordered curfew to help her keep Bobby in at night. At age fifteen, he began dealing drugs. For Isabel, Bobby's adolescence was a slow and losing battle. She was working full-time to provide for her boys, Bobby was out on the streets at night, and she had little idea what he was up to. His father was largely absent from Bobby's life. As he put it, "My mother's my father. My dad's been in jail my whole life."

Isabel shouldered much of the responsibility for her son before he went to prison. Apart from a brief stint working at Target, Bobby had never held a legitimate job. He got arrested, and his earnings from drug dealing dwindled as his case dragged on. He was unemployed, twenty-two years old, and living at home when his sentence was handed down. Isabel was largely supporting him, providing housing, food, clothing, and transport and covering his health insurance.

Besides all this, as a single mother of an incarcerated son, Isabel also helped take care of Bobby's daughter. Like Isabel, Bobby became a parent young, at age eighteen. His daughter Sofia was four years old and in preschool when Bobby began his prison sentence.

Many of the people we spoke to had relied throughout their lives on their mothers, not just for a place to stay and financial help, but for help in navigating the courts and prison. One respondent, Shana, came into the reentry study through a parole violation and was spending thirty days at MCI Framingham when we first met her. She had been arrested a number of times, mostly for shoplifting and other thefts, and had been a regular heroin user. She listed bipolar disorder and post-traumatic stress among her health problems.

An African American woman in her midthirties, Shana had grown up in the Midwest. She was raised by her older sisters and her mother, Ralene. Her father had not been a presence in her life since she was five years old. Ralene told us that Shana had an unexceptional childhood. She "never had any problems coming up. . . . She was a real quiet kid." Shana's conflicts with the law began later, when the family moved to Massachusetts when she was twenty years old. It was then that she first smoked marijuana. Later, she would start using heroin. Shana was arrested for the first time in Massachusetts the following year. The year after that, she was put on probation after illegally using a credit card.

Although Shana's drug problems and arrests did not begin until relatively late, her childhood was troubled. Her older sister was raped when Shana was eight years old, and she thinks her sister suffered from depression while they were growing up. When Shana was fifteen, Ralene left home to get treatment for her own cocaine addiction and Shana went to live with her godparents for a year. She completed twelfth grade, but did not pass the state exam required for a high school diploma. Just as challenging perhaps was the presence of other relatives who had contended with schizophrenia, drug addiction, and criminal convictions.

Ralene was in her early sixties at the time of the reentry study. A cocaine addict, she had maintained sobriety for over thirty years. She spoke to us about the helplessness she felt in the face of her child's addiction, a feeling echoed by several of the parents we interviewed. When Shana returned to Framingham on the parole violation, Ralene had long decided that she would support her daughter financially, but she could no longer live at home. Shana's children were welcome at the house, and they regularly stayed over at weekends. (Shana's third child was given up to adoption.)

Family support was crucial, but many of the mothers and grandmothers we interviewed had known hardship themselves even before housing and feeding their children and grandchildren just released from incarceration. Sam, at age thirty, relied on his mother, Queenie, for a place to stay and a little cash immediately after his release. He'd grown up with his mother, sister, and two brothers. Sam didn't come to know his father until later in his life, but his mother lived with two long-term partners each of whom was an important influence in his own way. The first was abusive. When he was "really young," Sam told us, his mother's boyfriend would beat her—until Sam, at age eleven, threatened to give him a beating of his own with a two-by-four. Sam described the second man, who would become Queenie's husband, as his father figure who "saved" his mother and was present in Sam's life from his teenage years.

Queenie raised four children with only intermittent support from the men in her life. When Sam was thirteen, Queenie was struggling financially, and he was sent to live with his grandmother. Missing his mother, Sam moved back in with her after a few months. By the time Sam turned fourteen, the family had lived in ten different places. They had doubled up with Sam's grandmother several times and had also been homeless on the street.

The family battled poverty when Sam was young, but he was not unusually troublesome at school. He told us that he got in a few fights, the first in middle school, and he was suspended twice. But, he said, he wasn't involved in crime when he was young. "Growing up, my friends weren't really into the streets like that," Sam said. "We played a lot of basketball and stuff." He finished high school and completed a year of college before withdrawing because he could not afford tuition.

Sam got involved in street life relatively late. When he was twenty-two, his older brother was shot in the head in a club in a gang-related killing. Queenie said that Sam began to change after his brother's murder. At the funeral, he sat not with her, but with his friends. He felt threatened and began to carry a gun around. "I was hanging around my brother, my cousins. The way we were living at that time made me have it. . . . It was for safety," he said. Later that year, Sam was arrested for the first time, for carrying a firearm, and he served an eighteen-month sentence.

Two years after his release, he was picked up again, this time on gun and drug charges. He served another two years in state prison. While he was in prison, Queenie and Sam talked on the phone each day, and she visited him a few times during his two-year sentence. He was released in the fall from a minimum-security prison and picked up by his siblings, who drove him home to Mattapan. He lived with Queenie, her husband, and his younger brother for the next year. Every weekend, Sam's six-year-old son, Little Sam, stayed over with the family at Queenie's place.

For Bobby, Shana, and Sam, and for the reentry sample as a whole, family support was provided by women, mostly mothers, but also by grandmothers, sisters, and aunts. At one week after prison release, just under half the sample (55 out of 122) were staying with family members, and most of those (40 out of 55) were staying with a female relative. In contrast, only 2 out of 55 reported staying with a father, and another 2 out of 55 reported staying with both parents in the first week after prison release. Staying with a partner was also relatively unusual: only 10 out of 122 respondents were living with a wife or a girlfriend immediately after incarceration.

Although incarceration was often just the most recent in a lifetime of challenges for some families, news of a prison sentence and the incarceration itself were often exhausting and demoralizing. Isabel was in court when Bobby was sentenced. She had been going to all his court dates and knew that prison time was the likely outcome. Nevertheless, when the sentence was announced, "I was devastated," she said.

When we asked Isabel what she felt when Bobby was incarcerated, she spoke about her exhaustion and anger. Initially she visited each week, and Bobby would also call home every few days. It was a demanding routine:

> It caused stress for me and also my other son. It was just us as a household. It was just me, my two kids. I've raised them by myself. It was tough. Having Bobby in there. And in my mind, it was just like, I have to visit my son, I have to see him all the time. I was running—ragged. I don't even know how to say it.

Isabel felt that she had little choice but to visit Bobby in prison, but it also made her angry. She described her conflicting feelings:

> I wanted to be there for both of my sons and for Bobby not to feel like he was alone, and at the same time I was mad at him. Because I would make sure that he knew that I was mad that I had to come visit. At the same time, I would never leave him. I would support him. I would visit him.

Bobby began serving his time in March. That December, Isabel was diagnosed with cancer. She had surgery at the end of the month and began chemotherapy in January. She shared the news of her diagnosis with Bobby on one of her visits, explaining the changes he would see in her as she went through her treatment. Once the chemotherapy started, Isabel would call ahead to the prison each time to make sure they would let her keep her wig on as she passed through the metal detectors to the visiting room.

Isabel usually visited the prison on her own. "I was happy to be able to give him a hug," she said. "Talking on the phone is not the same." At the start of each visit, she would say, "Let's get some food," then go over to the vending machine to buy snacks and soda. They'd pull out a board game or a pack of cards and play while trying to start the conversation. Bobby would talk about the programs he had enrolled in and the "good time" that would be taken off his sentence. Visiting hours were 6:00 to 9:00 p.m. Isabel would leave around 7:30, before it got too dark, so that she could get ready for work the next morning.

Bobby's daughter, Sofia, was four when he was first sent to prison. He kept in touch with her regularly by phone, calling Isabel two or three times a week when Sofia was staying over. Sofia regularly stayed overnight before Bobby was incarcerated, and this continued after he went to prison. Isabel worked hard on her son's relationship with his daughter while he was in prison. Besides the many phone calls, Isabel also took Sofia to visit her father in prison a few times. She made a photo album with pictures of her son that Sofia kept in her backpack and carried with her everywhere.

Like Bobby, Sam stayed in close contact with his children through his mother. Sam was living with his mother just before he was incarcerated. Mother and son were very close, Queenie said. When asked what kinds of support she typically gave Sam before he went to prison, she mentioned food, housing, clothing, transportation, and emotional support. "Any other support?" we asked. "With love," Queenie replied. Sam's two boys, Little Sam and Donte, were often over at Queenie's house before their father was incarcerated, and they would continue to be regular visitors for the two years he was in prison.

Sam's incarceration sent Queenie into a long depression. She stopped spending time with her friends and never spoke to them about what she was going through. "When Sam went in," she said, "it really broke my heart. When Sam wasn't around, you didn't want to do anything. I could see the sadness in my boys [Sam's younger brothers]. It's so hard to explain. We'd just sit here, just to hear the phone ring."

Queenie had endured a depression once before and recognized the symptoms. When we spoke to her nearly a year after Sam's release, she said it was still "all bottled up." She remained withdrawn from her friends and often cried, thinking about Sam's time in prison.

Sam was incarcerated for two years, and Queenie visited him four times in prison. The visits were emotionally draining, and Queenie found it hard to keep them up. "It takes so much out of me just to leave without him," she said. The visits themselves were quite long, starting in early afternoon and continuing until 6:00 p.m. Conversations during those prison visits were always positive, and focused on the family's activities.

Although Queenie found it hard to visit Sam in prison, she regularly supported him in other ways. They spoke on the phone nearly every day, and she regularly sent money for his canteen account to cover the cost of the calls. During his incarceration, Sam also spent money on a television, clothes, a fan for his cell, and food from the canteen. Queenie estimates that during his two-year incarceration she sent her son about $800 for clothes and about $1,500 in total.

During his incarceration, Queenie also took care of Sam's sons. Little Sam would regularly spend weekends with Queenie, and Sam called his son each week. Queenie also helped out Little Sam's mother financially. Sam was not as close to his younger son, Donte. Donte's paternity was uncertain, at least in Sam's mind. Donte was also just a baby when his father was sent to prison and was not yet a large presence in Sam's life. Still, Donte would sometimes stay with Queenie, and Queenie would help out Donte's mother, much as she did for Little Sam's mother. Like Little Sam, Donte visited his father just once during Sam's incarceration.

If Queenie was crushed by Sam's incarceration, Shana's mother, Ralene, was relieved by the news that her daughter was going to prison. "I knew that she was safe," Ralene said. "I knew exactly where she was." In the six months before her incarceration, Shana was staying with a friend but had also spent time in police lockups and a drug treatment program. She was using heroin a few times a week and was supported financially by her parents. Her incarceration at Framingham for thirty days on a parole violation brought to an end the latest slide back into addiction. While in prison, Shana made plans for her move to a residential drug program for women in the Roxbury neighborhood.

We asked Ralene if things changed much for the family when Shana was locked up. "No," she said. "People continued on with their lives."

Ralene kept in touch with Shana by mail, but she did not visit or call. "I don't believe in visiting prisons," Ralene told us. "I'm not a criminal. I don't want to be searched. As an addict, I don't go to jails to speak to people. . . . I don't want to be touched. I don't want them going through my purse. None of that. . . . I just don't like going to those places." Phone calls, too, were out. "No collect calls," she said. "Can't afford it."

Before her incarceration, Shana was in touch with two of her three children every few months. Their father had custody of the kids and lived outside Boston, but the two children would visit regularly with Ralene. Shana did not have contact with her children during her incarceration. As Ralene explained it to us:

> It's been difficult for Shana to take care of any kid. She's just not that. . . . Some people just aren't mothers. They don't have that in them. And she's one that doesn't. I told her that good mothers are mothers that say, "I can't take care of my kids. Can you help me?" Those are good mothers too. It doesn't make you a bad mother because you can't take care of your kids. Bad mothers are the ones that keep their children knowing they can't take care of them. And things wind up happening.

When parents spoke to us about their children's incarceration, they described a variety of strong emotions that often included sadness, disappointment, and anger. Many times, it was difficult for parents to talk about their children's incarceration without crying. Many told us that, although they were deeply anxious about their children going to prison, they had rarely shared these thoughts with anyone. None of the parents we interviewed had sought professional help to address the anxiety and depression they experienced because of their child's incarceration. Perhaps incarceration caused them to feel shame and embarrassment and made them reluctant to discuss the issue with anyone but close family and friends. It is just as possible that the low-income mothers among the parents of our respondents had too little time or money for therapists or psychiatry.

For the parents of long-term addicts—like Shana's mother Ralene—incarceration was not as much a source of anxiety and sadness as it was for most others. For these parents, incarceration at least provided a chance for their children to get sober and have their whereabouts accounted for. Compared to the overdoses, car accidents, and emergency room visits, prison was relatively predictable and offered the possibility of a fresh start.

In addition to the psychological toll of incarceration, families also paid for food, clothing, and other necessities through prison canteen accounts, covered the costs of calls and visits, and took care of children whose mother or father was in prison. It's difficult to estimate how much incarceration added to the financial burden carried by mothers, sisters, and grandmothers, but their own economic hardship was clear. Among the thirty-six mothers we interviewed, around one-third were single and not living with a partner, just over half were unemployed, and nearly two-thirds were on public assistance. The direct economic costs of supporting an incarcerated family member were borne by those with little capacity to pay.[1]

Incarceration's burden on families continued after prison release. When Bobby was released and returned to live with his mother Isabel, she was supporting both her son, now twenty-four, and his daughter Sofia, who continued to stay at the house two or three nights a week. The day Bobby got out of prison, Isabel could not get off work to pick him up, but she saw him later that day at a family gathering. Isabel's sisters had seen her struggle to visit him in prison and take care of Sofia even as she was going through chemotherapy and holding down a job. Now they rose to her defense at the "welcome home" party, urging Bobby to clean up his life. Bobby's return home, Isabel said, had been difficult, and his younger brother had been moody. "We were all going through these mixed feelings together," she said.

Nearly all of Bobby's financial support in his first few months after release was provided by his mother. She gave him around $200 each month, which he mostly spent on food and public transportation. Isabel also paid Bobby's monthly cell-phone fee of $50 and his monthly probation fee of $65.

Bobby could not find work in the year after his release. A few weeks out of prison, his probation officer gave him a well-worn list of CORI-friendly employers that were thought to hire job-seekers with criminal records. Still, his job search was long and unproductive. Isabel, who was closely involved in his job search, reflected on Bobby's year of unemployment:

> I'm frustrated, and he's frustrated, about this whole job thing. We've applied. I have Internet at home, and we sat down and put together whenever he worked . . . you know, put our dates together so he can apply. And it's frustrating. Whatever job we think of, no one calls him. And he's frustrated and I'm frustrated.

Bobby's employment problems also kept him at his mother's place. We asked Isabel how long she thought Bobby would be living with her. "Oh Lord, I don't know," she said. "He says, 'I'm grown. I'm going to leave one day.' And I say, 'Okay, I'm waiting.'"

Shana had made plans with her mother Ralene to move into a women's sober house after leaving Framingham. Over the next year, Ralene and her husband, Joshua, covered Shana's rent ($400 a month, twice as much as her food stamps benefit) and gave her money for food, clothing, and transportation. Shana would sometimes stay with Ralene and Joshua on weekends, and often her children would stay over too. During these visits, Ralene helped Shana work on her computer skills and prepare a résumé. Shana never worked during the year that we met with her, and she changed housing programs several times. It seemed that staying clean was a full-time job and, without Ralene and Joshua's financial support, stable housing and other necessities would have been out of her reach.

Shana's children were in their father's custody, but Ralene had them at her house every other weekend, and she managed the kids' visits with their mother. Ralene kept up with their progress at school, and when they came over, they played with other children in the neighborhood. The kids liked spending time with their mother, but understood, Ralene said, why they could not live with Shana. "I talk to [the kids] about mental illness and depression," she said. Although Shana did not see the children frequently, she stayed in touch with weekly calls. Ralene thought that this was a workable arrangement for her daughter: "I don't think Shana worries about [not seeing them]. She's okay as long as we see them. She doesn't have that motherly attachment."

Queenie was at work when Sam got released, and she saw him later that day at her place in Mattapan. "I was so happy to see him. All I could do was hug him," Queenie said. "Sam is the sunshine around here." They talked about the other incarcerated men Queenie had got to know from Sam's phone calls. During that first week back, Sam enrolled in food stamps and also got some money from his younger brothers. He also saw both his children that first week back. When Little Sam came over to Queenie's place, father and son played video games. The next day Sam took Little Sam to a Celtics game at the big sports arena downtown.

Like Bobby and Shana, Sam was unemployed in his first months back from prison, but he did eventually find work. At our six-month interview, we asked Sam what the best thing was about his life. "Finally getting a job," he answered. Sam estimated that he had submitted dozens of job applications in the six months he was unemployed, and he had also talked to friends and relatives about finding work. It was his stepfather's many connections through his own small business, a small West Indian diner, that finally landed Sam a steady job. A few weeks earlier, his stepfather was meeting with a supplier who sold soda to local restaurants The soda wholesaler said that he needed someone for a warehouse job, and Sam's stepfather put him in touch with Sam. The job paid $9 an hour for a forty-hour week.

Family support after incarceration takes many forms. Most commonly, families provide a place to stay and some ready cash, at least for the first few weeks back in society. Taken together, these supports greatly exceed the value of public assistance, chiefly obtained through food stamps and SSI. About half of the respondents who were staying with their mother or a sister after their first week out of prison were continuing to live with family a year later. Many of these supportive family members were stably employed, like Isabel, who worked as a school administrator, or Queenie, who worked at a hospital. Family supporters were often solidly working class, but they were also frequently helping other family members—other sons or daughters and their children—who had not gotten in trouble with the law.

Because family support was so gendered—chiefly coming from mothers, sisters, and grandmothers—the varieties of support were also gendered. Respondents told us that they had received not only food, clothing, and housing but also emotional encouragement. Most striking perhaps was the involvement of grandmothers in the lives of small children with incarcerated parents. Many of the mothers we spoke with were taking care of two generations: their sons recently returned from prison, and their sons' children who stayed over at weekends.

It was harder for older women in particular to find job opportunities for their children. Isabel worked tirelessly on Bobby's job search, but could do little beyond helping with his résumé and online applications. Job referrals and introductions for manual unskilled work were mostly provided by older men—friends, stepfathers, fathers-in-law—but such men were in short supply for those coming out of prison. Among Bobby, Shana, and Sam, only Sam found steady work, and that was through a connection provided by his stepfather.

For low-income families with few sources of support themselves, helping a loved one after incarceration often strained material and emotional resources. Isabel housed and helped her two boys and her granddaughter on an office administrator's salary while going through cancer treatment. Queenie's hospital job supported Sam and his younger brother, even as she battled her own depression, which had set in while Sam was incarcerated.

Research on the family lives of men and women released from prison has focused on wives and girlfriends and on children with incarcerated parents.[2] As sources of material support, the romantic partners of the reentry study respondents played a relatively small role during the year after incarceration.

They loomed large, however, as gatekeepers for formerly incarcerated men and women who wanted a role in their children's lives.

We can illustrate the shape of these relationships with family trees drawn in figures 7.1 to 7.3. Older generations appear at the top of the figure, with younger generations below them. Males are depicted with triangles and females with circles. Blood relations between mother and child and among siblings are indicated with solid lines, and marriages are shown with an equals sign (=). To capture some of the complexity of family relationships in the reentry study, parents who were on good terms but not romantically involved are shown as "approximately equals" (≈), and parents who no longer have any relationship with each other are "not equals" (≠). Family members who live together at least periodically are shown with a broken line. Although the figures depict only a small piece of the kinship structure, they do show the residence of the children and their relationships with their formerly incarcerated parents.

Kay was pregnant with Sofia when Bobby got arrested (figure 7.1). Bobby was eighteen and living half the time with Kay and half with his mother Isabel. He was making a good living selling drugs and enjoying the lifestyle of a successful drug dealer. By some measures, Bobby might have been a nonresident father after his release from prison. But Sofia regularly stayed with him and her grandmother for several nights each week, and on other nights, when Sofia was with her mother, Bobby would regularly stay over. Sofia had become as much a presence in her grandmother's life as in Bobby's. When Bobby was in prison, Isabel made sure the two talked on the phone.

By the time of Bobby's incarceration, his relationship with Kay had evolved into something more like a friendship. The couple went "back and forth," said Bobby. On the day Bobby was released, Kay came by with Sofia to pick him up from the prison and drive him to Isabel's place, an hour away. There a family cookout was planned to mark Bobby's return. That first week home, Bobby stayed mostly with his mother, but he also spent a night with Kay and Sofia, and another night with a girl he met.

A few months later, Bobby had settled into a routine. He was living with his mother but stayed in touch with Sofia every day, and his daughter, now seven, stayed over with Isabel and Bobby two days a week. Now, in the summer, Bobby was taking Sofia to camp and, largely with Isabel's help, providing some financial support for his daughter.

Over the course of the year, Bobby had relationships with a number of women but was continuously in contact with Kay. Despite these casual re-

Figure 7.1 *Bobby's Family*

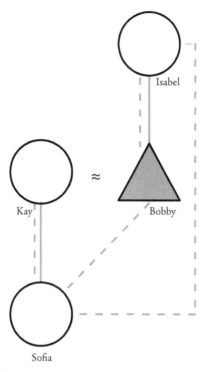

Isabel

Kay ≈ Bobby

Sofia

Source: Author's compilation.
Note: Bobby (shaded) lived with his mother, Isabel, after incarceration and was on good terms with Kay, the mother of his child Sofia, who divided her time between Kay's place and Isabel's.

lationships, Bobby said he talked only with Kay and Isabel about things that were important to him. Through the first six months out of prison, he described his relationship with Kay as "just friends." But by the end of the year, Bobby seemed more strongly committed to her. When we asked about Kay at the final interview, Bobby said, "That's my girl." He was spending most nights with her and no longer reporting any involvement with other women. The other women, he said, were getting "too clingy. It was turning into a using thing."

Shana was more distant from her three children, and the subject often seemed painful and difficult for her to talk about. Joanna and Seth were ages eight and six and lived with their father. Shana had been pregnant with her third child, Sasha, when she was incarcerated five years earlier. Sasha was put up for adoption and lived with her adoptive parents. Shana had

Figure 7.2 *Shana's Family*

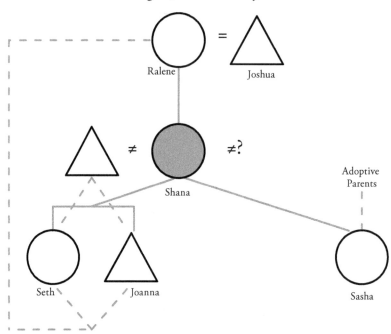

Source: Author's compilation.
Note: Shana (shaded), Ralene's daughter, had no relationship with the fathers of her three children. Two of the children, Seth and Joanna, lived with their father but visited their grandmother Ralene about once a month. Shana's other daughter, Sasha, was adopted at an early age, and Shana rarely spoke of her or her father.

never had contact with the adoptive parents and was never in a relationship with Sasha's father (figure 7.2).

Prior to her most recent incarceration, Shana was in contact with Joanna and Seth every few months. She was living in a residential drug treatment program and would sometimes visit the children on weekends when they were with Ralene and Joshua, or she would speak to them by phone. The children did not know that Shana had been incarcerated. Ralene had just told them that their mother had gone away for a while. Shana entered a sober house program when she was released and spent her first week attending meetings. A few months out of prison, Shana had seen Joanna with the children's father. By her second month out of prison, Shana had formed a new romantic relationship with a man she met at a drug rehabilitation meeting.

Shana got into more regular contact with her children as the year pro-

Figure 7.3 *Sam's Family*

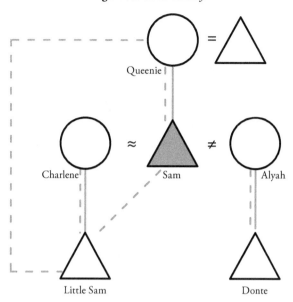

Source: Author's compilation.
Note: Sam (shaded) lived with his mother, Queenie, and his stepfather. He was good friends with Little Sam's mother, Charlene, but had a strained relationship with Alyah, the mother of his younger son, Donte. Little Sam would often stay over at Queenie's place, but Donte did not. Sam's primary relationship, with Britney, is not shown.

gressed. She saw them every month or so on weekends when they stayed with her parents. She also spoke with the children regularly on the phone. Still, she told us, being away from them so much was one of the most difficult things for her. At six months out of prison, Shana had ended her relationship, just telling us it was "because he lied." Over the next six months, Shana sank into a lengthy depression. She rarely left her room at the treatment program. The cloud had begun to lift when we met for the final interview. She sounded like she had woken up from a long sleep. Throughout it all, Shana had stayed in regular contact with Joanna and Seth.

Sam and Charlene were living together when Little Sam was born. Donte was born two years later to Alyah, with whom, Sam said, he was "just friends." In any case, he was not completely sure the child was his. At the time he was arrested, Sam was living with Charlene in a household that included Charlene's father and brother and Little Sam. Describing Sam's relationship with his two sons, Queenie told us, "Little Sam is always the one he holds closer," because of his close relationship with Charlene (figure 7.3).

By the end of his prison sentence, Sam was in contact with the mothers of both of his children, though he was no longer romantically involved with either of them. Sam was hopeful that he and Charlene might get back together, but Donte's birth had caused a rift between them. He suspected that she had started seeing someone else while he was in prison. Even as Sam and Charlene took stock of their relationship during the first month after Sam was back, he was in weekly contact with Little Sam and speaking on the phone every few weeks with Donte and Alyah. Two months after he left incarceration, he had spoken periodically to Charlene and Alyah and described both women as "just friends." At that point, his feelings toward Alyah were a little more positive and he was hurt that Charlene had not wanted to continue their relationship.

After he had been out of prison for a few weeks, Sam became involved with Britney. Britney worked as a home health aide and had known Sam since before his incarceration. She had two children of her own. Sam and Britney were getting on well in the first few weeks of their relationship, but he was frustrated that he could not contribute financially when they went out to the movies or to eat.

Over the remainder of his first year out of prison, Sam spent time with Little Sam once a week when the boy stayed with Queenie on weekends, but he had less consistent contact with Donte. At this point, Sam was not in touch with the children's mothers very much, but he still described both women as friends and said he viewed them both positively. Sam would talk to Little Sam every day, and he provided what financial support he could. Sam saw Donte much less frequently. Queenie said that Alyah felt rejected by Sam and was less willing to let Donte see his father. Still, Sam helped out with $40 each week for Donte.

We met Little Sam at our final interview with Sam, at his stepfather's diner. When Sam showed us a video on his phone of his son playing baseball, we recognized Little Sam as the small boy playing at the back of the diner, by the kitchen, with the eight-year-old son of Sam's stepfather. After being back home for some time, Sam had grown closer to the other children in his family, including his stepfather's young son and his sister's eight-year-old daughter.

Sam's relationship with Britney continued throughout his first year out of prison. Britney lived near Sam's warehouse job with the soda company, and he was spending a lot of time there. Although Sam told us that he lived at his mother's place and kept many of his clothes and belongings there,

Queenie said that he really lived with Britney. "He's always over there," she said. "Just give me a phone call. That's all I ask for."

Researchers who study the relationships of poor mothers and fathers often point to "family complexity" as a danger to the well-being of their children.[3] "Family complexity" usually refers to fathers who do not live with their children and may provide little social or financial support. Family complexity is magnified by "multiple partner fertility," where one parent (either a mother or a father) has children with several other partners. The idea of family complexity helps explain the economic insecurity and socially unstable environments of low-income children. At the same time, family complexity raises the possibility that fathers who are not living with their children, nor paying a child support order, are often doing more to support their children than statistics on single-parenthood suggest.

Most of the relationships between the reentry study respondents and their partners and children met the demographic definition of family complexity. Although the fathers and mothers of the reentry study rarely lived with their children in the first year after prison release, they were regularly in contact. Only about 10 percent of the parents in the study lived with their children at any point in the year after incarceration, but about 60 percent were in contact with their children at least once a week. Multiple partner fertility was the norm. Over half of parents with at least two biological children had had those children with two or more partners.[4]

For the mothers and fathers in the reentry sample, the custodial parent was the gatekeeper who determined the terms of contact between the children and their parent just released from prison. Sam and Charlene got on reasonably well, and Little Sam was a regular presence in his father's life after he got out of prison. Bobby, too, was able to be a father to his daughter after getting back together with her mother after his release from prison. But just as important as these partners were supportive mothers like Isabel, Ralene, and Queenie. These women were the key intermediaries that provided a place for their grandchildren to stay when they visited. They also maintained relationships with their grandchildren's guardians when their own children were incarcerated.

The complexity of family life makes it difficult to define a single effect of incarceration on parenting and children. Some men recently released from prison may be close to one child and one mother, but estranged from another child and his or her mother. Overlaid on family relationships characterized by multiple partner fertility, incarceration expands the challenge for parents of maintaining strong and consistent relationships with their children.

The fundamental importance of gender is often overlooked in research and commentary on mass incarceration. It is well understood that the prison population is mostly male, and that the negative effects of incarceration— lost earnings, poor health—are concentrated among men. Not as well documented is the caring work that helps to repair families disrupted by incarceration. This work is done primarily by older women—the mothers, grandmothers, and sisters of those who go to prison. These older women visit their loved ones, talk to them by phone, offer food and housing after release, and often help take care of their children. In the reentry study sample, the average age of the mothers who housed their son or daughter after prison was fifty-two, and the average age of their children was thirty. Research on incarceration and families has focused on the effects of parental incarceration on young children.[5] Such effects are enormously important, but they fail to reflect the greatest family effect of mass incarceration: the pressure on older women in poor communities to continue their role as caregivers to their children well past midlife.

The biographies of these older women often do not look very different from those of their children and their children's partners. Isabel grew up in a poor immigrant family and had a child at eighteen with a man who abused and then deserted her. Ralene also grew up poor and struggled with addiction until she got clean in her twenties. Queenie was a poor single mother with four children who spent time with them homeless and on the streets. In time, all three of these women found reasonably steady work, and in their forties, fifties, and sixties, they became critical sources of support not just for their children after incarceration but also for their grandchildren and other family members.

The gendered character of family support explains how the burdens of incarceration are distributed across family members. We can obtain a rough sense by estimating the rental value of the housing provided by different family members in the year after prison release. Assume respondents had lived continuously in the household they reported at each wave of the survey and each month of housing cost $500 in rent on the open market.[6] On this assumption, mothers in the sample are estimated to have provided a total of $118,000 in housing support over the year, compared to $14,000 provided by fathers. Partners are estimated to have provided $71,000 in housing support, which slightly exceeds the $50,500 in support provided by sisters. About 30 percent of the sample lived with their mother at some point in the year after release. These respondents received an average of $3,400 in housing support compared to their median income of $10,500. In short, housing support from mothers alone equaled about one-third of the total income received by these respondents from employment and government benefits. These figures underestimate the total level of maternal support and are only suggestive, indicating the relative levels of social support provided by different family members. Such quantification also glosses over the many other kinds of burdens borne by families when faced with the incarceration of kin.

The critical role of older women in maintaining economic and social stability also tells us something about the social structure of poor communities. In communities with high levels of poverty and violence, such women become the anchors of social life. They provide material support to their adult children and help sustain fragile social bonds among parents in the generation after them. Men's place in the structure of social life in these poor communities is more tenuous. Like more than half the reentry study sample, neither Bobby nor Sam really knew their father. Isabel raised Bobby on her own, just as Queenie raised Sam. It is hard to predict the roles that Bobby and Sam will play in the lives of their own children. A year out of prison, Bobby was a close and involved parent to Sofia, but he had been unemployed for that whole year and involved with other women. Sofia's mother, Kay, may well find better options or choose to raise Sofia alone. Sam saw Little Sam at least every weekend, but he saw Donte much less. In families like these, much of the care and support of children falls on older women, whose employment and households are relatively stable.

Debates about poor families are often suffused in a moral language that classifies parents as either good or bad, supportive or neglectful.[7] Bobby, Shana, and Sam played their roles as parents and children in poor and desperate circumstances that resist such easy judgments. In Ralene's view, Shana's bravest act of motherhood—as a heroin addict struggling to get clean—may have been to give up her youngest daughter for adoption. Bobby was a loving father, even while he played the field just out of prison and for a year could not find work to support his daughter. Sam was a proud father to Little Sam, who thrived in the web of family ties that revolved around his stepgrandfather's diner in Dorchester, yet Sam's other son Donte was rarely there.

Poverty and its multiplex social context make it hard to be a supportive parent. The separation from children during incarceration and the adjustment after release make it harder still. Yet loving support could be seen everywhere in how mothers took care of their adult children just out of prison. A mother's steady job, a stable home, and successful recovery nourished the bonds of social and financial support. Besides providing material assistance, the families with the strongest ties refused to make unforgiving moral judgments that might cloud the patient practice of compassion and love.

....

CHAPTER 8

Back to Jail

The first interview of the reentry study was conducted in a medium-security prison with Sean, about a week before his release. He felt optimistic about leaving prison, especially, he said, if he could stay sober. Sean's mother and one of his brothers had struggled with addiction, and he himself had been an alcoholic since his early teenage years. A white man in his midforties with an open and friendly face, Sean had worked as a house painter in the brief periods he was out of jail. Shortly after his release, he went to work for his brother painting houses on Cape Cod.

It was summer when Sean got out, and the Cape was busy with vacationers staying in the small fishing towns on the crescent-shaped stretch of land in Massachusetts Bay. On a warm and sunny day, Sean was offered a cold beer by a neighbor. His supply of Antabuse—an alcohol aversion drug—from prison had run out, and one beer quickly led to another. These few drinks ignited a three-day binge that also involved crack and heroin use. The bender ended abruptly when Sean went into a bank in Cambridge, exhausted, desperate, and armed only with a note demanding money. The teller handed over bags of cash, and Sean made his escape by bus. While Sean rode away from the crime scene, police cruisers inched up, tipped off by a tracking device planted in the packets of money from the bank. Easily apprehended, Sean went back to prison for the unarmed robbery. We interviewed him a few weeks later back in MCI Concord. The reentry study's first respondent was reincarcerated within three weeks of his release.

By the time our field period was over, 38 of our 122 respondents had returned to custody, 27 within twelve months of release. Twenty-two times we returned to prisons and county jails for reincarceration interviews. Some respondents were locked up for just a week or so awaiting a court date. Others went back to state prison to serve long sentences for new and sometimes serious crimes.

Returning to jail after incarceration is often the yardstick by which the transition from prison to community is measured. Reincarceration is viewed as a failed reentry. The offender has failed by returning to crime. The penal institution has failed by doing too little to deter or rehabilitate. The focus of experts and practitioners in the field on reincarceration accompanies an overriding concern for reducing recidivism. Indeed, the entire correctional project—prison programs, community supervision, transitional services— has the reduction of recidivism as a central goal. In this world, an offender who avoids reincarceration is clearly signaling that he has turned his life around and is now abiding by the law.

Reincarceration, however, is many things and not just a marker of failure. Often, as in Sean's case, it is relapse to addiction. Sometimes it is living under the suspicion of a parole officer with a full caseload and little time. Sometimes it is just living poor in a bad neighborhood. The overwhelming focus on reincarceration in research and policy can misunderstand the process by which people return to prison and the capacity of criminal justice institutions to foster a productive life in free society. Tracing the paths back to incarceration can help us define a richer set of objectives for our criminal justice institutions and redefine the elusive goal of rehabilitation that has motivated the correctional project with limited success since its inception.

The latest recidivism study from the U.S. Bureau of Justice Statistics reported that 18 percent of state prisoners nationwide return to incarceration within twelve months of release—a rate almost identical to the level of reincarceration in the Boston Reentry Study.[1] In Boston, women were just as likely to return to custody as men, reincarceration among blacks was no higher than among whites, and recidivists were not especially likely to be unemployed, unstably housed, or lacking in family support. Instead, we found that just three factors among many were closely associated with a return to incarceration: relapsing to addiction, being on probation or parole, and being younger than average. These risk factors describe different aspects of the social context of recidivism.

The correlation between drug relapse and a return to custody was the strongest in our analysis of recidivism. When we first met people in prison, over half told us that they previously had problems with drugs or alcohol, and they cited their regular use of cocaine, heroin, and alcohol. (Respondents with drug problems were also regular marijuana users, but marijuana use was even more common among those reporting no history of drug problems.) Of these drug-vulnerable respondents, half reported using drugs or alcohol over the twelve months after prison release. We categorized respondents with a history of drug problems who used drugs after prison release as relapsing to addiction. The reincarceration rate among these respondents was more than double the rate for the rest of the sample (56 versus 22 percent), and more than triple the rate for those who had a history of addiction but who stayed clean after prison release (12 percent).

Sharon was one of a handful of respondents whose final interview, like her first, was conducted in prison. We learned about her return to custody from the Department of Correction, which sent us regular updates on arrests and incarcerations of the reentry study sample. The note on Sharon read: "Sharon David has a Violation Notice on 12/22/12. On 12/22/12 she was committed as a new court commitment at MCI-Framingham on F93887 as a parole violator, first time serving on her 2008 offenses. She is in DOC custody."

Back in prison, Sharon—a white woman in her late twenties—was bright and self-assured. She talked about how the prison was starting a softball league as the summer moved into August. "Hopefully I won't be so competitive that I get in any fights," she said. In our interviews, we asked a lot of questions about respondents' childhoods. From Sharon we learned that her father was an alcoholic who was sometimes violent at home before he left after a contentious divorce. When we spoke with Sharon at Framingham, her father had been sober for nineteen years. Sharon herself started drinking at age eleven. She tried pills and cocaine around the age of thirteen, then heroin when she was seventeen. "I obviously liked just being out of myself. I've never not liked anything I've done with drugs or drinking," she said. Sharon used heroin with her boyfriend, Liam, and both of them spent her seventeenth year in a cycle of heroin use and drug treatment ("in and out, in and out").

Like many of the people with drug problems whom we spoke to, Sharon said that staying sober was the key to her successful departure from prison. At the time of her release from prison at the age of twenty-eight, she had been clean a full a year for the first time since she was fifteen. Her mother had been her main supporter from childhood and through the many periods of institutionalization, in both prison and treatment programs. Her mother had picked up Sharon from prison the last time, given her a place to stay, and helped her out financially in the first months after incarceration. Sharon also helped herself, pursuing services at community reentry programs and going to Narcotics Anonymous meetings. By two months after release, she was working full-time, although her bartending job might have presented some risks. Her parole required that she remain drug- and alcohol-free, attend a treatment program, and undergo drug testing.

Sobriety was fragile for many of those with a history of addiction. Sharon, who had absorbed much of the language of addiction and recovery, reflected on how addiction tested her willpower:

> Right now I'm sober. So if I go and say I had a bad day, I'm going to go and get high. I know better, but once I start, it's no holds barred. If I don't pick up the phone when I'm having a bad day and call up somebody, then that's on me. It's hard, and at the same time it's not. It's a simple program. You gotta work the program. Here I am telling you all this, but I can't get a year of sobriety.

Besides their own craving for drugs, people with drug problems are often surrounded by friends and intimate partners who are also drug users. On a June day, one week out of prison, Sharon told us that heroin and alcohol remained strong temptations. By the time of her release, she and Liam had been together on and off for twelve years. They had been through cycles of using and detox, but had so far survived a tumultuous passage from adolescence to adulthood. Within months of getting out, Sharon was pregnant, her second time with Liam, after the first had ended in a miscarriage.

In October, four months after her release, she miscarried again. Events followed quickly after that. She and Liam began fighting, and other girls started to visit him at his residential treatment program. Sharon started using again, and the couple broke up. She began to see an ex-boyfriend, who was receiving treatment in a methadone program. Hearing that Sharon was using again, Liam also started getting high and was thrown out of his program. With Liam back in circulation, Sharon would sneak him into her mother's house, where the couple would shoot heroin together. By November, Sharon had stopped working and she and Liam were applying themselves full-time to buying and using heroin.

That phase ended suddenly after Sharon went to detox in November. She started using again straight after detox, however, and was using at the time of her court date in early December. The next week after court, she told her probation officer that she had gone to detox. Her heroin use was revealed—a violation of a condition of her release. Parole was revoked, and Sharon was going back to prison. She expected to get ninety days. "The judge cried when she gave me a year," Sharon said. "I knew I'd go to jail, but I didn't think it would be a year."

Sharon returned to prison fully absorbed by her addiction. She smuggled drugs in for herself and other prisoners, who subsequently tested positive for drugs and disclosed Sharon as their source. She was sent to solitary confinement, locked down for twenty-three hours each day. When we talked to her at Framingham shortly after her return to incarceration, though visibly tired and sad, she acknowledged that prison had at least given her a chance to stop using drugs and get healthy. She said that she needed to stay away from Liam, that they brought each other down.

A few months later, Liam had gotten clean but was battling other health problems. He died from complications related to a heart condition while Sharon was back inside. Sharon was grieving when we met her at Framingham for her final interview. Around her neck with her prison ID she wore a photo of herself and Liam, arms around each other, smiling. She told us that she was so used to being in and out of prison that it didn't get to her anymore. She was disappointed, she said, that she could not be more of a success story for the study.

Addiction charts many paths back to jail. Besides dealing drugs, people may steal cars or rob passersby for fast money to support a habit or just to make ends meet. Some may get into fights, fueled by alcoholic rages. Still others, like Sharon, may fail a drug test or otherwise disclose their drug use, violating the conditions of community release. Among the reentry study sample, relapse was often a response to the temptation of drugs or alcohol that became available immediately after release. The appetite for drugs was also sharpened in the presence of friends and partners who were users themselves. Sharon told us that by the time she was twenty-eight, most of her friends were heroin addicts. In addition to managing the craving, perhaps in the risky company of friends who were also addicted, drugs were also used to cope with tragedy or pain. Sharon's heroin use escalated following her miscarriage. A number of other heroin addicts also told us about using drugs following the deaths of friends or family members.

Whatever the precise sequence of events leading to a relapse, criminal responsibility in the eyes of the court is undiminished by addiction. About half of all respondents who gave no indications of drug problems and were charged for a new offense after prison returned to incarceration (seventeen out of thirty-two cases). For those who relapsed and picked up new charges, the odds of being sent back to prison were nearly identical (ten out of seventeen). In short, new charges, relapse or not, make reincarceration a strong possibility.

In Sharon's case, reincarceration resulted from a parole violation, not a conviction for a new offense. Community supervision—parole and probation—plays its own role in the process of reincarceration. Probation and parole were Progressive-era innovations in correctional policy, emerging in the first decades of the twentieth century. Probation was a court function. Probation officers were to write detailed pre-sentence reports on criminal defendants that would help judges decide whether to impose a prison sentence. If the probation officer reported sufficient potential for reform, the judge would return the defendant to the community, but under the supervision of the probation officer, who would help with rehabilitation. Parole was an executive function: after a period of incarceration, the parole board would review a prisoner's application for early release. If parole was granted, the prisoner would be released to the supervision of a parole officer, who would assist in the transition from incarceration to community. In both cases, community supervision was designed as part oversight and part social work. In fulfilling their oversight function, probation and parole officers could recommend that their clients be removed from the community and incarcerated if they violated the conditions of their release.[2]

Modern community supervision has drifted away from its rehabilitative origins. Probation and parole officers now spend much of their time monitoring compliance with the many conditions of release, which commonly include refraining from drug use, staying away from victims and those with criminal records, and participating in programs. Joan Petersilia writes that "parole agents have become less 'kind and gentle.' Parole departments in most large urban areas have a prevailing culture that emphasizes surveillance over services."[3] As "community corrections"—the collective term for probation and parole—looks more like policing, officers more often carry firearms and the day-to-day work is focused on surveillance activities such as drug testing, monitoring curfews, and collecting fees.

Contemporary probation and parole is an uneasy mix of crime prevention and strict punishment. Rigorous regimens of drug-testing and curfews are intended to deter crime, but when supervision is disrupted or rules are violated, probation and parole officers appear to have few remedies besides incarceration.[4] The success of the crime preventive effect was reflected in the low level of drug use among probationers and parolees. Counting drug use, only one-quarter of respondents on community supervision reported illegal activity compared to half of those who were not on supervision. Despite the low crime rate, the reincarceration rate was twice as high for probationers and parolees compared with the rate for respondents who had completed their sentences and were unsupervised (28 percent versus 13 percent). For those respondents who reported illegal activity, about half returned to incarceration regardless of supervision status. The key difference was for those who said that they were not involved in illegal activity. Virtually none of the unsupervised respondents went back to jail if they were not involved in crime, but 20 percent of those under supervision were reincarcerated, even when they reported no involvement in crime. Reincarceration in these cases usually resulted from a technical violation of the conditions of supervision. Thus, the reentry study reveals a strange paradox: probationers and parolees committed less crime, but more often went back to prison.

In the Boston study, 60 percent of respondents were released to the community under the supervision of a probation or parole officer.[5] The criminal justice term "community supervision" conveys more involvement by probation or parole officers than we typically observed. Parole and probation generally require regular reporting to an officer in the community. For our respondents, meetings with probation officers tended to be quite brief, often lasting less than thirty minutes, and were focused on providing proof of residence and employment (for those who were working) and sometimes drug testing. As in many jurisdictions, Boston-area community supervision also imposes monthly supervision fees. These would sometimes be waived in return for community service, but nonpayment could also result in a violation.

Charles was a twenty-three-year-old African American man who had served four and a half years on gun charges. He had a long history of arrests, mostly for weapons offenses, and he had been incarcerated as a child with the Department of Youth Services. He was a high school graduate, and his first real employment was during incarceration, learning auto-body repair on a work-release program. He had two daughters and told us that he was on good terms with both their mothers, though his criminal record showed that a restraining order had been taken out three years earlier by one mother on behalf of herself and her child. Charles told us that he had been in regular contact with both daughters during his incarceration.

Not uncommon in Massachusetts, Charles was released to both parole and probation supervision, on separate charges, and had to report regularly to officers at each agency. He was required to avoid drugs and alcohol, stay away from gang members, and find employment. In his first week after release from prison, he said that supervision might be useful, to keep a check on him, but two months later he told us that parole had "nothing to offer but a jail cell." Each month he owed probation $65 and parole another $85, fees he had trouble paying as he searched for work.

Four months after his release we received an update from the Department of Correction: "Charles Sampson received violation notices on 5/21/2013 for 4 charges out of Suffolk Superior Court." These charges referred to his original offenses, prior to his incarceration. "As of 7/9/13 he has status of warrant for these 4 charges. On 7/10/13 he was committed on a parole detainer under number W308421. His parole was revoked on 7/10/13."

Charles was incarcerated in July for the parole violation, and we talked to him the following month. He told us that he had been visiting with his daughter one evening in early July and returned early to his mother's place so that he could be home in time for his parole curfew. Late that night, a friend got arrested. The police report identified Charles fleeing the scene of the crime "clutching his waist," indicating possession of a gun. The following day Charles's parole officer told him to come into the office or a warrant would go out for his arrest. At the parole office the next day, he was met by a state trooper who handcuffed him and took him directly into custody. His parole was revoked, and he was to serve fifty-five days for the violation. Charles called his mother. She began to cry on hearing the news. He reassured her that he "wasn't in his old ways." "It sucks to say this," he said, "but coming back to prison doesn't really have an effect on me. Been doing this since I was eleven. Just let them put the cuffs on me. Just fifty-five days."

At a parole hearing back in prison, Charles learned that the charge that triggered his parole revocation was assault and battery on a police officer. He also had violations for associating with known criminals, failing to report contact with police, and nonpayment of parole fees. Charles was told that he could answer the charges at a subsequent hearing in sixty days. His incarceration was for only fifty-five days, so he waived his right to a second hearing. The assault and battery charge was dropped and never appeared on his criminal record. Indeed, no arrests or any other court actions appear on Charles's record after the gun charges from five years before. In September, fifty-five days after his parole revocation, Charles was released from prison and the violations were withdrawn.

We met with Charles for the last time the following February, sixteen months after our initial interview in prison. He was living with the mother of his oldest daughter. He also had custody of his younger daughter while her mother served two years at Framingham. He was out of work, as he had been for most of the previous year, and received $167 a month in food stamps, which he gave to his girlfriend. His expenses exceeded his income, so it is possible that he was making money illegally, as he did before he initially went to prison. Still, in the five months since coming out of prison, Charles had no new charges and had not been stopped by police.

In Charles's account of events, being mistakenly identified in a police report while on parole made him arrestable and subject to reincarceration. Whatever the exact facts, there was no case to answer, and no charges were pressed.

What do fifty-five days of reincarceration mean in this context? None of the classic purposes of incarceration—incapacitation, deterrence, or rehabilitation—have been meaningfully advanced. No programs are available for someone back in prison on a fifty-five-day parole detainer, and any removal from street life is short-lived. Nor is there evidence of deterrence. With his long history of institutionalization and current unemployment, Charles seemed relatively unconcerned about these two months of confinement. It is not even clear whether reincarceration in his case was a sign of new criminal behavior.

Charles's case shows how the logic of community supervision can lead to reincarceration. Of the twenty-six cases of return to custody of parolees and probationers in the reentry study sample, nine reported no illegal activity and six had received no new criminal charges. Of course, violations of parole and probation conditions might reflect criminal behavior that is missed by our surveys or by arrest records. The cases of people being returned to custody without clear indications of criminal behavior point to a gray area. Reincarceration resulting from a police report or an arrest can be brief and perhaps largely a procedural matter for busy agencies whose default perspective is suspicious, risk-averse, and little enchanted with the sacredness of liberty for the formerly incarcerated. Although the numbers in the reentry study are small, the data on self-reported crime, arrests, and reincarceration suggest that Charles's case is not exceptional.

Probation and parole are surveillance bureaucracies whose many conditions are accompanied by procedures to monitor compliance. Much of the work of community corrections officers revolves around regular drug tests, frequent meetings with the men and women on their caseloads, and scans of police and court databases. With dozens of people to supervise, each officer has only a few tools with which to manage inevitable disruptions, and reincarceration is chief among them. Men with long criminal histories are well known to the police, and they are often stopped and their names run to check for warrants and supervision status.[6] The environment of surveillance is primed for the possibility of violation. For men and women who are poor and often unemployed, monthly supervision fees simply add to the risk of noncompliance. Charles experienced probation and parole largely as an intrusive system of oversight that required monthly payments and threatened him with incarceration. He told us that he was unaware of his parole violation, and the schedule of parole hearings offered no opportunity to answer the charges against him, which were later dropped in any case. Fifty-five days was disruptive, but not exceptional. In Charles's case, parole revocation was a bureaucratically organized deprivation of liberty that seemed purposeless and unaccountable.

The most basic social fact of criminology is that, after adolescence, criminal involvement declines as people get older. Reincarceration follows a similar pattern. One-third of all reentry study respondents under age thirty returned to incarceration, but less than one-quarter of those age fifty or older were reincarcerated. The relationship between age and reincarceration reflects not just people's decreasing involvement in crime but also their social context. Spending time with young friends and family members raises the risks of running into police, making arrest and return to custody more likely.

Juney was twenty-five years old when we first spoke to him at Concord Farm a week before his release. He was a member of the long-standing Cape Verdean community in Dorchester whose older residents still spoke the native creole of the rocky islands off the coast of Senegal. Juney's parents came to the United States when he was four, renting a house for a family that would swell to include four boys. Juney's father was strict and abusive and often beat his lively young son, who chafed at being kept inside. The tense and violent climate at home was relieved when Juney's father abruptly told their landlord that he was returning to Cape Verde, leaving the family behind. "I leave tomorrow. I'm not here anymore," said Juney's mother, recalling her husband's departure.

Juney had been attending eighth grade at St. Patrick's, but the family's abandonment left them unable to pay tuition fees. In the struggle for housing and financial stability, he missed a year of school, and his school attendance would remain irregular in the following years. With his mother spending long days at work, Juney ran the neighborhood with the older boys on his block. At sixteen, he began dealing drugs and cycled in and out of juvenile incarceration throughout the rest of his teenage years. He first served adult jail time at eighteen, was arrested for gun possession, and began a four-year prison sentence for trafficking cocaine at age twenty. Removed from the street life by prison, Juney found his interest in education rekindled. He completed his GED while incarcerated and was one of the few respondents we interviewed who completed college credits during his reimprisonment.

With his release from prison a week away, Juney was determined to make changes in his life. He told us that his biggest challenges were finding work and keeping away from old friends. Instead of moving back with his mother, he moved in with his cousin and her young family to avoid his old neighborhood. A few weeks out of prison, Juney was on probation and parole for separate charges. His obligations to his supervising officers had become his largest concern. Each agency imposed its own conditions, and the conflicting demands made compliance difficult. Parole imposed a 10:00 p.m. curfew and required Juney to find a job. Probation, on the other hand, required Juney to attend a drug treatment program each day from 8:00 a.m. to 2:30 p.m. We asked about the treatment program: "It's pointless there. They have me do GED classes and stuff like that. I already have a GED. They still make me do it. Drug rehab classes. I don't even do drugs. Alcohol stuff. A whole bunch of classes I don't really need."

Since he was busy during the day with the probation program, Juney's only option for finding work was a night shift. Parole, he said, would remove his curfew if he could find a night job. Despite the conflicting mandates, Juney picked up a few hours' work in the afternoons as a trainer at a local gym. After a few months, he was making around $200 a week and juggling his time between the gym and the drug treatment program. Spending his spare time mostly with family, he was following his plan to stay out of trouble and avoid his old friends, who remained involved in the gangs and drug trade that had led to many of Juney's arrests in his teenage years.

Juney had been able to avoid the police, and in the first months after his prison release he was stopped only once—while riding in a car with his cousin because, a police officer said, they "fit the description" of suspects in a nearby shooting. A few months later—now about five months after his release—we received word from his cousin that Juney was arrested and back in prison. Over the following six months, we received several updates from the Department of Correction on Juney's case:

> Juney Duarte was returned to DOC custody on A928365 on 10/11/1012. He has 3 arraignments on 10/10/2012 for drug charges, 2 dismissed and 1 found guilty and sentenced to 2 years in a HOC suspended on 1/22/2013 and continued to 1/19/2015. He went to court on 4/9/13 and did not return to the A928365 number, but instead he returned as a parole violator to number W47644. His final revocation hearing is scheduled for 5/28/2013. His other cases were continued to 6/9/13.

This terse summary of the criminal record database conveys the slow-moving nature of a legal process in which a string of courtroom delays—the "continued" dates—kept Juney locked up for over a year.

The events leading up to his arrest had passed much more quickly. One afternoon Juney's younger brother, twenty-year-old Tone, was seen by a neighbor in what appeared to be a drug deal on the street. The neighbor called the police, and Tone was quickly stopped and sat down on the sidewalk for questioning. Juney was just leaving his probation program when he received a text from his brother saying that he was in trouble. Juney was close by and said he would walk right over. Coming up on the scene, Juney was stopped by a police officer. In rapid-fire questions, the officer asked what his relationship was to Tone and whether he was the man who sold Tone drugs. Juney explained that he was Tone's older brother and that he'd received a text from him saying he had been arrested. The officer asked Juney for his identification, and a check on his name revealed that he was on parole. The officer quickly became more suspicious. He took Juney's phone and scrolled through his text messages. The officer said that there was enough there to charge him with conspiracy. Juney and his brother were both arrested, though only Juney, still on parole, was sent to prison.

A few months later, Tone received a noncustodial probation sentence of eighteen months. Two of the charges against Juney were dismissed, but he agreed to a plea for unsupervised probation for distributing a controlled substance. The probation charge did not require prison time, but it did result in a parole violation, which kept Juney locked up for most of the following year.

Back in prison, he was upset, angry at Tone for calling for help without considering that he would be putting Juney at risk. But he quickly returned to the prison routine with its meals, head counts, gym, and reading. Juney's mother, after his many arrests and incarcerations, was tearful at her son's return to incarceration. But, she said, she loved him and she would continue to visit "wherever they put him." Mother and son spoke on the phone each day, and every few weeks she would add another $25 to his phone account.

Juney was released a year after he was arrested. As with his previous release, he was mandated to a drug treatment program. This time he stayed at a halfway house that housed mostly older men with a long history of drug addiction. Through a cousin, Juney found regular work at a supermarket, training to be a butcher. Five months later, he completed the drug program and moved to a small town in the southern part of the state. He found a job working as a personal care assistant, mostly for elderly women and patients with cerebral palsy. A long way from Boston, he felt safe from the police and far from the influence of the street gangs of his youth.

The reentry study research team came to know Juney well. He was a thoughtful young man who spoke honestly about his criminal involvement, but also about the challenges his family faced as new immigrants raised by a single mother. He helped us understand the life of gangs, drugs, money, and jail that sweeps up many of the boys of inner-city Boston.

Putting together his story from conversations with him and his family, as well as from the official criminal record, we saw that Juney had resolved to stay out of crime when we first met him at the time of his first release. As a young man with a criminal history, he understood the risks of staying closely connected to other young men from his neighborhood. He could be tempted back into the drug trade, and he could be stopped by police while riding in a car with other young men, which in fact happened. Or he could run into the police by responding to a friend in trouble. In this case, his friend was his brother. Police contact at a crime scene is perilous for young men on parole. They are viewed suspiciously, and the likelihood of their arrest is elevated. Once arrested, they are subject to a criminal justice process that moves forward with a momentum all its own, from court dates to plea agreements and revocation hearings.

Juney's return to prison appeared to result more from his connection to his younger brother than from any criminal conduct of his own. The new arrests and reincarceration of other men in their midtwenties with whom we spoke were precipitated more directly by involvement in crime. Around 30 percent of the young men in our sample under the age of thirty reported to us their involvement in crime, and over 40 percent of the young men on community supervision reported to us their parole or probation violations. But as Juney's case illustrates, the social context of even young men not directly involved in criminal activity makes their reincarceration more likely, because they are in contact with other young men who may be involved in crime and are viewed suspiciously by police. Juney's youth combined with his parole and probation supervision to make his reincarceration overwhelmingly likely, even though there were few indications of his continuing involvement in crime.

Shortly after we first interviewed Juney at Concord Farm, we spoke to Peter, who, at forty-six, was more than twenty years older than Juney and had been incarcerated for about two-thirds of his adult life. He had served four different prison sentences for drug dealing, property crimes, and violence. Throughout his life, he had dealt drugs, stolen cars, and gotten in fights.

We saw earlier that Peter brought to his transition from prison the experience of prior prison releases and a strong motivation to be present in the lives of his two young children. He attacked his reentry with great energy, quickly enrolling in food stamps, seeking out a therapist, getting work clothes from a reentry program, meeting with his children's teachers, and buying them school supplies. Experience and motivation enabled him to use a variety of strategies small and large, for staying out of trouble.

For the first year after prison, Peter got from place to place by mass transit and walking. He was concerned that riding in a car with friends might get him arrested. If the car was stopped by police and his probation status came up, a violation might be triggered if other passengers had felony convictions or if drugs or guns were discovered. He also went without a cell phone, which would have made him more available to friends and associates who might lead him astray.

Finding a job was an urgent priority. Peter told us that work improved his sense of self-worth and allowed him to provide for his children. He could not find work initially, but he enrolled in employment programs doing maintenance and operating machines. The programs paid less than minimum wage, but Peter thought it was important to get into a daily routine. For eight months in the work programs, he would rise at 5:00 a.m., be ready to start at 7:30 a.m., and work through to 3:00 p.m. At age forty-six, and with no recent work history, Peter struggled to make the jump from job programs to the labor market. He thought his criminal record was the main obstacle. He would do well in interviews until a criminal background check was requested. Ten months out of prison, he finally found work through a temp agency at a laundry, where he worked, at age forty-seven, for the minimum wage. Although the work was consistent, it offered no benefits or any prospect of advancement.

Peter reported to probation in his first year out of prison. He couldn't afford the $65 monthly fee, so he would do community service on weekends. With his long experience in the criminal justice system, he had a good understanding with his probation officer, an older woman who was prepared to meet less frequently than the usual two-week cycle. "I'm kind of glad I got probation. That's like a reminder," he said, referring to his determination to stay out of prison. Probation created the risk of a violation and a return to incarceration, but older probationers were less likely to receive violation notices and more likely, like Peter, to describe their relationships with probation officers as supportive.

Under conditions of material hardship and amid a swirl of family relationships, Peter took steps to maintain a work routine, avoid drugs and alcohol, and stay in regular contact with his children that seemed almost heroic. As with most older men, Peter took a long time to find work. He spoke often of the importance of sobriety, but that was tested when he stayed with his father, who sometimes drank heavily. He also wanted to get closer to his children, but this intention was complicated by his daughter's mother, who wanted to have a romantic relationship with Peter. Employment, sobriety, and positive family relationships were all works in progress that required significant effort.

Researchers sometimes describe the "turning points," such as a steady job or a good marriage, that can help people desist from crime and move into mainstream social roles.[7] For many of our older respondents, who were often unemployed and alone, staying away from drugs, violence, and other crime seemed to grow out of reflection on their lives. They would talk about being tired—tired of prison and tired of street life. Tiring of prison was sometimes accompanied by a renewed sense of the importance of family or the significance of their own mortality.

Peter's turning point sprang from tragedy rather than a marriage or a good job. A few years before Peter was sent to prison, a boy was shot and killed in Boston on his way to school, a bystander caught in a gang rivalry.

The boy was Peter's stepson, his son's brother. Shortly after the shooting, Peter drove to New York with his son to get him a suit for the funeral of his brother:

> I was taking my son to New York, my younger son to New York, to get him a suit to go to his brother's funeral. My mother called me because she had found out what happened. And I cried all the way to New York. My son was in the backseat sleeping. I could see that he was going through it mentally, he was going through it mentally. And I cried and I cried. And I asked my mother, I told my mother, "Ma, if I change my life, will he take care of us?" And she was like, "Who?" And I was like, "God. If I change my life, is he gonna take care of us?" She was like, "Yeah," she said, "Yeah, trust and believe and he'll take care of you." And so I made a decision to change my life, and he's taking care of us. He's taking care of us.

Peter said that taking care of his son was his first priority. He had a good relationship with his son's mother, and when he was first released from prison, he was able to see the boy every day. With the help of a good lawyer, Peter ultimately moved into his own apartment with a Section 8 federal housing voucher. His son then began to stay with him three nights each week. After a while, Peter began taking him to the local gym for boxing lessons.

Much of Peter's determination to provide for his children and be present in their lives seemed to be linked to the murder of his son's brother. Senseless tragedy appeared to not so much present a bolt of realization but begin a process of reflection. "I felt that I'd been so loyal to the streets, and the streets took something from me," he said, talking about the anger that immediately consumed him when the boy died. He would get arrested again after that event and serve another three years before he would be released from Concord Farm. Even from prison, he saw that his son was becoming withdrawn and struggling at school after his brother was killed. As Peter told it, his reflection began while he was in prison, and he became determined to be a positive presence in the lives of his children.

"I understand that this is my last chance," Peter said. "I'm getting older. I'll be forty-seven. The judge told me, if I come before him again, I'll never get out. Yeah, so, I'm all set. You know how the system takes its toll on you, you get to the point where you're like. . . ." He trailed off and sighed deeply. "I want to see my kids get older."

What was the significance of Peter's age during the year he stayed out of prison? In his late forties, living with his sister and resuming contact with his parents, he was surrounded by older family members who were less involved in crime than the young brothers and cousins of the respondents who were still in their twenties. In his late forties, he was also better able to develop an understanding with his probation officer that made revocation less likely. He developed many small strategies to stay out of trouble: sticking to a daily routine, avoiding cars and phones and the friends and associates they attracted, seeking mental health treatment, and participating in programs. As he reflected on his children, and particularly the tragedy in his son's life, Peter also said he had decided to put street life behind him. Time was running out on his life goals. Even though his perspective on life had changed, his daily challenges as an older man were formidable. Jobs were hard to find. Independent housing seemed unattainable. The determination of many older men in our sample was strong, but the families to whom they returned were less supportive. Although older men were more likely to stay out of jail, they often did so only with great effort.

Drug relapse, community supervision, and youth were all associated in the Boston Reentry Study with going back to jail. Over half of those who relapsed, one-third of those on probation or parole, and one-third of those under age forty-five returned to custody. In carrying out their core mission of preventing a return to custody, correctional authorities are armed with rehabilitative programs that aim to correct distorted thinking, remedy the deficits of education and job training, and promote sobriety. Correctional programs such as cognitive therapies, GED preparation, and transitional jobs are judged by their capacity to reduce recidivism. Recidivism is often thought of as a behavioral event where crime is chosen over obedience to the law.

The experiences of the reentry study respondents with reincarceration show the shortcomings of a purely behavioral conception of recidivism. Drug addicts may resume drug use for many reasons. Sometimes drugs offer a way of coping with personal tragedy in a network of friends and family for whom tragedy has become commonplace. Sometimes that network comprises mostly other addicts whose daily lives revolve around buying drugs and getting high. The powerful impact of social context on the likelihood of relapse is one reason why intermittent relapse seems characteristic of attaining long-term sobriety. But drug use by itself is often not the only cause of reincarceration. The return to addiction sometimes triggers furious benders in which crime is the ultimate outcome. In such cases, going back to jail certainly reflects new offending, but it's not so much the choice of crime over obedience to the law but the predictable outcome of uncontrolled drug use that often began in early adolescence.

Drug addiction can also precipitate reincarceration when drug use violates the conditions of parole or probation. Indeed, we found that community supervision was associated with less crime (mostly less drug use) but more incarceration. Probation and parole officers are often weakly equipped to assess compliance with the conditions of supervision, and they appeared to have few tools besides reincarceration to deal with violations. Thus, Sharon was sent back to prison when she told her parole officer that she'd started using heroin again. Also, with their wide discretion in street interactions, police may be more likely to arrest a probationer or parolee, whose status covers them under a veil of suspicion. A parole violation and reincarceration may be triggered even if charges are dismissed. When Juney went to his brother who had been arrested, his parole status raised a flag for the police officer, who scanned Juney's phone for incriminating messages. Policing in this case lacked parsimony, a determined effort to use state power minimally.[8] Finally, young men like Charles may well have been continuing their criminal involvement after release from prison, but social context matters even here: Charles was returning to a network of young male friends who remained involved in crime.

Often the association between age and desistance from crime is traced to the prosocial roles of worker and spouse, which routinize and monitor social life. People leaving incarceration fit uneasily into this story about going straight, in part because most other people who are thirty to forty years old ended their involvement in crime a decade or two before. Age is an important factor for men in their forties leaving incarceration because they are less likely to be stopped by police, they are familiar with the routines of reentry—enrolling in services and programs—and their peers are older and less likely to be involved in crime. But more than this, respondents often described an evolving life perspective. Their own mortality now weighed on their life choices, and their intimate relationships with partners and children had gained new priority. This changed perspective describes Peter's weary determination to hold on to a job and to be a parent to his children. But even for Peter and others of his generation, and even with a revised outlook on life, the possibility of going back to jail never fully disappears, and the avoidance of incarceration is an ongoing project that must be managed from day to day.

CHAPTER 9

....

Women

Men are much more likely than women to be arrested and more likely to have a criminal conviction. Nine out of ten state prisoners are men. The overrepresentation of men in the criminal justice system is closely related to the vast gender gap in serious crime. Men are more involved in violence than women, they get involved in crime at younger ages, and they stay criminally active for longer.[1] Although women are much less involved in crime, their imprisonment rate has grown more quickly than men's in the thirty-five years since 1980. By the 2000s, the United States incarcerated more women than any other country in the world. So large was the number of women in U.S. prisons and jails that the female incarceration rate was approximately equal to the overall Western European incarceration rate for men and women together.

Women chart a distinctive path into prison, and a distinctive path out.[2] They are less likely than men to be serving time for violent offenses and more likely to have been convicted for drug crimes.[3] When women enter prison, they have accumulated long histories as victims of sexual and other violence and are also more likely than men to have serious drug problems. Family often looms larger in their lives than it does for men, but is also more vexed. In Boston, we found that women were generally younger than men when they had children and had often relinquished custody of their children before incarceration. After prison, they were much more likely than men to be living with family. Finding work was a leading challenge for men after incarceration, but for women employment often took a backseat to staying clean and rebuilding family relationships.

Women's incarceration, more than men's, highlights the role of prison as a social policy agency of last resort. Prisons house those who wrestle with poverty, family chaos, mental illness, addiction, and histories of trauma and abuse—problems that, in combination, are too large and intractable to be adequately addressed by the flimsy American safety net. Women, who are often more closely tied to their parents and children, reveal the fundamental fact of incarceration as an enduring separation from the bonds of family and community. Women's incarceration and its rapid expansion through the prison boom also reflect a zeal for punishment that wastes little time on the moral ambiguity presented by offenders with biographies of serious victimization. In short, women's incarceration throws the injustices of imprisonment into sharp relief. Most clearly for women, punishment is not just the outcome of crime, but also of lifetimes of mental illness, drug addiction, and victimization.

Carré had a short shock of magenta hair that announced her youth and individuality. At age twenty, she had been arrested half a dozen times, usually for thefts but also for a few assaults. When we first interviewed Carré in prison, she was pregnant by her boyfriend, Benny. Ricardo, the father of her eighteen-month-old daughter, was in immigrant detention facing deportation. And she thought (incorrectly) that her mother, Bebe, was also locked up.

An African American woman, Carré was raised mostly by her grandmother, Lovelie. Carré had lived with her mother when she was very young, but after a few years the Massachusetts Department of Social Services, with the help of the police, removed Carré from her mother's house and asked Lovelie to take custody of her five-year-old granddaughter. Bebe had a drinking problem and a long history with abusive men; she was also periodically homeless. Carré would begin school after moving in with Lovelie, and for the next few years she lived with both Lovelie and her grandmother on her father's side. Some fifteen years later, Lovelie would also take custody of Bebe's new baby boy and then Carré's own baby daughter. Lovelie by then was in her seventies and living in public housing in Cambridge.

As a teenager, Carré had found it hard to concentrate in the classroom. She suffered from anxiety, and her mood would swing from day to day. "She goes up and then she comes down," Lovelie would say. As her mental health worsened, Carré was sent to a school in the suburbs for children with learning disabilities. She had trouble fitting in and would try to win over the other students with small gifts that she would steal from home. "She was just stealing, stealing, stealing," said Lovelie.

Despite her efforts, her classmates would tease her about her race and her weight, and Carré's anxiety deepened. She was diagnosed with attention deficit disorder and post-traumatic stress. Later she would tell us that she had also been diagnosed with bipolar disorder. Taking care of Carré was difficult for Lovelie. Her granddaughter had stolen cell phones and a laptop computer from Lovelie, and she had also wrecked two cars along the way. "I bought a new CRV," Lovelie said. "I only had it four days. She crashed it. Then she got my other car. A Civic. She just demolished it." In eleventh grade, Carré was expelled and never returned to school. Shortly after that, at age seventeen, she started getting in trouble with the law. Lovelie would bail her out each time. "Five hundred dollars. Five hundred dollars. Five hundred dollars. I just bought a Sony. A new flat screen. I sold it for $240 to get her out of [jail]. I didn't want her to spend a night [there]."

At eighteen, Carré was living with Ricardo when she gave birth to their daughter, Kayla. Ricardo was Haitian, in his midtwenties, and had been living in Boston without immigration papers. The couple struggled to take care of their newborn child. They would fight, and one time when they were arguing over changing the baby's diaper, Ricardo burned the baby's legs and bottom in boiling water. Kayla was six months old and weighed less than eleven pounds. Shortly after that, Lovelie took custody of the child. Ricardo was detained by immigration authorities and then sent back to Haiti. Years later, the skin on Kayla's legs was still pink from where it had peeled away.

At age nineteen, Carré was sent to MCI Framingham to serve several months after being picked up for shoplifting. After her release from prison, she went to live with Bebe. Carré struggled financially after getting out of prison. She reported no income in the months after she left Framingham and could not find work. She qualified for SSI but was reluctant to go to therapy, as the program required. Within months, she began smoking marijuana and drinking again and staying out late with her friends. "Gradually I'm slipping back into my old ways. It's all starting back up again. I have a very hard time staying out of trouble," she said. Bebe had problems of her own and got in fights with her boyfriend, who also lived in the house. Two months after Carré's release from prison, Bebe kicked her out, and her daughter was homeless for the next few months. She slept on a sofa at a friend's place and sometimes stayed with Lovelie and Kayla.

Pregnant by Benny while incarcerated in Framingham, Carré had an abortion just after leaving prison. She explained that she didn't feel ready for the baby. She was also concerned that Benny wouldn't have helped support his child. "I can't raise another baby by myself," she said. And then there was the prospect of Ricardo someday returning to Boston from Haiti. "I can't have a baby by nobody else right now, because when he comes back, he'll probably rip my head off."

As the year after incarceration wore on Carré moved between friends and Lovelie's place. She got into fights with Bebe and Lovelie and cited family conflict as her biggest challenge since she'd been released. Kayla had been living with Lovelie, but Carré remained in close contact with her daughter. She read to Kayla and played with her. Some days Lovelie would return to her house to find that Carré had filled it with flowers or brought gifts for her daughter and grandmother. By all accounts, Kayla at two years old was strong-willed and forthright. Carré wondered if her own anger during her pregnancy had somehow rubbed off on the baby.

> Me and my daughter got anger problems. Because my doctor just told me, when you're pregnant with your child, the way you act develops their personality when you're pregnant with them. No lie. I was really angry when I was pregnant with her. I would just be angry. She's angry. She's an angry baby. She hits you, she'll punch you. She'll swear at you. I'm just like, that's how I was when I was pregnant!

By the end of her first full year after incarceration, Carré was enrolled in food stamps. She had been unemployed for the whole year, hadn't looked for work for months, and got most of her income from Lovelie. Her grandmother, she said, was the most supportive adult in her life.

A few months after our final interview, and just after her twenty-first birthday, we learned that Carré had been arrested again, this time with another girl at one o'clock in the morning for an alleged assault while trying to steal a car.

Celia grew up in Boston's Roxbury neighborhood, the daughter of a Puerto Rican mother and African American father. She was small and slight, with her mother's light skin and gray eyes. She lived with both her parents, but her father was abusive and the household was often violent. Celia's mother described her relationship with Celia's father:

I was a battered woman for thirteen years. He used to beat me up. It started to get so bad that I was like, you know, this man could kill me. He used to beat me up for our relationship. But I managed to save money on the side. Because I was raised the old-school way, like, you stick with your kids' father no matter what. But it started to get so bad that I was like, this man is able to kill me. It was bad. The beatings were bad and what not. So one day I waited for him to leave the house and I told my neighbor to help me out. You know, and I rented a truck and loaded it. And I took the highway.

Celia was four years old when her mother took her away. They lived for four years without any contact with her father or the family in Boston. They returned to Roxbury when she was eight.

From age twelve and throughout her teenage years, Celia lived at different times with her mother and her grandmother. She had a stormy relationship with her mother and a tumultuous time as a teenager. Celia would run the streets. She got in fights and was suspended dozens of times. At thirteen, her mother filed an application to the juvenile court to get help with her daughter's behavior. At fourteen, Celia got pregnant by her boyfriend, Tommy, and had her first child at fifteen. Some months later, she left her baby in the care of her younger sister. In a panic, Celia's mother called the Department of Social Services to intervene. At sixteen, Celia found herself in the emergency room after a fight, and later for a concussion after a car accident.

A year later, in the tenth grade, Celia dropped out of high school. She got her own apartment in Dorchester and lived by herself at age seventeen. The next year, she was pregnant again. This time the father was her new boyfriend, Eric. At nineteen, she got into a fight with another girl and spent time in jail, charged with assault and battery. At twenty, she and Eric had another daughter, Celia's third. Her mother remembered Celia sporting black eyes around this time, and she worried that Eric was beating her up. Celia lost custody of her three children when she was arrested later that same year. While she spent six months in jail, her children stayed with her mother for a while, until she herself lost custody to Celia's grandmother. The following year, back out of jail, twenty-one-year-old Celia had her fourth child, her third with Eric.

Over the next two years, Celia's relationship with her mother deteriorated and the two were seldom in contact. Celia lived at times with her grandmother and at times on her own. Her grandmother had custody of the kids, but Celia was regularly involved in their lives. Her mother described Celia as "the greatest mom" when she was with her kids, but often she was not. "They love her. The first three ones know that she's really their mom. It's just that when she does stay away from them, she stays away from them."

By age twenty-two, Celia had accumulated a long list of drug charges. Her mother said that Celia didn't use drugs, she just liked making money from them. She picked up a felony drug charge that year and was sent to Framingham. In prison, Celia got into fights and spent time in solitary confinement. But she also passed her GED, took college courses and vocational training, and worked in the prison kitchen. Celia rarely saw a doctor on the outside, but had periodic checkups at Framingham. There she was diagnosed with depression, which she attributed to her incarceration.

Celia's kids were living with her grandmother during this time. Celia would call them every other day and also kept in regular contact with her mother, who took the kids on the forty-five-minute drive to visit Celia in Framingham a few times. "They thought she was in training school," her mother said. Celia's brother was also incarcerated at this time. By the time of her release, Celia had been in prison a total of thirty months and was twenty-five years old.

When Celia was released, she first went to live with her mother, but the optimism that often surrounds prison release soon evaporated and mother and daughter were fighting within a month. Like many of the women we interviewed, Celia had male and female romantic partners. A few months after release, Celia had formed a relationship with a young woman who lived in a town just outside of Boston. The couple moved in together after Celia left her mother's house. She stayed there for about three months, until a house fire forced her out and into a shelter. After a month in the shelter, Celia moved in with her grandmother. A month after that, she was living with friends back in Boston.

Throughout her first year out, Celia's three oldest children were living with Celia's grandmother. Aged six to eleven, the kids saw their mother regularly, but their daily care was provided by their great-grandmother. She also helped Celia out financially. Celia's youngest child lived separately from his siblings, with Celia's mother. Because Celia and her mother were not getting on well, she saw less of her five-year-old son than the older children. Still, she told us, she saw him once a week. In the year after her release from

Framingham, Celia was not in contact with the two fathers of her children. The youngest three, however, saw their father every other weekend or so.

Back in Boston, Celia would ultimately move back in with her grandmother and live with her three oldest children. Her youngest would stay with Celia's mother. She was out of work for her first year after Framingham, but she took a seven-month course to become a beautician, attending school full-time. After graduating, she found part-time work that paid $9 an hour. Celia was known as a drug dealer around her old neighborhood and may have made the balance of her income that way.

Our final interview with Celia was on a hot sticky day nearly two years after she was released from prison. She was sitting out in front of her house on a lawn chair, braiding her daughters' hair. One of the kids was being bullied at school, and Celia had been going into the school that spring to arrange to have her daughter transferred. "I need my daughters to be safe," she said. Celia shared the daily care of her oldest three children with her grandmother. She was still seeing less of her youngest, who remained in the custody of her mother. Celia's relationship with her mother was strained, as it had been for most of her life. Celia had grown up mostly with her grandmother, and her mother had been locked up, on the streets, and had brought violence into Celia's childhood home. Celia's voice would tighten when the subject of her mother came up, but the two were occasionally in contact.

As our interview continued, the summer quiet was disturbed by the sound of a car crash. Shots were fired. Celia's youngest daughter ran inside, frightened by the commotion. "Make sure the girls are okay," Celia called out to her sister. Minutes later, sirens announced the arrival of an ambulance. "There's been a lot of shootings this summer," Celia said. A lot of people had been hurt. "The baby, you see she ran right upstairs. I'm on them all day. I'm like, I need to see you. This is not where you can play. This is not okay around here." We asked Celia about her biggest challenge since her release. "I'm just trying to stay away from the negativity. The violence, everything."

Women in the reentry study were much more likely to report combined histories of drug addiction and mental illness compared to the men. Nine of the 15 women (60 percent) we interviewed had a history of drug and mental health problems, compared to 31 out of 107 men (29 percent). Carolina began using drugs relatively late in life, but by the time we first interviewed her, at age fifty-two, she had been using cocaine and heroin for fifteen years. She had also been diagnosed with depression and had been taking antidepressants while she was incarcerated.

Carolina grew up in Puerto Rico. Her father had a steady job as a janitor and her mother worked as a seamstress in a factory. Despite the financial stability of her working-class family, Carolina's childhood home was chaotic and violent. Her older sister and brother both drank and used drugs heavily. Both would die young, her brother in a car accident when Carolina was seven, and her sister from AIDS when Carolina was nineteen. Between the ages of seven and twelve, Carolina was sexually abused by several family members when her parents were working and away from the house. "Oh my God, I was so scared," she said. "I stayed under my bed or locked my room." Her abusers threatened to kill her if she said anything. One, her uncle, was an alcoholic, and he would molest Carolina when he was drunk. She remembered him cutting open his chest with a knife during a drunken rage when she was eight or nine. Her aunt doused herself in gasoline and set herself on fire. "I saw that like it was today," she told us. Amid this violence, Carolina would retreat to her church, where she often stayed.

At age seventeen, Carolina learned that her mother was cheating on her father. Worried that Carolina would say something, her mother sent her to Boston to live. It was arranged that Carolina would live in Boston with an uncle and his family. After arriving in Boston, Carolina worked for the next fourteen years as a seamstress, like her mother, sewing clothes in a garment factory.

In her midthirties, Carolina began seeing a therapist to talk about her history of family violence and sexual abuse. Carolina also started seeing a woman around that time, but that relationship quickly turned abusive. "I gave her money," said Carolina. "Every single day. I start getting mad, 'cause I spend a lot of money just like that. And I start to argue and argue. And she say, 'You'll love it. I want you to try this.'" Carolina began using drugs for the first time. At age thirty-six, she picked up her first case, for shoplifting and for possession of a syringe. Over the next few years, she was arrested on a string of drug possession charges involving cocaine and heroin. Finally, she was arrested for heroin possession coming off a plane at Logan airport in Boston. She was sent to Framingham, where she served four years.

During her time in prison, Carolina committed herself to a drug treatment program and to her church attendance. She also got involved in a group for survivors of sexual abuse, and she spoke with pride about her work making flags in prison. She took GED classes, but was released before she could take the test. Like nearly all the older women we spoke to, Carolina struggled with an array of health problems, including painful joints, a liver condition, hepatitis C, and debilitating depression. Prolonged heroin use lay behind much of her chronic pain and disease and added greatly to the challenge of successfully leaving incarceration. Throughout her four-year incarceration, Carolina regularly wrote to her family and called them.

We first met Carolina on her fiftieth birthday. Heavy-set with close-cropped hair and a laugh that came from deep in her belly, she was about to leave prison and planned to stay with her cousin in Boston. Like many of those we spoke to who struggled with drug addiction, she told us that her biggest challenge would be staying clean.

Carolina left prison early in the summer with $300 and a thirty-day supply of medication to treat her depression, joint pain, and migraine headaches. She planned to return to Puerto Rico, but for now she would stay at her cousin's place, living in his basement, until she got back on her feet. In her first week out of prison, she mostly stayed at home, wrote letters, and watched television. She ventured out one time in that first week, to go to church.

Carolina saw a doctor in her first month out of prison, but she was eager to see a psychiatrist, as she had at Framingham, and was becoming anxious that nothing was organized. Her medications were running out, and her new doctor was still waiting for her medical records from Framingham to arrive. She called us several times a few weeks later. Now coping without antidepressants, and in pain with a bad knee, Carolina was in tears and close to relapse to heroin use. Her cousin was trying to talk her out of it, but she was reaching a crisis point. A week later, Carolina called in again. She still hadn't received her medical records from the Department of Correction, but sounded relieved that she had a new prescription for antidepressants. And more important, she was seeing a doctor she liked.

As her medical care was getting organized, Carolina was becoming concerned about her housing. She had been living in her cousin's basement for three months and had visited a prisoner reentry program to get a housing referral. They recommended that she go to a homeless shelter, but Carolina was frightened at the prospect. "I saw a lot of girls there from Framingham," she said. "They're all still getting high. For every five, only one is clean." Carolina's housing situation was becoming urgent. With October approaching and no heating in her cousin's basement, she needed a new place before the winter. A few weeks later, she called us again. "Looking, looking everywhere," she said about her housing search. "I see people all messed up in the street. I don't want to be like that."

Through all these calls, we heard Carolina struggling with her drug addiction under the pressures of her depression and her housing situation. Her housing search put her in the company of heroin users as she visited reentry services and transitional housing programs. Some people were getting high, and others, like Carolina, were trying to stay sober. She enrolled in a lottery for public housing, applied to several transitional housing programs, and asked her cousin to write a letter supporting her applications. By November, she still had not found any strong leads.

As winter arrived, Carolina found another solution to her housing problem. She bought a ticket to Puerto Rico and returned home. We heard from her early in the new year after she made the move to San Juan. She was living with her sister's family. Things were coming together. She had found a doctor, was going to church regularly, and was staying away from drugs. Carolina was happy to be close to her immediate family. "I never realized how much my family loves me," she said.

Over the next few months, she fulfilled one of the most elusive goals of her reentry. She found her own place, a small apartment where she lived by herself. Her medical problems presented an ongoing challenge, but her history of employment (rare among the reentry study respondents) provided her with health coverage through Social Security Disability Insurance (SSDI), Social Security's disability program. SSDI also provided a monthly benefit of $900, enough to cover her rent and utilities, leaving about $150 for groceries. In the week we spoke to Carolina, she'd also just sent $30 back to two women still incarcerated at Framingham. She was volunteering at her church and writing about her experiences as a survivor of sexual violence.

Carolina's year out of prison traced a long arc. In the first months, even with her cousin's significant help, she felt frightened and insecure in her mental health and about her housing. She was often tearful and uncertain about her future. Moving back to Puerto Rico to live with her sister proved pivotal. She found her own place to live, enrolled in SSDI, and became active in her church, attending services and volunteering in programs. Having started at the distant margins of her community, Carolina had now become a support for others. Her childhood was turbulent, but it was family relationships, those with her cousin and her sister, that were critical to her successfully leaving incarceration. Nevertheless, family problems remained.

Carolina herself had found a place in her family that allowed her to flourish, but her nephew, for instance, used drugs and Carolina would not let him in her house. "I love him," she said. "But that's it."

Heroin use was twice as common among women as men. Forty percent of the women in the sample (six out of fifteen) used heroin in the six months before incarceration compared to 19 percent of the men (twenty out of 107). Heroin correlated not just with gender but also with depression, chronic pain, the company you kept, and the long journey traveled by those who struggled with addiction and their families.

Maria had been a heroin user since she was seventeen. With a thoughtful face and intense brown eyes, she was a master storyteller who painted a vivid picture of her addiction. Unlike most of the formerly incarcerated women we interviewed, Maria was white and grew up middle class; she had been raised and supported financially by both her parents for her whole life.

Maria began using drugs young, drinking at twelve and smoking marijuana at thirteen. That year she was scheduled to have her tonsils out, but the operation was canceled. Nevertheless, she eagerly took the preoperative medication. At fourteen, and just starting high school, Maria was bullied and suffered anxiety. A psychiatrist prescribed a strong anti-anxiety medication, Klonopin, a habit-forming drug that Maria began abusing almost immediately. Maria was drawn to drugs. As a teenager, she told us, she used ecstasy (MDMA), angel dust (PCP), special K (ketamine), and acid (LSD). She was admitted to her first detox at seventeen, but resumed drug use shortly after that.

Maria's heavy drug use in high school was surrounded by turmoil. She was raped twice, once by a man she was smoking angel dust with, and another time at a party. She began dealing prescription drugs, and she saw her boyfriend get stabbed when a drug deal went bad. By age sixteen, Maria was using the prescription opioid Oxycontin and had been suspended from school for fighting.

At seventeen, her grandmother became ill and was admitted to the hospital. Maria had been going out of state to buy Oxycontin, but with her grandmother in hospital, she was reluctant to leave town for any length of time. Heroin was available locally, so Maria tried it, using it for the first time with her boyfriend, who injected her. Later that year, high on crystal meth, Maria beat up a friend whom she learned had sex with her boyfriend. She was expelled from school just months before graduation.

In Maria's telling, the next decade of her life was a series of catastrophes and brushes with death. She was behind the wheel in two serious car accidents. She overdosed, contracted infections from dirty needles, and was hospitalized for a serious lung problem. Her parents had her committed to a hospital three different times. She was also arrested a number of times for drug possession and shoplifting.

For Maria's parents, much of their life became about "chasing her, trying to protect her," said her mother. Parental support for a daughter with a heroin addiction took many forms. Maria's mother extended unrelenting love in the face of a disease she had little power to control. Her father, less reconciled to the inevitability of addiction, desperately tried to control Maria's drug use, and at times her life. In the six months before her incarceration, Maria was using cocaine and heroin daily. Mostly living with her parents, she was also hospitalized, living out of her car, crashing with friends, and staying in hotels, police lockups, and treatment facilities. As her life spiraled, her father resolved that significant action was needed, and he reported Maria's drug use to her probation officer. With few tools besides incarceration to keep Maria safe, the officer was determined that she would not die under her supervision. A probation violation was entered, and Maria was sent to prison for eighteen months.

While in prison, Maria went to twelve-step meetings, saw a counselor, and attended a church group. She had just been hospitalized before her incarceration, and in prison she now received treatment for seizures, hepatitis, and depression. Her parents were committed to protecting their daughter during her incarceration. "Our routine was to see her every single Saturday," said her mother, "to make sure that she had emotional support, to make sure that she had money in her canteen." As for many of the parents we spoke to, incarceration was wrenching for Maria's mother. "It's like a death you go through. A grieving period," she told us.

When Maria was released, like Carolina and about half of all heroin users in our sample, she told us that staying clean would be her biggest challenge. At age thirty-two, she returned to live with her parents, as she had since childhood. Maria was picked up from prison by her mother and father, and straight from prison the family went for a cup of coffee and a cigarette, followed by a lobster dinner.

Maria was chain-smoking Newports when she told us about her fear and anxiety in the first few months after incarceration. Sometimes she wanted to be back in jail: "It was easier to live. I got up in the morning. I went to work. I worked for $21 a week." Out of prison, she was still adjusting to meeting new people and the jostling of crowds. Maria relied for support in adjusting to life out of prison on a network of female friends she had known from prison and halfway houses. Her girlfriend was still in prison, and this relationship would dwindle over the coming months. All of her close friends, she said, had been in prison. Still, her parents were clearly her main supporters. Unlike nearly all our other respondents, Maria experienced no financial hardship. She received some income support from disability, and the rest came from her parents. "If something happened to one of my parents, I'd be fucked," she observed.

Perhaps because of the stress of transition, Maria used heroin a couple of times in the first few months out of prison. This aggravated her lung condition and sent her back to the hospital for a week. Heroin remained a strong temptation during the year after her prison release. About eight months out of prison, a close friend was released from incarceration only to die weeks later from a heroin overdose. Maria was devastated and close to relapse. She used Klonopin instead to try to control her mood. Shortly after that, she enrolled in a Suboxone clinic for recovering heroin addicts. While enrolled at the clinic, she reduced her Klonopin use and ultimately stayed clean for the rest of the year.

As she struggled to stay away from drugs, health problems dogged Maria's first year out. Years of heroin use had left her with hepatitis and serious respiratory problems. A gall bladder infection put her back in the hospital for surgery. A few months later, Maria arrived at an interview with a black eye, a painful back, and cuts on her hand. She had been mugged late one night in downtown Boston. Besides her physical ailments, she also had diagnoses of depression, post-traumatic stress, and attention deficit disorder. Her physical and mental illnesses were accompanied by an array of medications that included Adderall, Klonopin, and Suboxone. When asked how she rated her health, she replied, "I get sick a lot."

Like Carolina, Maria found the transition from prison to community immensely difficult for the first few months. But by the end of her year out of prison, Maria had begun a carpentry program and was working on a crew and carrying the tools of her trade with confidence. She felt good about the skills she was developing. She was also seeing a therapist regularly, and she spoke warmly about a relationship she had begun with a man, also formerly incarcerated, who was working as an advocate for men in prison. Her mother was relieved to have her home and out of prison. "I don't have to worry about her getting into fights with crazy girls," her mother said.

Addiction and criminal involvement are tightly linked for women who use heroin. In Maria's case, her parents and probation officer hoped that prison would be a safe haven as her life became increasingly chaotic. Maria brought to her imprisonment a history of victimization and sexual violence that we rarely saw among men. Her body was weakened by lung disease and infection, and her mind was clouded by depression. The prison is fundamentally an institution of punishment, but for women who use heroin, it sometimes heads off self-destruction. What is just, what can be deterred, and what can be incapacitated all appear to be in doubt when confronting the social reality of women's incarceration.

A woman's path to prison is different from a man's, and so is her path out. Although violence was common in the lives of our respondents, the women among them were much less likely to have been perpetrators of serious violence than the men. Nearly all the women in our sample reported getting in fights in adolescence, but few reported committing acts of serious violence in adulthood. Among the reentry study respondents, only 20 percent of the women were convicted of violent offenses, compared to 40 percent of the men. The men also accounted for all the firearms offenses in the sample (11 out of 122). While men were more involved in violent offending, women spoke more about their victimization in violent confrontations with family members and partners. Men were more likely to tell us that they were hit by their parents in childhood. When women reported being hit by adults in the family, nearly all reported that they were also sexually abused. Indeed, the rate of childhood sexual abuse was twice as high among the women in the study than among the men (29 versus 14 percent). Although the sample of women was very small, these results are similar to those found by other researchers reporting serious victimization among incarcerated women.[4] The Boston life-history data also show that such victimization can continue for decades, from childhood to adulthood.

Among the reentry study women, a childhood history of sexual abuse and family violence is closely associated with heroin and other serious drug use in adulthood, but the associations are much weaker for men. Among women, heroin use correlated at 0.4 with childhood sexual abuse, and 0.6 with being hit by parents (N = 14), compared to correlations of 0.2 and 0.1

for men (N = 95). Sample size is very small for women, but the gender differences are large. Too many factors are at work to conclude that family violence and abuse cause heroin use, but clearly family violence, abuse, and heroin are tightly bundled for women who have been incarcerated. Heroin produces a powerful physical dependence, but it also draws its users, like Carolina and Maria, into a social network of addicts who know each other and build relationships through copping dope, using, being incarcerated, and getting clean.[5] Both Carolina and Maria recognized other heroin users from Framingham as they made their rounds through reentry programs, transitional housing, and other social service programs. Maria's close support network was made up of women she had come to know through treatment and detox. A network of heroin users also makes sobriety more challenging, however, particularly in the face of tragedy, such as the death of a friend, or untreated health problems.

Heroin use was also correlated with chronic pain and mental illness, and the heroin users among the women in our sample were generally in worse physical and mental health than the men. Their physical symptoms were often related to long histories of using heroin and other drugs. Forty percent of the women had back pain compared to 18 percent of the men. The anxiety and post-traumatic stress described by Carré were common among these women and reported less often by the men in the sample. Depression, which Celia related to her incarceration, was almost universally reported by the women (80 percent) compared to less than one-third of the men (32 percent). Women's rate of anxiety, as measured in prison, was double that for men (27 versus 13 percent), and the women's rate of post-traumatic stress was five times higher than it was for the men (33 versus 7 percent).

The social context of women's incarceration is also distinguished by the depths of family distress in their lives. Mothers' custody of children is woven into our economic and social institutions, the welfare system, law, and our cultural expectations of family life. In a social context that considers maternal custody of children profoundly normal, mothers who go to prison struggle to maintain a constant custodial relationship with their children, and incarceration disables such a relationship entirely. Prior to their incarceration, none of the mothers in the reentry study had full custody of their children. Most children had been taken in by other women in the family, though in a few cases, children lived with their fathers or their father's family. A few were in the custody of foster or adoptive parents. Although women's custody of their children was often tenuous, children could help smooth out contentious family relationships. The caregiving role played by grand-mothers and great-grandmothers tended to draw incarcerated mothers into networks of family support. As a result, we find that women were much more likely than men to be living with family after incarceration.

While some family members proved to be important sources of emo-tional and material support for formerly incarcerated women, their male partners could be violent and abusive. Some women, like Maria, having tired of the instability and conflict they had encountered with men, gravi-tated to the company of other women and formed romantic attachments and other close bonds with them.

More generally, the social process of leaving prison is fundamentally gen-dered. Struggles with sobriety and physical and mental health are wide-spread but greater for women than for men. The imperative to restore rela-tionships with children and other family were more urgent. Because women have greater family support than men but poor physical and mental health, women were faced with larger obstacles to employment but less financial necessity. While formerly incarcerated men frequently struggled to find a firm place in the labor market, formerly incarcerated women struggled for a place in their families.

Where girls grow up under conditions of poverty, subject to sexual abuse and other violence in an environment where drug addiction and mental illness are hopelessly entangled and children are neglected or taken away, the prison emerges as a bad solution to many problems. Carré's mood swings and economic insecurity lay in the background of her shoplifting convic-tion. For a girl who had an abusive father, moved frequently in childhood, and got into fights as a teenager, Celia could pay the rent with her street-corner drug dealing and keep close to her children, without the supervisors and time clocks of a regular job. Carolina was absorbed into a community of heroin users and dealt drugs to support her addiction. Finally, Maria vio-lated her probation by using heroin, but her father hoped that incarceration would keep her alive as her life spun out of control. In each case, incarcera-tion was not ordered according to any well-laid plan to deter crime or render justice. Prison simply lay at the end of the road after a series of failures of support for mental health, drug treatment, stable housing, and child well-being.

For women who live with poverty, mental and physical illness, family violence, sexual abuse, and addiction, incarceration is a poor instrument for justice. Punishment often adds suffering to the lives of those who have been victimized, and for our female respondents, victimization had already been unusually severe and often produced in their intimate relationships with partners and family members in the form of sexual violence. As a type of punishment, incarceration carries a special burden for women who are mothers, dividing them from the children with whom they have lived. Moreover, with women, the punitive sentiment behind incarceration is being applied to those who are, on average, only slightly involved in serious violence.

The crime preventive effects of prison are also less convincing for women. Theory says that incarceration deters crime when the pain of lost liberty exceeds the pleasures of crime. In the real world of criminally involved women, punishment's deterrent effect is compromised by the strongly correlated adversities that accompany women's incarceration. The relative hardship of punishment is reduced by harsh conditions of life faced by women who go to prison. Indeed, for some, like Maria, daily life in the grip of addiction became so dangerous that imprisonment offered a respite from chaos and self-destruction. MCI Framingham is not a particularly humane institution, but it wound up being a superior alternative to an addiction careening out of control.

As closely as imprisonment is linked to serious crime, it is equally a social policy intervention responding to the conflict and disorder that accompany the failures of the American safety net. For women who go to prison, the safety net as it now stands is inadequate to repair lives that have gone wrong in a dozen ways. Incarceration is ordered because no alternative exists, and an institution that is intended to produce justice through punishment perversely has the reverse effect.

CHAPTER 10

Race and Racism

Mass incarceration has been called "the new Jim Crow," the latest chapter in a history of oppression that has for centuries marginalized African Americans in American society. In this perspective, race relations have passed through a series of stages: from slavery to Jim Crow segregation in the South, followed by the northern ghetto and then mass incarceration. The institutions have changed, but the fact of racial confinement is inscribed on each.[1]

The idea of the new Jim Crow captures the kernel of a new racial inequality that emerged with mass incarceration. Scholars in the fields of history, politics, and sociology together describe aspects of a deep racial division in three main parts: a political history invoking black criminality, a large racial disparity in incarceration rates, and a range of negative socioeconomic effects disproportionately felt in black communities. Social and economic progress, especially for the poor, has been stalled by this new racial inequality. Hopes for full African American citizenship that grew out of the civil rights era have been disappointed.

This chapter places the experience of the reentry study respondents in the context of the new racial inequality. We found that the relationship between poverty and incarceration was different for different racial groups. For whites, incarceration and its aftermath were closely tied to addiction, mental health problems, and failure to receive adequate health care. Incarceration for blacks and Latinos was more closely linked to school dropout and poor job prospects. Despite better health and stronger family support, blacks and Latinos suffered higher unemployment and lower wages after prison release. These results suggest that racial disparities do more than transmit the negative effects of incarceration mostly to communities of color. For blacks and Latinos, incarceration is closely linked to deficits of economic opportunity. As a result, incarceration is more extensive for blacks and Latinos, and finding economic independence through the labor market after incarceration is more challenging for them.

Prejudices about black criminality have deep historical roots that long pre-date mass incarceration. Statistical and social science studies of the late nineteenth century viewed black men as immune to the influence of social environment, and violence among them as the product of internal traits. As one pioneering analysis of black criminality put it in 1896, until "the negro . . . learns to believe in the value of personal morality . . . criminal tendencies . . . will increase."[2]

Ideas about the criminality of black men shaped data collection, social research, and policy throughout the twentieth century. By the 1960s, amid backlash to the civil rights movement, conservative politicians were conjuring the specter of black violence in political talk about crime. Politicians and commentators likened minority neighborhoods to jungles filled with violent young men unconstrained by conscience or self-control. Republican senator Barry Goldwater, running for president in 1964, despaired of the "mob and the jungle." Alabama governor George Wallace, running in defense of southern segregation in the 1968 presidential election, described Washington, D.C., as a "jungle where citizens fear to walk the streets at night." In that same election, the Republican candidate, Richard Nixon, warned that the "city jungle" and "the brutal society that now flourishes in the core cities will annex the affluent suburbs."[3] As president, Nixon declared wars on crime and drugs in the early 1970s, and President Ronald Reagan declared another drug war a decade later. Drug arrest rates escalated in the 1980s, and much faster for blacks than whites. In the states—where most crime policy is written—long sentences were adopted in the 1980s and 1990s for violence and for defendants with prior felonies. Being more likely to be convicted of violence than whites, blacks began serving lengthy terms of imprisonment. Academics played a part in this story by rejecting rehabilitation as a goal for crime policy and arguing instead for incarceration to deter and warehouse ("incapacitate") criminal offenders.[4]

Tough-on-crime politics stoked fears of black violence and helped to produce a vast penal system whose defining feature was its large racial disparity. At the peak of racial disparity, African Americans were eight times more likely to be incarcerated than whites. Serving prison time became a common experience for black men without a college education. Among black males born since the late 1970s who had no more than a high school diploma, 36 percent served time in prison, compared to just 12 percent a generation earlier. Incarceration rates grew so high that black men born since the late 1960s were more likely to go to prison than to finish college with a four-year degree.[5]

Black men occupy a special place in the new racial inequality. The effects of the racial disparity in incarceration have not been confined to the loss of liberty. A whole generation of black men carry the stigma of a prison record that limits their social and economic opportunities. Incarceration reduces employment and earnings, relegating black men to minimum-wage jobs and economic insecurity. In addition, families have been torn apart as children are separated from their fathers and mothers and shamed by the stigma of parental incarceration. Researchers have found that following the incarceration of a parent, children act out, become depressed, and do poorly at school. These effects cut across racial lines, but because the racial disparity in incarceration is so large, economic and family life are distorted for blacks much more than for whites.[6]

The new racial inequality described in recent scholarship focuses largely on blacks and whites. Latinos fit uneasily into this picture. Many Latinos, including those in Boston, share a recent history dating from the growth of non-European immigration since the mid-1960s. Latino incarceration rates at the national level are about twice as high as those for whites, but much lower than incarceration rates for blacks. Incarceration rates also vary across different groups, being highest in long-standing communities from Puerto Rico and Mexico and much lower among recent arrivals from South America.[7] Still, the social conditions prevalent in some Latino communities—poverty, poor schooling, and segregation—resemble the conditions in African American neighborhoods where incarceration rates have skyrocketed. Latin American immigrants have also faced escalating rates of immigrant detention and deportation. In Boston (and in the reentry study sample), most Latinos are U.S. citizens of Puerto Rican descent and have largely avoided the effects of coercive immigration policy.

Massachusetts is a low-incarceration state, but like many states with a small minority population, racial disparity in incarceration is unusually large. A report by Marc Mauer and Ryan King at the Sentencing Project calculated total prison and jail incarceration rates for blacks, whites, and

Latinos in each of the fifty states in 2005. In Massachusetts, the African American incarceration rate was 1,635 per 100,000 of the population; thus, on an average day in 2005, about 1.6 percent of the entire African American population in the state was behind bars. The incarceration rate for whites was 235 per 100,000. Both rates of incarceration were below the national average. Still, African Americans in Massachusetts were seven times more likely to be incarcerated than whites, a disparity that was nearly 50 percent higher than the national average at the time.[8] The high rate of African American incarceration is reflected in the large number of black respondents in the reentry study. African Americans make up about 8 percent of Boston-area residents, but over 50 percent of the reentry study sample.

The Latino-to-white disparity is even larger compared to the national standard. Nationwide, Latinos are 1.8 times more likely to be incarcerated than whites, but the Latino-to-white disparity in Massachusetts is 6.1, the second-highest ethnic disparity among the fifty states, second only to Connecticut. Just as African Americans are overrepresented in the reentry study sample, Latinos account for 10 percent of Boston-area residents but made up 20 percent of the reentry study sample.

The history of Boston race relations lay close to the surface for the older participants in the reentry study. For people in their forties and fifties, racial violence of the 1970s in Boston was a focal point in their descriptions of childhood. Boston's recent history of racial conflict is vivid and virulent. Dating from the 1960s, historically Catholic and Jewish neighborhoods in Roxbury, Dorchester, and Mattapan saw increases in their African American and Latino populations and corresponding declines in the numbers of whites. From 1970 to 1980, the city of Boston declined in population from 640,000 to 560,000, a decline due entirely to shrinking numbers of white residents. In Dorchester, Roxbury, and Mattapan, the white population declined by 75,000, the black population increased by 13,000, and the Latino population increased by about 9,000.[9] In this transitional decade, historically white neighborhoods were transformed into centers of African American and Latino life.

Many explanations have been offered for the racial and ethnic transformation of inner-city neighborhoods, not just in Boston but in cities throughout the Northeast and the Midwest. Rising crime rates, civil disturbances throughout the 1960s, and federal antidiscrimination efforts have all been associated with the exodus of white inner-city residents and the influx of African Americans. In Boston, local land developers and banks drove neighborhood change in part to capture federal mortgage guarantees. Incoming black and Latino residents were redlined into Dorchester and Mattapan, replacing the Jewish residents, who were chased off by real estate brokers with horror stories of black crime and declining property values. "Do you want your child knifed or killed by those colored hoodlums?" one Mattapan resident was asked by an agent in 1971. "Sell now, you can still get your price."[10] Mortgage defaults among new minority homeowners undermined the economic vitality of the emerging minority neighborhoods. Under these conditions, the rapid emergence of black and Latino enclaves in Boston's inner city provided a context for the neighborhood poverty and racial violence that increased through the 1970s.

Following a period of rapid racial succession in Boston neighborhoods, the city's public schools entered a period of court-ordered desegregation from 1974 to 1976. During this time, black students were bused in to what had become strongholds of Boston's white working class in Charlestown, East Boston, and South Boston. White students were bused to schools with large African American populations in Roxbury. The *Boston Globe* related the story of one driver, James "Little" Richardson, on the first day of busing, when he was bringing a group of black children to a school in South Boston:

> He could hear people outside yelling racial slurs. He could hear the children on the bus, crying harder. He took a left, trying to find a way out. He drove to the end of West Eighth Street and ran into D Street. There, at the corner, he realized his mistake. They were surrounded by another crowd, bigger and more furious than the first. Bricks were flying, with few windows left to stop them. Richardson told the kids to lie down on the floor, but the kids were lying down already.[11]

The demonstrations, violence, and hostility directed at the black students added another layer of complexity to national understanding of American racism. Newspaper photographs and newsreel footage of white parents in the Irish enclaves of Charlestown and South Boston recalled similar images of segregationists in the South in the 1950s and '60s.[12] We interviewed a black man in his late forties who talked about the "basic racial fights" of this period taking place alongside the car accidents, overdoses, and muggings in his childhood neighborhood. A white man of similar age told us that "back then," when he was twelve, "it was busing days, so I was fightin' black kids."

These large historical changes formed part of the context in which the older respondents were exposed to violence during adolescence. The neighborhoods that were then being formed became the segregated social environments in which the younger men and women we interviewed were raised.

Peter's teenage years were spent in the 1970s and early 1980s in the largely African American housing projects of Roxbury. He ran the streets as a young man, sometimes escaping to New York in a stolen car to listen to the beats of a new kind of music called hip-hop that was performed in the parks of Harlem by Grandmaster Flash and Afrika Bambaataa. Like many of the older men we interviewed, Peter had a deep folk knowledge of Boston. He knew the city's bus routes, its neighborhoods, and many of its housing projects. Visiting the university in Cambridge, Peter would wear his Red Sox cap to avoid trouble. We often met him at a diner in Mattapan, not far from where he spent late nights as a boy out with his friends.

In one conversation with Peter about his childhood, he pointed to a scar on his face from a brawl when he was fourteen or fifteen. He had been playing dice on the sidewalk with friends near Mattapan Square late one night and was walking home with his cousin. "Back then [in the late 1970s], blacks weren't really allowed up here on this side of the street," he said.

> They used to have a bar on the corner, and we used to gamble over there on the other side of River Street, and one night we was walking home to catch the bus right here. And two white men, brothers, approached us and wanted to fight, so when we pulled out our knives, they went into the Irish pub to get their father and their uncle, and we got into a big fight right here in Mattapan Square.

Peter was hit in the eye with a crowbar, and the white men were stabbed. "There was a lot of racial tension back then," he said. Interracial violence was common on that borderline of neighborhoods in flux. "You still have racism today," said Peter. "But it's not like it was back in the seventies and the eighties."

Older white men who had grown up in Charlestown and South Boston in the 1970s and 1980s also had memories of racial violence. Brian was thirteen years old and living in Charlestown in the first year of busing. Charlestown was fiercely Irish and included a mix of working-class and poor residents. Violence was common around the Charlestown housing projects, Brian told us. Young men regularly got into fights, and Brian remembered seeing two stabbings and a shooting while he was growing up.

The year busing began, Brian told us, a group of black students from Philadelphia were visiting the Bunker Hill Monument. Looking for the bus stop, they were sent in the direction of the housing projects at the bottom of the hill. Four young residents of Charlestown, white men around age eighteen, drove past Brian in their car toward the black students from Philadelphia.

> I saw five black kids from Philadelphia get beaten with golf clubs and a bat during busing. I was thirteen years old, it was the first year of busing in Charlestown, and unfortunately, that group of kids from Philadelphia, on a tour, went to the Bunker Hill Monument, and they got misdirected, and they went down towards the projects to wait for the bus to go back towards Boston, and I can remember the car driving by, there were four kids [in the car]. . . . Two out of four them were later killed, and umm, they get out, went to the trunk, and opened the trunk up, and three of them had golf clubs and one of them had a bat and started beating them pretty bad.

For the older men of the reentry study, racial violence marked territory, asserting white control over South Boston and Charlestown and the lines of contest in the rapidly changing neighborhoods of Roxbury, Dorchester, and Mattapan. Mass incarceration had not yet emerged in the 1970s, but the demographic transformation of America's inner cities and the racial violence that often followed provided an important part of the social context in which tough-on-crime politics would flourish.

These neighborhoods were the stage on which the transition from prison to community would play out in the reentry study decades later. The city of Boston has twenty-three neighborhood areas. Reflecting the large racial disparity in incarceration in Massachusetts, about half (55 out of 122) of the reentry study sample lived in just four of those neighborhoods prior to their incarceration—the largely African American sections of Roxbury, Dorchester, and Mattapan and the adjacent neighborhood of Hyde Park.

After incarceration, a similar proportion of the sample returned to just those four areas and remained there for the year after prison release. Within these neighborhoods, the reentry study sample returned to the blocks with the highest rates of poverty, unemployment, and racial segregation. By one year after prison release, African American respondents were living in neighborhoods with an average poverty rate of 20 percent, while Latino respondents were living in 27 percent poverty, compared to an average neighborhood poverty rate of 14 percent for white respondents. Neighborhood rates of female-headed households and unemployment were also about twice as high for black and Latino respondents compared to whites.[13] So much of the city's experience with residents' return from prison unfolds in a handful of neighborhoods where the poorest minority population resides.

For white respondents, neighborhood return looked very different, as they dispersed more widely across the greater Boston area. About one-third returned to the historically white working-class areas of Charlestown, the North End, South Boston, and East Boston. The rest of the white respondents were spread out from the southern shore towns, to northern beaches, and west toward central Massachusetts. White respondents returned to communities that were whiter, more affluent, and less urban than the neighborhoods to which their black and Latino counterparts returned.

While older black and white men had all lived through a period of violent racial conflict, they differed socially and demographically. Looking at the common markers of socioeconomic disadvantage, African Americans just out of prison shared some of the demographic disadvantage of the general black population. Only one-quarter of black respondents had lived with both parents at age fourteen, compared to about half of white respondents and one-third of Latinos.[14] Black respondents were also more likely to have changed schools while they were growing up (82 percent) compared to whites (65 percent) or Latinos (52 percent). Interrupted schooling was associated with a relatively high rate of high school dropout for blacks compared to whites: 38 percent of blacks we interviewed had failed to complete high school, compared to 27 percent of whites. Similar to the general population and the national prison population, Latino respondents in the reentry study had low levels of schooling, with 61 percent having failed to complete high school.

By common demographic measures, white respondents in the reentry study were more advantaged than blacks or Latinos. However, whites faced more serious troubles of other kinds. Formerly incarcerated whites tended to be older than their black counterparts, with an average age of forty-one; most were in their forties and fifties. African Americans in the reentry study were younger, age thirty-five on average; most were in their twenties and thirties. Latinos were the youngest with an average age of thirty-four.

The relative ages of whites, blacks, and Latinos leaving prison reflects differences in their life trajectories. In addition to being older, whites were more socially isolated, more likely to be disconnected from family, and also more likely to have a long history of drug use and mental illness. Half of all whites reported a history of mental illness and drug problems, compared to one-quarter of blacks and Latinos. Whites also reported higher rates of depression, anxiety, and chronic pain. Over one-third of whites told us that they had used heroin in the six months before they were incarcerated, compared to 13 percent of blacks and 21 percent of Latinos. These patterns follow national prison statistics in which whites in state prison tend to be somewhat older than blacks, to be in worse physical and mental health, and to have a history of serious drug use.[15]

Before they were incarcerated, whites were also more isolated from their families than black or Latino respondents. Whereas half of all blacks and Latinos strongly agreed that they felt close to their family prior to incarceration, only 20 percent of whites said that they felt close to family. Similarly, 40 percent of black respondents and 30 percent of Latinos strongly agreed that their families were a source of support, compared to 27 percent of whites. We also asked respondents how many family members they felt close to. African Americans felt close to an average of six people in their family, compared to just three for white respondents. Whites were also less likely to be living with family prior to incarceration and more likely to be living in unstable housing. During incarceration, 58 percent of Latinos and 54 percent of blacks were in regular contact with their family, through visits or phone calls. Only 38 percent of whites said that they were in touch with family members more than once a week while in prison. In short, family bonds appeared relatively weak for whites compared to blacks and Latinos.

These statistics reflect the different types and different extent of disadvantage associated with incarceration for the three racial-ethnic groups. Most white respondents had been struggling with lifelong drug and mental health problems, often into their forties and fifties, and these sustained problems had contributed to lifelong incarceration. Whites lived precariously prior to incarceration and were sometimes homeless, with only weak connections to their families. Blacks and Latinos were younger, in better physical and mental health, less likely to be dependent on drugs, and more likely to be involved with their family prior to incarceration. Being younger than the white men and women of the reentry study, blacks appeared to have had more short-lived involvement in crime and the criminal justice system.

The crimes for which the respondents were convicted also help show how incarceration operates in the lives of blacks, Latinos, and whites. Over half of all whites we interviewed were convicted of violent offenses, and only 10 percent were convicted on drug charges. Drug convictions were much more common among black respondents (24 percent), and blacks accounted for ten of the eleven firearms offenses in the sample. (Latinos had relatively high rates of violent offenses and drug offenses.) At least two reasons may explain why whites, who disproportionately report serious drug and mental health problems, have few drug convictions but high rates of conviction for violent offenses: robberies conducted to support drug habits, and fights waged in the furious phases of alcoholism.

Brian, raised in the Irish American stronghold of Charlestown, pulled armed robberies at pharmacies in search of the prescription painkillers to which he'd become addicted. Sean, also Irish American, had struggled with alcoholism from the age of twelve and held up a bank, as he had in the past, on the third day of a bender on alcohol and cocaine. John, raised in the housing projects of South Boston, was in his midforties when we spoke to him. A violent drunk, like his father, he would beat people up when he'd been drinking and was pessimistic about his chances of staying out of prison. Justin grew up in Charlestown; in his late twenties, he was younger than most of the other white men we interviewed. He began drinking at fourteen, and alcohol and violence had been closely linked throughout his life. After his release from prison, he got work as a bouncer, played in a local football league, and was arrested and returned to jail following a bar fight.

For black respondents, the large number of drug convictions and firearms offenses (accounting for a total of 40 percent of all black respondents) reflects their greater involvement in drug dealing and neighborhood gangs, as well as a sentencing regime that imposes prison time for drug offenses. Although violent convictions were less common among black respondents, many of the younger African American and Latino men we interviewed were close to Boston's gun violence, which is overwhelmingly concentrated in the largely African American neighborhoods of Roxbury, Dorchester, and Mattapan. Shooters and shooting victims in Boston are also mostly African American or Latino, reflecting the heavy concentration of serious street violence in these areas.[16]

Khalil was the son of Jamaican parents and grew up in Dorchester. He described himself as a "high-energy kid" growing up, with little time for school. Khalil accumulated a few small drug busts and weapons offenses before his imprisonment. After he was stopped by police for failing to use his turn signal and he and his friends were caught with two dozen bags of marijuana hidden in their clothes, he was sent to prison for six years. Sadiq was a little older among the African American respondents. A jovial man in his forties, he would braid his hair elaborately for special occasions and boast to us of his high tolerance for quality marijuana. A drug dealer all his adult life, until his most recent prison release, he was reliably high at every interview. We met other black and Latino men convicted of drug and gun charges in earlier chapters. Juney, in his midtwenties, grew up in a Cape Verdean family in Dorchester. Not a drug user himself, he had picked up a long list of drug possession and firearms charges. He spoke knowledgeably about the men in his neighborhood swaggering when they were carrying guns concealed in their clothes, a sign that invited trouble, he said. Peter had also been a drug dealer, but built up a long criminal history that also included hijacking trucks and assaults. More than a year after his prison release, nearly fifty years old, he found steady work at a suburban gym. Hector, a soft-spoken Puerto Rican man, served time for weapons and drug offenses in his midtwenties. After coming out of prison in his early thirties, he worked continuously in several food service jobs before getting construction work through his father-in-law. By the end of the year, he and his wife had a baby and they had moved into their own place.

Most of these black and Latino men had little employment in their background before their most recent incarceration. They had stopped going to school regularly around the age of sixteen, and none had finished high school. They were often involved in gangs as teenagers and got into drug dealing as a way of making money quickly. Most found a path to steady work after they got out of prison, mostly in low-wage jobs that required little training, and all received financial help and housing from their families.

We can think of the experience of different racial groups as stemming from different kinds of social inequality. Poor whites, mostly men, with mental health and drug use disorders came into conflict with the law repeatedly over their lifetime and returned to prison even in their forties and fifties. Black and Latino men were mostly younger, had histories of educational difficulties or learning problems, and faced poor economic opportunities in neighborhoods with high rates of poverty and unemployment. These men became involved in the drug trade and other street life and went to prison in their twenties and thirties.

The paths from poverty to prison worked in two distinct ways. Among whites, we saw a public health crisis in which drug use and mental illness were uncontrolled and felony convictions followed. The white men and women of the reentry study faced deficits of support for health problems that dogged them over a lifetime. Among blacks and Latinos, and the men in particular, we saw an economic crisis in which drug dealing and gang involvement presented a significant alternative to joblessness and minimum-wage employment. Because the threshold for incarceration was linked to the employment problems that broadly affected all young African American men with little schooling, it was especially low for black men. The deficits of opportunity faced by the black men we spoke to had clearly denied them access to a stable working-class life.

Whites, blacks, and Latinos began the transition from prison from different starting points. White respondents—older, with histories of drug addiction and mental illness and little family support—left prison with little money, just $200 at the median. Black and Latino respondents—younger, healthier, but without strong histories of employment—left prison with more money, a median of $340 for blacks and $450 for Latinos. In their first week after prison release, around 50 percent of all whites were in unstable housing—either a shelter, several residences, or a transitional housing program. By comparison, only 38 percent of Latinos and 28 percent of blacks were unstably housed immediately out of prison and were more likely to be living with family (52 percent of blacks and 43 percent of Latinos) than whites (33 percent).

Differences in housing are foreshadowed by differences in social isolation in the first week after incarceration. We constructed a scale to measure social isolation in the first week after incarceration, recording whether respondents spent time on their own and whether they spent time doing nothing. The measure of isolation was strongly associated with housing instability six months later.[17] Whites scored nearly half a standard deviation higher than blacks and Latinos on the scale of social isolation. Thus, not only were whites released with less money and to more unstable housing, but they were also more likely to be alone and idle immediately after prison release.

Isolation in the first week of community return was also associated with a relatively low likelihood of living with family later in the year. At six months after prison release, just over one-third of whites were living with family, compared to half of blacks. By twelve months after incarceration, 23 percent of whites were housed with family, compared to one-third of all blacks. Latinos provide a mixed case: they reported a low rate of housing with family, but also a low rate of unstable housing. The black men and women, but not the whites, also reported high levels of financial support from family members after incarceration.

The family support received by the black respondents coupled with the large racial disparity in incarceration suggests how the African American community is drawn into contact with the penal system. Even beyond the racial disparity in incarceration, black families were more likely to visit a relative in prison, pay for collect calls, and then house their relative after release. Black children were more likely to visit their incarcerated parent and more likely to be in contact with that parent after incarceration.

Isolation from family among whites was associated with continuing drug use after incarceration. Consistent with the life path of heavy drug users, whites leaving prison were much more likely to report heroin or cocaine use after incarceration than blacks or Latinos were. Around one in five whites were using heroin or cocaine over the year, compared to around 5 percent of blacks and Latinos.

Because of the disadvantages of the whites in the reentry study—their poor health and disconnection from family—we would expect them to do worse economically than black and Latino respondents. This was not the case. Despite serious drug use among the white respondents, both their rates of employment and their wages were higher than those of blacks and Latinos. Incomes for nearly all those we spoke to were very low, below the poverty line, but there were still clear racial differences. Median annual income from all sources (including jobs, government benefits, illegal income, and family support) totaled $10,200 for whites, compared to $7,300 for Latinos and only $4,700 for blacks.

Employment rates were initially highest among whites, and whites readily used their social networks to find work. Latino men also found work through friends and family, but most of the jobs they found paid close to the minimum wage. Some of the white men we interviewed were able to find union jobs after incarceration, many of them after reinstating their union cards with the help of friends or family members who were also union members. Only two of the black respondents, and none of the Latinos, were union members. (One black respondent worked for his brother's company, and another worked for a supermarket chain that was newly organized by the Teamsters.) The black men we interviewed were the most likely to use formal methods of job search: applying for jobs online or cold-calling employers. Jobless rates for black men were higher than for whites or Latinos, and black men were much more likely to report that they encountered discrimination because of their criminal record.[18] While the black and Latino workers we interviewed were most commonly working in fast-food restaurants and other service industry jobs, white workers were more likely to be working in relatively well-paying jobs in the construction industry.

Because white respondents earned more and were more likely to be employed, they were less dependent on government benefits. A year after prison release, 45 percent of whites were enrolled in food stamps, compared to 55 percent of blacks. Latinos were unusual in reporting very low rates of enrollment in government programs. Only one-third of Latino respondents were receiving food stamps a year after release from incarceration.

Life trajectories varied across the three racial groups, but not in any way associated with patterns of recidivism. Whites were somewhat more likely to get new charges compared to blacks (41 percent versus 32 percent). Only one-quarter of Latinos were rearrested. Reincarceration rates were virtually identical for blacks and whites: one-quarter of each racial group returned to custody at some point in the year. Reincarceration for Latinos was somewhat lower at 13 percent.

In sum, incarceration for whites was tied to the bodily hardships of illness, homelessness, and isolation from family. Coping with mental illness and addiction under conditions of poverty, white men and women disproportionately went to prison, often for violent crimes, in the grip of a bender that they had been powerless to stop. While black and Latino incarceration was connected to the deficits of opportunity rooted in segregation, neighborhood unemployment, and poverty, white incarceration was connected to the deficits of support for the health problems of mental illness and drug addiction.

Mass incarceration has been the vehicle for a new racial inequality. Historically high rates of incarceration have grown out of a racially charged politics that imposes harsh sentences and produces high rates of incarceration among minority men with little schooling. The unemployment and family disruption that follow incarceration are concentrated in poor black and Latino communities, where the footprint of the justice system is largest. These communities themselves emerged from the racial conflict and discrimination that infuse tough-on-crime politics. Boston has its own version of this history. Black and Latino residents of the city have long been segregated through discriminatory lending and housing development. Clashes between blacks and whites amid the virulent busing crisis of the 1970s hardened racial divisions between neighborhoods.

The new racial inequality is associated with racial disparity in incarceration rates. In Massachusetts, despite a low rate of incarceration typical of the New England states, the minority-white incarceration ratio is much higher than the national average. The negative effects of incarceration—not only the loss of liberty but the socioeconomic disadvantages that follow imprisonment—are disproportionately felt by blacks and Latinos. In Massachusetts as elsewhere, however, racial disparity in incarceration is only part of the story.

The new racial inequality emerged from the intimate connection between incarceration and poverty. Black poverty, particularly in urban areas, is different from white poverty. Black poverty is built into the structure of neighborhoods and labor markets. Sociologists have described how the neighborhood environments of low-income blacks are unusually disadvantaged compared to the neighborhood environments of other racial groups.[19] Being black and poor relegates one to living with other poor people in a racially segregated neighborhood where the local unemployment rate is high, families are more likely to be led by single mothers, and street crime is common. Economic dislocation is extensive, and street life and the drug trade present inviting alternatives for young men in their twenties and thirties who have dropped out of school. White poverty that touches the criminal justice system—concentrated among men who are loosely connected to families—is closer to skid row, rooted in mental illness, drug addiction, and the scarcity of treatment services. Black and brown incarceration is *extensive*. Serving a prison term is a regular part of life for many in recent cohorts of young African American and Latino men who have dropped out of school. White incarceration is *intensive,* narrowly focused on those whose multiple infirmities have landed them on the bottom rung of the social ladder—or lower.

For young whites, school failure followed by unemployment by themselves were not sufficient causes of incarceration. The young white men of the reentry study were familiar with drug dealing and gang life, but the drug trade and street life were not sewn into the fabric of their neighborhoods, as they were in the poorest blocks of Roxbury, Dorchester, and Mattapan. For whites in the study, it was mental illness and addiction, and ultimately estrangement from family, that linked poverty to incarceration.

The social structure of the economic disadvantage and lack of opportunity in minority neighborhoods compared to white neighborhoods shaped fortunes after prison release. Blacks and Latinos released from incarceration encountered significant obstacles to the kind of stable and well-paying jobs that were more readily available to whites. Blacks and Latinos also tended to be close to family. In fact, racial differences in family support had the perverse effect of drawing entire black and Latino kin networks into the orbit of the prison system. Visitation during incarceration and family support in its aftermath became common experiences for black and Latino mothers with incarcerated sons and daughters, and minority children often visited their incarcerated fathers. The social isolation of whites after incarceration, together with their low incarceration rates, prevented a broad spillover effect of mass incarceration among poor whites and their families.

For the men and women of the reentry study, incarceration was extensive among blacks and Latinos but limited in the life course—that is, recidivism was lower for blacks and Latinos in their forties and fifties compared to those in their twenties and thirties. For whites, returns to custody were largely unrelated to age. As recidivism declined with age for blacks, their employment increased, but for whites, plagued by addiction and mental illness and lacking family support, criminal justice contact was sustained over the life course. Nevertheless, despite their continuing recidivism, economic forces ran so strongly in favor of white men that when they came out of prison they had higher wages and less unemployment than young men of color who were in better health and had greater family support.

What are the ethical implications of the new racial inequality? In public conversation and in policy debates, we often resist the idea of racism in our social institutions. Defenders of prisons and the courts argue that our criminal justice system is not racist. Instead, disparities in incarceration or sentencing can be explained by racial differences in crime or the criminal histories of defendants. "Racist," in this argument, describes police, judges, and prosecutors who personally harbor a special animus against black and brown people and treat them harshly on the street and in court. Studies of the racial disparity in imprisonment have tried to assess the extent of such individualized racism that causes some people to treat minorities worse than similarly situated whites. Researchers distinguish between the "warranted" racial disparities that are attributable to crime and the "unwarranted disparities" that remain after crime rates have been taken into account. These studies show that more than half the racial disparity in imprisonment is "warranted" in this sense.[20]

But racism can work in other ways. Racial hierarchy can be built into the design of institutions, their regulations, and their procedures. Institutional racism of this kind does not depend on the individual animus of police or judges. Instead, it is inscribed on a sentencing policy that adds prison time for offenses for which black and Latino defendants are likely to be arrested. The sentencing shifts of the prison boom—expanding incarceration for drugs, violence, and repeat offenders—are racist in this institutional sense of disproportionately affecting blacks and Latinos.

Even more fundamentally, lawmakers have embraced tough-on-crime policy to manage the outcomes of the harsh conditions of American poverty, which compounds violence, disorder, and other disadvantages in segregated black and Latino neighborhoods. Focused criminalization in those neighborhoods is equally a failure of social policy to offer some path to the mainstream of American society to young men whose way has been diverted by school failure and fighting. This, fundamentally, is the nature of racism in the criminal justice system—that the economic marginality of young black and brown men, and all the antisocial behavior that follows, was answered with incarceration.[21] Punitive crime policy generates disparities in incarceration not primarily because police and judges are biased against young minority men, but because imprisonment has been chosen as the policy response to the kinds of crime and disruption in which these young men are involved. The transition from prison to community for the black and Latino men we interviewed was littered with obstacles because of deficits of education and economic opportunity. The punitive function of incarceration had failed because punishment was applied, not to cases of individual moral failure, but to moral failures that occurred in contexts of deep neighborhood and economic disadvantage.

Whereas antidiscrimination measures—staff training or limits on discretion, for example—may reduce the individualized racism among police and in the courts, institutional racism requires a different response. Policy change that weighs and then seeks to minimize the risk of racial disparities in incarceration represents one approach. For example, recent measures to reduce disparities in federal drug sentencing for crack cocaine (used more by blacks) and powder (used more by whites) aim to address institutional racism. However, the injuries incurred through the institutional racism of mass incarceration are historic and collective: the harms of the prison boom have accumulated over decades and affected entire groups of the population. Just as the harms of mass incarceration are historic and collective, so too is the injustice.

Thus, mass incarceration has not just created a new racial inequality: it has also created a new moral challenge to seek racial justice. Answering the challenge will involve acknowledging the harms delivered over decades through the agency of the state, in keeping with a long history of racial oppression. Some may object that a project for achieving racial justice relieves the perpetrators of crime in poor minority communities of moral responsibility. While the residents of poor black and Latino neighborhoods act with full moral agency no less than anyone else, their neighborhood conditions make the consequences of their agency ominous. Under these conditions that leave so little room for error, the imperative for racial justice is even more urgent.

CHAPTER 11

Criminal Justice as Social Justice

A man was raised by his mother in a poor African American section of Dorchester. He was stabbed three different times during his teenage years, and by the onset of his schizophrenia, he had accumulated a long list of juvenile convictions. Eddie was an army veteran and had been a crack addict for most of his adult life. He worked periodically, but in the year after incarceration he lived mostly off his veteran's benefits and street scams. Patrick's mother was a heroin addict who died of AIDS when he was seventeen. A heroin user himself, Patrick had been a witness and victim of serious violence since early childhood. Carla was also a heavy drug user whose life was suffused by violence. Before she went to prison, she made a living by prostitution, selling drugs, and a government disability check for a bad back injured in a prison brawl. Juney was abandoned by his father and raised by his mother, left school at sixteen, and completed his GED in prison. Juney's parole was revoked when his brother got arrested and called him to the scene to help out. Celia was raised by her mother, who had fled an abusive husband who battered her for years. Celia periodically lived with her grandmother, but left home for good at age seventeen. Like her mother, Celia was a victim of domestic violence as a young parent of twenty and made her living as a drug dealer. Peter grew up in the housing projects of Roxbury, with a mother who was addicted to drugs and an abusive father. He was a runaway from the age of eleven. At fourteen, his head was split open with a crowbar in a racial brawl. From the age of seventeen, he spent more than half his life in prison.

These many different starting points all led to Massachusetts prisons, and then to prison release. Life after incarceration was followed by stress and material hardship. Older men in their fifties and sixties and those who had battled mental illness and addiction were often socially isolated and supported by government programs. AJ, Mike, Patrick, Peter, and many other respondents were nervous in crowds. They avoided the bus and the subway when they first got out. After incarceration, two-thirds of the sample had poverty-level incomes, and half made less than $6,000, a level that researchers describe as deep poverty. Food stamps, paying an average of $200 each month, were the most common source of steady income. People lived with their mothers and grandmothers or in shelters or sober houses. Only a handful had their own housing. Their health was poor, and chronic pain and disease were common among them. More than half the people we spoke to were African Americans and Latinos who lived in the historically low-income minority neighborhoods of Roxbury and Dorchester that grew out of redlining and Boston's white flight of the 1960s and 1970s.

This is the world in which the criminal justice system operates. Certainly, justice is urgently needed here. Violence is abundant. Harms stack up like mail at a vacant address. Among the incarcerated, their families, and their neighbors, few have escaped victimization. There is a role for agencies of justice, but in the era of mass incarceration they have come to rely on one tool: the deprivation of liberty through imprisonment.

The social world of incarceration is rich in racial inequality, poverty, and violence. The criminal justice meted out in poor African American communities is rooted in the centuries-long contest over black citizenship. The nation's constitutive flaw of slavery, followed by Jim Crow and the modern ghetto, institutionalized an impassable racial divide. Even after the civil rights reforms of the 1960s that outlawed segregation and racial discrimination in housing, true freedom of residence for African Americans has been unattainable. The racial divide only deepened when, in the early 1970s, a historic expansion of the scale of incarceration commenced in the name of crime control.[1]

Racial inequality is a dominating reality for the criminal justice system. African Americans are six to seven times more likely to be incarcerated than whites, and Latinos are about twice as likely. Because of racial segregation in housing and the concentration of poverty in minority neighborhoods, jail time, parole appointments, and police interactions have come to be a regular part of life in very disadvantaged areas.[2]

Some commentators saw little injustice in the racial disparities in incarceration. High rates of incarceration among African Americans, they argued, were simply a reflection of racial disparities in crime. As John DiIulio wrote in 1996, "If blacks are overrepresented in the ranks of the imprisoned, it is because blacks are overrepresented in the criminal ranks—and the violent criminal ranks, at that."[3] But this naturalizes the link between crime and incarceration. Of all the different ways in which policymakers could have responded to the problem of crime, they chose a course that massively curtailed the liberty of a segment of the population who have had to fight for their freedom from the beginning.

In Boston, African Americans and Latinos make up less than one-quarter of the city's population but were about 75 percent of the formerly incarcerated sample of the reentry study. The white respondents we interviewed were mostly in their forties or older, were high school graduates, and had histories of addiction, mental illness, and homelessness.[4] The black and Latino respondents were more often in their twenties and more likely to be high school dropouts with little work history. They experienced more unemployment, and their incomes were only half the incomes of whites after incarceration. Because kin connections were stronger among black and brown respondents compared to whites, black and brown families were drawn into the orbit of the prison through visits, phone calls, canteen payments, and the provision of housing after release. In short, the new racial inequality was visible in Boston through the association between the incarceration of young black men and the deep economic disadvantage woven into the structure of their economic opportunities.

Extreme poverty was as common as racial inequality among the reentry study respondents. Most had grown up poor in poor neighborhoods. After incarceration, their incomes were not only low but well below the poverty line. Their only steady income was government support, and they kept their heads above water only with help from family. The income poverty of people who have been to prison is only one marker of the greater challenge of correlated adversity. Multiple disadvantages—untreated mental illness, addiction, poor physical health, housing insecurity—accumulate among people involved in the criminal justice system. Two-thirds of those we interviewed had a history of mental illness or addiction to drugs or alcohol. Depression was common among them—and nearly universal among the women—and anxiety and post-traumatic stress were also frequently reported. Twenty percent of respondents used heroin or cocaine in the year after prison release, and about half of those with a history of addiction experienced a relapse to drug use, which regularly preceded a return to prison. Most of the regular users were the children of addicts.

Lifetimes of poorly treated addiction and mental illness under conditions of social and economic insecurity had taken a physical toll. Over 40 percent of the reentry study sample lived with chronic disease, like diabetes or hepatitis, and another one-third reported chronic pain, often related to accidents, fights, or heavy drug use. In the social world of incarceration, poverty is accompanied by human frailty.

Finally, violence. By the time we interviewed them, the men and women of the reentry study had survived abusive childhood homes, grown up through teenage years filled with fighting, been stabbed or shot, and delivered their own share of violence too. Researchers claim that prison has an "incapacitative" effect that reduces violence by removing it from society. But this claim assumes that prisons themselves are safe and secure and that whatever occurs within their walls need not be counted in statistics on violent crime. Respondents reported that the prison environment was tense with the possibility of beatings, stabbings, and retaliation. Fighting was common in some facilities and barely contained by prison staff.

Violence is a lifetime reality for people who go to prison. It grows out of the chaotic context of poverty and its accompanying disadvantages. In the world of incarceration, order emerges less from the informal bonds of community than through the coercion of the group home, the county jail, and the state prison. Living in such contexts further exposes incarcerated men and women to violence. Given the contextual character of violence, the roles of victim, witness, and perpetrator are not neatly divided among individuals. Instead, one comes to play all these parts as the life course unfolds. A key implication is that those with a long history of offending have been victims and witnesses to violence for even longer.

Racial inequality (rooted in generations of confinement), extreme poverty (magnified by human frailty), and violence (lifelong, contextual, and saturated with victimization) define the social space where the criminal justice system does its work. Mass incarceration has only hardened the connections between racial inequality, harsh poverty, and violence. High rates of incarceration have deepened racial exclusion and undermined economic opportunity. Whatever public safety gained through mass incarceration was offset by incarceration's negative social effects.

Adopted in the name of public safety, perhaps the most critical test of mass incarceration is its effects on violence. It is true that crime rates fell dramatically from the early 1990s while incarceration rates increased. By 2015, the murder rate was at a historically low level. The great decline in American violence did significantly improve the quality of life in disadvantaged communities, but the growth in incarceration appears to have played only a small role in the decline. Researchers have been unable to find compelling evidence that high and demographically concentrated rates of incarceration produced large and long-term reductions in violent crime. Dozens of studies have tried to calculate the effects of the prison boom on crime. Estimating the effects of prison population growth on crime is difficult because crime itself is a cause of incarceration. There are several excellent summaries of this research, but most conclude that the fourfold growth in incarceration rates from the 1970s to the 2000s reduced crime only slightly, accounting for perhaps just 10 percent of the 1990s crime decline.[5]

Whatever the precise reduction in crime from increased incarceration, none of the research considers the larger patterns we see in the reentry study. Assessments of the value of incarceration overlook the costly transitions from prison back to community, the lost employment, the costs to families of visitation and reentry, the separation of children from parents, or the cynicism that grows in heavily policed communities. Neither does the research weigh the injustice of imprisonment that is concentrated among people who themselves have been seriously victimized by crime, who are poor, and who are mostly African American or Latino. Finally, even the crime reductions that incarceration can take credit for should be judged against alternative approaches, not against the politically impossible option of doing nothing. For all these reasons, mass incarceration has failed to clearly bring justice and safety to America's poorest and most troubled communities.

The overpowering social reality in which incarceration operates challenges us to think about justice in new ways. Discussions of the ethics of punishment are usually abstract and ignore the social conditions that surround the courts and prisons.

Philosophers and legal theorists usually start by acknowledging that punishment—the state-sanctioned imposition of suffering—is an evil that requires justification for its legitimacy. One of two justifications for punishment are usually presented. First, punishment can be justified as retribution, where the state is leveling the moral playing field by returning to an offender the injury he inflicted on a victim. A whole jurisprudence of proportionality in sentencing has grown from the theory of punishment as retribution. The second common justification for punishment points to its consequences: punishment can both warn would-be criminals (deterrence) and remove dangerous people from free society (incapacitation). Thus, deterrence and incapacitation became the leading justifications for harsh punishment in the period of mass incarceration.

Today the main justifications of punishment—retribution, incapacitation, and deterrence—assume that crime is caused by an individual disposition that resists rehabilitation. The policy analyst James Q. Wilson famously described this disposition as belonging to "wicked people" as well as to those who are merely "watchful, dissembling, and calculating."[6] In this view, both types deserve the retribution of incarceration. The wicked can be incapacitated in prison. The calculating can be deterred by long and mandatory sentences. Writing in the 1970s, Wilson's analysis abandoned rehabilitation and looked to punishment as the primary instrument for crime control.

Wilson lent academic authority to the punitive thrust of crime policy in the 1970s, and today's reformers have absorbed many of the same ideas. Reform initiatives are now focused on so-called nonviolent drug offenders and seek to reduce sentences for drug convictions.[7] In 2015, for example, Congress considered a proposal to reduce mandatory minimum sentences for first-time defendants tried for drug crimes. The Smarter Sentencing Act was intended to concentrate "limited Federal resources on the most serious offenders." Relaxing mandatory sentences for drug offenses, the bill promised, in the words of its sponsor, Republican congressman Raúl Labrador, to "improve safety by enabling the justice system to focus on the most violent offenders."[8] A concern about harsh drug sentences was echoed by President Barack Obama in his *Harvard Law Review* article published in the waning days of his presidency. "Too many, especially nonviolent drug offenders, serve unnecessarily long sentences," he wrote.[9] In line with this view, initiatives to reduce sentences for drugs, but not for violence, are advancing around the country. These efforts aim to identify those deserving of leniency (people convicted of drug crimes) and reserve retribution and incapacitation for "dangerous offenders."

Reforming sentences for "nonviolent drug offenders" only goes a small way. Fewer than one in five state prisoners are serving time for drug offenses. Reducing drug-related incarceration will only produce a small reduction in the overall prison population. We also know from the reentry interviews and a considerable body of research that the "nonviolent drug offender" is largely a mythic figure. The street trade in drugs is a dangerous business that must be protected from robberies and rival dealers. Guns and a willingness to use them are part of the business. The Boston respondents often carried guns, shot at their rivals, and were shot at themselves while selling drugs on the street. The fiction of the "nonviolent drug offender" denies the violence of the drug trade for people entangled in the criminal justice system.

Because violence is so prevalent in the social world of incarceration, the good and the bad, the wicked and the innocent, cannot be neatly differentiated. Instead, victims and perpetrators are often one and the same. Violence flares in contexts of family chaos, untreated addiction, and poverty. Having grown up in this context, people in prison have histories of trauma and abuse that date from early childhood. This is a world whose material conditions are shot through with ethical ambiguity. The great moral challenge is not to find the innocent among the guilty, but to treat with decency and compassion even those who have engaged in violence.

Instead of asking with the philosophers how and for whom state-imposed suffering can be justified, I take a different starting point. In a world where the social conditions of inequality are ripe with violence among the most disadvantaged, how can we promote justice for those who are harmed?

One proposal recognizes the necessity of punishment but argues for consideration of the poverty and other disadvantages of the defendants who come into the criminal courts. The legal scholar Michael Tonry calls this "social adversity mitigation."[10] Tonry argues that the context of criminal offending is formed in part by the harsh social conditions under which many defendants grew up. The reentry study richly demonstrates Tonry's argument. Well beyond poverty, the conditions of social adversity include family chaos in childhood, untreated addiction and mental illness, homelessness, and chronic disease and pain. All these parts of a defendant's biography are typically excluded from assessments of guilt or innocence and from sentencing decisions. Tonry argues that these conditions of social adversity should be considered as part of the cause of crime. Crimes are not simply failures to resist temptation, as theories of retribution and deterrence often claim. Instead, crimes "often result from the regrettable but understandable choices of people whose lives present few positive options and who are subject to extraordinary stress."[11] Arguing that these social contexts should influence our assessments of moral culpability, Tonry is answering the tough-minded philosophy of "do the crime, do the time." This philosophy, writes Tonry, "ignores and lacks empathy for the complex circumstances of the lives of deeply disadvantaged people. Proponents of a social disadvantage defense or of sentence mitigation are responding to that deficiency by searching for a better solution."[12]

Social adversity mitigation helps express our instincts of compassion and leniency. Reducing sentences for defendants who have lived with poverty, abuse, homelessness, and discrimination helps neutralize the retributive outrage embodied in mass incarceration. Social adversity mitigation admits the moral complexity of the social world and acknowledges that a defendant too has suffered harm. Still, weighing a defendant's life conditions offers only a small window on the many injustices where violence is tied to race, poverty, and its correlated adversities.

Opening the window wider requires that we ask why pervasive incarceration has failed to greatly reduce crime. It is not police, courts, and the threat of punishment that create public safety, but rather the bonds of community produced by a raft of social institutions—families, schools, employers, churches, and neighborhood groups. In regularizing social life and promoting daily routine, these institutions engage the attention of neighbors, co-workers, spouses, teachers, and employers, who monitor conduct and stand as a normative reminder of order. The social institutions of community life are also age-graded: as children grow into adolescence and then adulthood, they are socialized into the roles of spouse, worker, and citizen that help maintain regularity and routine in daily life. Movement through the life course has an important material component where growing up confers not just independence from family and school but also the means to sustain oneself and others.

Indeed, the reentry study respondents and their kin richly revealed the orderly and sustaining effects of family, education, work, and community life. Young men like Bobby and Sam were housed by their mothers after they got out of prison. The mothers also kept their sons in touch with their children during incarceration, and after prison both men maintained relationships with their babies' mothers. Although the path away from prison was not always straight, both men completed their first year back home without an arrest. Mike, in his midfifties, first lived in a sober house paid for by a reentry program. But by the end of the year he had started a household on the South Shore with his girlfriend. The work he found in demolition paid a living wage, well above poverty. Mike's experience shows the integrative power not just of work but of skilled work in particular. Hector lived with his girlfriend in her parents' house and worked continuously after prison. He first stayed on in his work-release job, then graduated to a construction job organized by his girlfriend's stepfather. He took pride in the birth of his daughter, and the guns and drug dealing that dotted his criminal record receded far into the distance as the year progressed. In total, two-thirds of the men and women in the reentry study—with the support of family, employers, and government assistance—got through their first year without a new arrest.

People with families, work, and other social supports enjoyed and added to a thick kind of public safety that brought order and predictability to their daily lives. This kind of public safety kept them not only free from bodily threats but materially secure in their housing, intimate relationships, and livelihoods. Thick public safety lengthens people's time horizons, allowing them to imagine a future in which it makes sense to invest in themselves and their children.

The restorative power of thick public safety contrasts with the political talk about crime in which a thin kind of public safety is threatened by strangers engaged in street violence. For pundits and policymakers who conjure up shadowy street criminals, protection is offered only by the deterrent and incapacitative force of punishment.[13] The harsh conditions of poverty and the close link between violence and poverty are largely missing from the thin conception of public safety. In reality, the violence that derails people's lives does not usually occur in random confrontations with menacing strangers. Instead it emerges in family homes and neighborhoods. Victims and perpetrators are known to each other. Violence—because it is endemic and attaches to conditions of poverty—is itself a type of deprivation.

Thick public safety is clearly in short supply in environments of racial inequality, poverty, and contextual violence. The great failure of mass incarceration is that it tends to weaken the social bonds that produce order and predictability in daily life. The removal of community residents by incarceration reverberates through families, and so does their return. Violence ruptures social bonds and creates the public policy challenge of their restoration for both victim and offender. Incarceration on a massive scale offers nothing to such a challenge.

Solutions to the problem of violence—both preventive and remedial after violence has taken place—must be socially integrative, helping to build the conditions of opportunity and future-orientation that underpin thick public safety. Where threats of violence and bodily harm are related less to the individual dispositions of offenders than to social environment, justice is more readily found in the abatement of violent environments than in the punishment of violent people. Here, criminal justice becomes social justice.

The principle of social justice demands that public policy not unduly burden any particular group and that it foster instead a fair distribution of rights, resources, and capacities for all groups in society.[14] Broadly promoting the capacities of all, under conditions of deep and destabilizing inequality, is thus central to the criminal justice function. Harsh punishment, particularly the community-eroding instrument of incarceration, has only a minor role in such a reimagined criminal justice. Instead, in the aftermath of violence, our courts and correctional agencies should help rebuild the social membership of both the victim and the offender, since both have been alienated from the social compact by violence. Such rebuilding will involve recognizing the histories of victimization and trauma of those who have most recently been offenders as well as attending directly to the harms suffered by victims, rather than through the convoluted conceit of punishing the offender. Besides their physical injuries, victims' mental trauma, economic losses, and the stigma of victimization must also be addressed.

Most importantly, however, a reimagined criminal justice will concede some jurisdiction over the policy task of public safety to other agencies—departments of housing, child services, public health, education, and labor. The reentry study shows that needs are most acute in three areas. First, for those coming out of prison, there remains an urgent need for transitional support in the first weeks after release. The stress of transition from prison to the community interferes with everyday tasks and can subvert even the most motivated efforts to find health care, housing, and a means of subsistence. One-stop shops, with staff who are knowledgeable and compassionate about the disorientation that follows incarceration, would smooth the path from prison to community. Second, continuity of medical and mental health care after incarceration is an urgent necessity for a population with high rates of disability and mental illness. At this writing, the future of an expanded Medicaid is uncertain, but it should be noted here that in Massachusetts, Medicaid enrollment prior to prison release greatly reduced social insecurity. Third, over the course of the entire reentry study, almost no one we interviewed managed to secure independent housing. Attending to the housing needs of the recently released, however, must go beyond improving the availability of safe and secure transitional beds for them to also support the families who provide them with a place to stay and financial assistance. A "returning citizen" tax credit for families who house and support adult relatives who have been institutionalized would help relieve the financial burden now imposed by public policy on private citizens.

Community programs also offer models for a justice policy aimed at social integration in the aftermath of crime. Roca, a youth antiviolence program in Massachusetts, works successfully with young men who have been involved in serious violence. Roca's approach is based on "relentless outreach"—an intensive style of case management that energetically offers support to young people even as they relapse and return to incarceration. As Roca staff take to the streets, visit homes, and go into police stations, courthouses, and jails, they proactively build relationships with clients over the years. ComALERT, a different kind of program in Brooklyn, New York, provides housing, drug treatment, and transitional employment to men and women on parole. Run by the Brooklyn district attorney, ComALERT, like Roca, engages with clients over a long period. Providing up to a year of employment and housing, ComALERT's assistance to a poor and largely homeless group of parolees has exceeded that of other reentry programs. In providing a full year of housing and transitional employment, the program is relatively expensive, but it is cheaper than incarceration. A third program, the Transitions Clinic in San Francisco, provides "complex care management"—a type of case management for people immediately after prison release. In addition to providing primary medical care, the Transitions Clinic helps patients manage chronic conditions and navigate the health care bureaucracies of clinics, hospitals, and insurance companies. Evaluations show that the Transitions Clinic greatly reduces emergency room visits for its patients in the year after incarceration.[15]

Each of these programs focuses on different needs and works with different kinds of clients and patients, but they share two important characteristics. First, they help improve the material well-being of those who are poor and frail and have come into conflict with the law. Their efforts reveal a realistic understanding of the conditions of poverty in which the criminal justice system operates. Second, programs also provide powerful personal advocacy for those who must negotiate countless bureaucracies and a suspicious justice system.

The reentry study findings show that there is no one path from prison to community but many. A single program or policy cannot meet the many challenges to achieving social integration after incarceration. The findings do suggest, however, that poverty and human frailty threaten individuals' community membership after they come into conflict with the law. Policies that improve material well-being and provide client advocacy help meet the challenges of poverty and human frailty. Designing social policy according to these principles will also help relieve the justice system of much its unwanted and ill-equipped responsibility for the consequences of the harsh conditions of American poverty.

Expanding social policy in environments currently dominated by police, courts, and prisons is crucial for reform, but there is an important role for criminal justice too. It will remain important to signal society's disapproval of violence in human affairs, publicly acknowledge the injuries of victims, and remind offenders of their responsibility for the harms they have caused. Pragmatically, too, incarceration will remain necessary for the small fraction who pose immediate risks to themselves and to those around them. But even in these cases, the penal principle of parsimony should be paramount. Incapacitation through incarceration should be confined to that minimal number of individuals who threaten public safety even in community settings properly designed for thick public safety.

The mission of social integration in the aftermath of crime creates a broad test for criminal justice policy: does it encourage community membership or does it deepen social exclusion? Many staples of American criminal justice fail this test. Fines and fees for cost recovery, pretrial detention for want of bail, criminal record disqualifications for government benefits, revocations of probation and parole for technical violations—all fail the test of social integration.

Criminal justice is a poor instrument for social policy because at its core, it is a blaming institution. Finding alternatives requires a shift in perspective. How can we do something different for people who are frail, homeless, poor, and often disruptive and antisocial? Expanding the social policy response to disorder and antisocial behavior is a shift in politics as much as a shift in policy. Reimagining the criminal justice function as restoring community life also departs from the standard moral script for victim and offender. We can at least complicate our moral judgment by placing people in the context of their social situation and biography. Bringing realism to the political conversation about crime not only calls for our most clear-headed thinking but also invokes our values. The problem of crime is thus humanized, and our bonds of mutual obligation underscored.

If we are going to reduce our prison populations, we must acknowledge that human frailty under conditions of poverty puts people at risk of simultaneously becoming both the perpetrator and the victim of violence. This moral complexity, where victims and offenders are often one and the same, is challenging for a justice system designed to assess guilt or innocence and mete out punishment. Historically, we have punished violence as an assault of the strong on the weak. The larger challenge now is to heal the frailty from which violence springs.

Policy researchers often propose correcting the error of bad public policy by adopting good policy going forward. But policy reform falls short as a remedy for the state violence of incarceration, which has become pervasively linked to conditions of poverty and human frailty, particularly in black and brown communities, and deformed the citizenship of society's most vulnerable members. Policy reform acknowledges none of the harms of the past suffered by communities and families as they became swamped by rising prison populations. The wholesale state-sanctioned deprivation of liberty in America's poorest communities of color is a collective and historic injustice—collective because incarceration has injured entire communities, affecting even those who have not been incarcerated themselves, and historic because mass incarceration has prolonged the centuries-long struggle of African Americans to be free.

The resolution of historic injustice is fundamentally a political question, but there are models for how to go about it. Reparations have been proposed to make whole again those who were injured. In making a compelling argument for reparations in relation to the historic injustice of Jim Crow, Ta-Nehisi Coates traces specific cases of the expropriation of property by whites from black landowners. Writing later, Coates asks if reparations are also due for the harms stemming from mass incarceration.[16]

Many other approaches, however, have been taken to help resolve the harms that flow from historic and collective injustice. Postcolonial societies have established special courts for war crimes, formed truth and reconciliation commissions, and issued official apologies. Opening museums, erecting monuments, sponsoring cultural events, introducing new school curricula, opening secret files to public access—all these actions have been taken to acknowledge the collective injuries suffered by entire communities. Some societies have adopted small rituals recognizing historic injustices against indigenous people as part of the etiquette of daily life. Public meetings in Australia and Canada, for example, regularly begin with what Australians call a "Welcome to Country" that acknowledges the traditional, indigenous occupants displaced by white settlement. Other efforts to respond to mass violence have emerged in postconflict societies where tribal or colonial divisions clearly mark the perpetrators and the victims. As Martha Minow observes in her catalog of these responses to mass violence: "These alternatives all share one feature. They depart from doing nothing."[17]

Attempts to address large-scale injustices affirm the human dignity of those who have suffered, but present a daunting political challenge for all those who have been harmed by mass incarceration. Incarceration denies the moral worth of the incarcerated, and the stigma of criminality often spreads to family members and neighbors. Blame in the criminal justice system is also attributed individually. The collective justice project—to deny blame and affirm the collective dignity of a whole segment of the population—flies in the face of criminal jurisprudence.

In the United States, pervasive incarceration remains a daily reality in poor and minority neighborhoods. Policymakers—elected officials, prosecutors, and correctional administrators—resist the idea that a historic and collective injury was suffered by the most vulnerable citizens in America's most disadvantaged communities. Justice institutions and the people who staff them will have a special role to play in this process. Acknowledging the past harms of the criminal justice system asks of police, prosecutors, judges, and correctional staff to understand the histories not just of their agencies but of the communities with which they interact. Terence Cunningham, president of the International Association of Chiefs of Police (IACP), began to address this challenge in 2016. Speaking in the context of several years of protest against racial bias in policing, Cunningham said:

> There have been times when law enforcement officers . . . have been the face of oppression for far too many of our fellow citizens. . . . This dark side of our shared history has created a multigenerational—almost inherited—mistrust between many communities of color and their law enforcement agencies. . . . For our part, the first step in this process is for law enforcement and

the IACP to acknowledge and apologize for the actions of the past and the role that our profession has played in society's historical mistreatment of communities of color.

Chief Cunningham's statement was brief and carefully focused on past injustice. But he argued that the deep mistrust of police in communities of color is a problem to be addressed deliberatively between police and community representatives. Apology by the police was central to those deliberations.

To acknowledge the injustice of incarceration and the pain of state violence heaped on the frail and the poor is a fundamentally humanistic step that begins to extend compassion and mutual understanding. It recognizes that public policy intended for the common good has in fact had the reverse effect. Millions have been removed from their families, friends, and communities in greater numbers and for longer periods than the common good can justify. And this would not have happened if those subject to the influence of the penal system were not mostly black, brown, poor, and sometimes broken and vulnerable in myriad ways. One task for the acknowledgment of harm is education—disseminating histories of oppression so that all those involved in the criminal justice system can gain real understanding of the conditions of life for the most disadvantaged. Education is a justice project.

However American society comes to recognize the historic mistake of mass incarceration and the collective injury to the poor and to communities of color, the immediate goal should be mutual understanding. Such understanding will reveal the lived conditions of American poverty, the historic weight of racial inequality, and the basic humanity of all those who are touched by America's massive network of penal institutions.

Redressing the historic injustice of mass incarceration does more than settle accounts with the past. Police, judges, and penal officials who acknowledge historic harms can begin to heal relationships and build trust with disadvantaged communities. But such efforts will feel hollow without real change. Under the harsh conditions of American poverty, the antidote to violence is not more punishment but restoring the institutions, social bonds, and well-being that enable order and predictability in daily life. I hope that recognizing historic harms might slow our reflex to punish and instead encourage socially integrative responses to crime. Criminal justice could then contribute to a thick public safety that allows even the poorest to live day to day with an eye on their future and the future of their children.

NOTES

....

Preface

1. Garland's panoramic view of crime policy in the period of "late modernity" is described in *The Culture of Control* (2001). Wacquant writes about social control under conditions of racial inequality and welfare state retrenchment in the United States and France in *Prisons of Poverty* (2009a), *Punishing the Poor* (2009b), and *Urban Outcasts* (2007). In *Locked Out* (2006), Manza and Uggen study the electoral effects of felon disenfranchisement. Pager, giving new life to audit studies, examines employer responses to job applicants with criminal records in her book *Marked* (2007). Pettit's *Invisible Men* (2012) analyzes the invisible inequality of mass incarceration. Wakefield and Wildeman estimate the effects of parental incarceration on children in *Children of the Prison Boom* (2013). The encyclopedic summary provided by the NAS report (Travis, Western, and Redburn 2014) does miss some of the most exciting work by young scholars. While the list is long, important contributions include Eason (2017), Goffman (2014), Kohler-Hausmann (2013), Miller (2014), Muller (2012), and Patterson (2010).

Chapter 1: Introduction

1. Garland 2001; Alexander 2010.
2. The research on the effects of incarceration is summarized by Travis, Western, and Redburn (2014). The Council of Economic Advisers (2016) estimates that by 2012 all criminal justice spending at the local, state, and federal levels totaled $274 billion. Correctional spending, which includes the costs of probation and parole, totaled $83 billion. The figure on the EITC is for 2013 (Falk and Crandall-Hollick 2016); the food stamps figure is for 2015 (USDA 2016). All spending figures are in 2015 dollars.
3. See, for example, Brooks et al. (2005) and Travis, Western, and Redburn (2014).
4. Rich et al. 2014; Food and Nutrition Service (2012).

Chapter 2: Learning About Life After Prison

1. Statisticians say that survey nonresponse is "non-ignorable" when it is related to the outcomes of interest. With the very high response rate in the BRS, we found that the

risk of nonresponse was strongly non-ignorable: a hypothetically high nonresponse rate, as obtained in earlier studies, would have created large statistical biases (Western et al. 2016).

2. Becky Pettit (2012) has written at length about the topic in her book *Invisible Men*.

3. Martin, Abreu, and Winters 2001; Harding et al. 2014.

4. John Warren and Andrew Halpern-Manners (2012) warn that repeated contact with interviewers can induce behavioral and attitudinal change and may even improve outcomes for respondents. Improved outcomes would be welcome news for released prisoners and policymakers, but the insignificant differences in recidivism between the BRS sample and the state as a whole suggest that participation in the BRS had few positive effects on our respondents.

5. Similar protocols were used in other studies of hard-to-reach populations by Harding et al. (2014), Farrington et al. (1990), and Desmond et al. (1995).

6. David Harding and his colleagues (2014) adopted a similar approach in their study of Michigan parolees.

7. See, for example, Teitler, Reichman, and Sprachman 2003.

8. Responsibility for the protection of confidential data ultimately lies with the researcher and the "Certificate of Confidentiality" may not carry much weight if data are subpoenaed. Leslie Wolf and her colleagues (2015) provide a good discussion.

9. Jerolmack and Murphy (2017) provide a useful review and discussion.

Chapter 3: Transitions

1. In his classic study on prisoner reentry, John Irwin (1970, 107) wrote about "withstanding the initial impact" of returning to society. He observed that the first weeks after incarceration could be filled with disorientation, disorganization, and difficulty with everyday interactions. Christy Visher and Jeremy Travis (2003, 96) also highlight the first weeks after incarceration—"the complex dynamic of the moment of release"— as critical to the reentry process.

2. Panel regressions with the reentry study data showed that an index of social isolation in the first week after release was related to family support, housing instability, and unemployment six months later after controlling for demographics, incarceration variables, time fixed effects, and mental illness and addiction (Western et al. 2015).

3. The bridge was found to be unsafe over the course of the study. The shelter was closed, and Long Island's residents were dispersed to shelters across the city.

4. Although Clemmer's (1940, 300) analysis is now archaic in some ways, his observation that incarceration produces "new habits of eating, dressing, working, [and] sleeping" remained relevant to our observations in Boston seventy years later.

5. Maruna and Toch 2005.

6. Irwin 1970, 115.

7. Six out of the twenty-eight respondents age forty-five or older reported a welcome-home event, compared to twenty out of the thirty-six respondents age thirty or younger.

8. Irwin 1970, 175. Recidivism also bears, of course, on the quality of community membership and is examined further in chapter 6.

9. Major studies of the effect of stable marriage on criminal desistance have been conducted by Robert Sampson and John Laub (1993) and by Mark Warr (1998). Compare the work of Andrea Leverentz (2011) and Jessica Wyse, David Harding, and Jeffrey Morenoff (2014), who find that formerly incarcerated women can be destabilized by the influence of partners who use drugs or are involved in crime. Megan Comfort (2008) describes the respite for women partnered with incarcerated men. Sara Wakefield and Christopher Wildeman (2013) provide an important quantitative analysis of the effects of parental incarceration on children. Chapter 7 explores the links between incarceration and family life in greater detail.

10. Martinez and Christian (2009) and Leverentz (2011) have also observed the supportive role of female relatives.

11. On postrelease housing in New York and Philadelphia, see Metraux, Roman, and Cho (2008) and Travis (2005, ch. 9). For Massachusetts figures on homelessness, see Metraux, Roman, and Cho (2008, 5). David Harding, Jeffrey Morenoff, and Claire Herbert (2013) provide an excellent large-scale analysis of housing and housing insecurity among Michigan parolees.

12. "Sober houses" are low-income group residences in Massachusetts that administer drug and alcohol testing and conduct rehabilitative programs.

13. In response to the open-ended question asked at the two-month interview about their biggest challenge since release, 40 out of 122 respondents mentioned employment or income. The next most common challenge mentioned (14 out of 122) was staying out of trouble or desisting from crime.

14. The pride, status, and routine accompanying steady work have been observed by Robert Sampson and John Laub (1993), Mercer Sullivan (1989), and Timothy Black (2010). Both Jeffrey Kling (2006) and I (Western 2006) have documented the low earnings after incarceration. Enrollment in public assistance is analyzed in Harding et al. (2014), and my colleagues and I (Western, Kling, and Weiman 2001) and Harry Holzer (2009) have reviewed the research on labor market outcomes after incarceration. The relationship between incarceration and the labor market is explored in greater detail in chapter 5.

15. According to the fifth edition of the *Diagnostic and Statistical Manual of Mental Disorders (DSM-5)*, intermittent explosive disorder is indicated by spells of verbal or physical aggression that cause distress and impairment of personal functioning (American Psychiatric Association 2013).

Chapter 4: Human Frailty

1. Timothy Smeeding, Irwin Garfinkel, and Ronald Mincy (2011, 13) write that "public income support policy in the United States has more or less ignored young unmarried men and fathers for several decades." Yonatan Ben-Shalom, Robert Moffitt, and John Karl Scholz (2011) report the large effects of antipoverty policy focused on single-parent families with children.

2. The physical and mental vulnerability of incarcerated people has been widely observed by health researchers (Skeem, Manchak, and Peterson 2011; Baillargeon et al. 2009;

Diamond et al. 2001; Côté and Hodgins 1990), who note the high prevalence of co-occurring disorders.

3. See, for example, Kuperberg and Caplan (2003).

4. Peter Lucas (2011) discusses *Titicut Follies*. In "A Death in Restraints After 'Standard Procedure'" (*Boston Globe*, February 16, 2014), Michael Rezendes reports that the inmate, Joshua Messier, was having a schizophrenic attack when he was fatally restrained by correctional officers in 2009.

5. Eaton, Chen, and Bromet 2011. High rates of schizophrenia among Afro-Caribbeans have been reported for U.K. samples.

6. The rate of severe mental illness in the general population was estimated by Ronald Kessler and his colleagues (1994), who measured severe mental illness by self-reports of a diagnosis of a psychotic condition.

7. Data on the average annual cost of a Massachusetts prison bed is from Mass.gov, "Frequently Asked Questions About the DOC," available at: www.mass.gov/eopss/agencies/doc/faqs-about-the-doc.html (accessed December 2, 2017). The average cost of incarceration in Massachusetts is approximately $53,000 per year for a prison bed, so Eddie's twenty-two years of incarceration cost the state approximately 22 × $55,3000 = $1.17 million.

8. Mumola and Karberg (2006).

9. Maruna 2000.

Chapter 5: Lifetimes of Violence

1. One of the most striking portraits of criminality in the tough-on-crime era is offered by William Bennett, John Dilulio, and John Walters (1996, 27) in their account of "superpredators": "radically impulsive, brutally remorseless youngsters . . . who murder, assault, rape, rob, burglarize, deal deadly drugs, join gun-toting gangs, and create serious communal disorders. . . . To these mean-street youngsters, the words 'right' and 'wrong' have no fixed moral meaning." Similarly, Dilulio (1995) quotes a district attorney on youth involved in violent crime: "They kill or maim on impulse, without any intelligible motive."

2. It is widely observed that U.S. crime trends are only weakly correlated with incarceration trends (see Travis, Western, and Redburn 2014, 42–60). Critics of punitive crime policy often conclude that there is no substantive relationship between crime and incarceration. Thus, Michelle Alexander (2010, 8) writes: "for reasons largely unrelated to actual crime trends, the American penal system has emerged as a system of social control unparalleled in world history." Other scholars suggest that, as a result of the disconnect between crime and incarceration, many people are now incarcerated who are uninvolved in violence. John Irwin and James Austin (1997, 54) write of their sample of state prisoners: "With the noted exception of the violent thugs [16 percent of a sample of habitual offenders] their crimes were petty and pathetic." Similarly, Loïc Wacquant (2009a, 31) writes that America's prisons are "overfull, not with 'violent predators,' but by [*sic*] nonviolent criminals and petty delinquents." Any attempt to link crime and incarceration, he says, "has no validity other than ideological" (158–59).

3. See Evans, Eckenrode, and Marcynyszyn 2010; Wachs and Evans 2010.

4. Evans 2004, 88.

5. See, for example, Gabarino and Sherman (1980), Panel on Research on Child Abuse and Neglect (1993, 126–36), Drake and Pandey (1996), Emery and Laumann-Billings (1998), and Paulle (2013). In their review of the research on the links between family poverty and the adverse development of young children, Jack Shonkoff and Deborah Phillips (2000, ch. 10) observe that common channels for the effect are maltreatment and neglect. In an important line of research, Cathy Widom (1989; Nikulina, Widom, and Czaja 2011) finds evidence for links between childhood poverty and maltreatment and adult criminal offending. For a review, see Widom and Nikulina (2012).

6. Sampson and Wilson 1995.

7. Ibid., 51.

8. On the spillover of violence into adjacent communities, see Peterson and Krivo (2010). On the violent effects of spatially concentrated social problems related to poverty, see Sampson (1987), Lee (2000), and Kubrin and Weitzer (2003). Harding (2010) offers an excellent discussion of youth violence in three Boston neighborhoods. Much of the violence among young African American men in Boston traces to long-standing neighborhood rivalries.

9. For example, Sampson 1986; Sampson, Raudenbush, and Earls 1997; Warner and Rountree 1997.

10. Sampson 1987.

11. Rylko-Bauer and Farmer 2016.

12. Scheper-Hughes 1992; Bourgois and Schonberg 2009, 19; Auyero et al. 2014.

13. For an analysis of the life-history data and an explanation of its limitations, see Western et al. (2015).

14. In this classification, robberies were grouped with assaults because we sometimes lacked the information to draw a clear distinction.

15. The negative effects on children of witnessing a killing and of close proximity to homicide have been studied by Patrick Sharkey and his colleagues (2010; Sharkey et al. 2012).

16. In his discussion of adolescent fighting in Boston, Harding (2010, 32) also views violence as an important source of masculinity: "Standing and fighting when challenged is the essence of manly behavior," he notes, among teenagers from poor, high-crime neighborhoods. Harding goes on to observe that youth violence in particular in Boston is often organized around the defense of neighborhood loyalties.

17. Georgia Carpenter and Ann Stacks (2009) review research on the effects of intimate partner violence on young children. Gaylal Margolin and Elana Gordis (2000) review studies of the psychological effects of family and community violence on children.

18. Recent public opinion data are reviewed by The Opportunity Agenda (2014).

19. Mary Pattillo and John Robinson (2016) review research on urban inequality, distinguishing approaches that emphasize the deficits of poor communities from those that focus on resilience. They argue for a third approach that underscores heterogeneity within these communities. Recent research on urban violence finds that most shootings in large cities are attributable to a small number of mostly young, gang-involved men (see, for example, Papachristos, Hureau, and Braga 2013). The ubiquity of the vio-

lence that we found among the reentry respondents results in part from our permissive definition, which includes family violence, assaults and fighting not involving firearms, and noncriminal forms of violence, including accidents and suicides.

Chapter 6: Income

1. See Waldfogel 1994; Pager 2003; Pager, Western, and Sugie 2009. Holzer (2009) reviews research on the effects of incarceration on labor market outcomes.
2. In their exceptional study, Harding and his colleagues (2014) describe the many sources of income obtained by a sample of Michigan parolees. The Boston Reentry Study sample faced similar economic challenges and, in this respect, also resembled the low-income mothers interviewed by Kathryn Edin and Laura Lein in *Making Ends Meet* (1997).
3. Supervision fees have recently gained attention as one of many financial burdens imposed on criminal defendants by courts (Harris 2016). We found that the collection of monthly probation and parole fees was associated with greater cynicism about the motives of the justice system. Interactions between probation and parole officers and the respondents were often focused on the collection of fees. Moreover, for respondents receiving financial assistance from family, supervision fees were regularly covered by family, undermining any sense of accountability the fees were intended to impose. Despite flaws in the system of supervision fees, community corrections officers did appear to be willing to replace fees with community service for very low-income clients.
4. Nearly thirty years earlier, the anthropologist Mercer Sullivan (1989) found that work experience among poor young black men in New York City consisted mostly of jobs programs. Although providing some income, the work provided few social connections to the adult labor market.
5. Freeman and Holzer 1986.
6. Sullivan's (1989) study of white, black, and Latino youth with criminal records traced superior employment among whites to stronger network ties to the labor market and better employment opportunities in the white neighborhoods of his New York field site. Sandra Smith (2007) found that formerly incarcerated African Americans were unlikely to be recommended for jobs by friends in case they were unreliable. Racial differences in the labor market are discussed further in chapter 10.
7. Maruna 2000; National Research Council 2008.

Chapter 7: Family

1. In a survey of women visiting prison, Olga Grinstead and her colleagues (2001) found that monthly expenditures on visits, phone calls, and delivery of packages totaled $292 in 2001, about 36 percent of the median income for her respondents. It was hard to get similarly accurate figures in the Boston Reentry Study because we relied on retrospective reports of visits and calls made sometimes years earlier.
2. Wakefield and Wildeman (2013) provide a book-length treatment on the effects of parental incarceration on child well-being. Qualitative studies include Braman (2004)

and Nurse (2002). For a study of marriage, divorce, and separation during and after men's incarceration, see Lopoo and Western (2005), and for a review of the literature, see Wildeman and Muller (2012).

3. Sykes and Pettit (2014).

4. Family structures and parent-child contact among the reentry study participants are examined quantitatively in Western and Smith (2018).

5. For example, Wakefield and Wildeman (2013).

6. Although assuming continuous household residence overestimates housing stability, this overestimate does not vary much across family members. The housing cost of $500 a month is roughly in line with the costs of private transitional housing.

7. The topic of the moral status of the poor is vast, extending from historical debates about the "deserving poor" to recent policy efforts to promote marriage, to the demographic analysis of family structures. Landmark contributions to the analysis of the dynamics and structure of poor families that also engage public debates on their moral status include Wilson (1987, ch. 3), McLanahan (2004), McLanahan and Sandefur (1994), and Edin and Kefalas (2005).

Chapter 8: Back to Jail

1. Durose, Cooper, and Snyder 2014, 16.

2. David Rothman (1980) describes the Progressive origins of probation and parole.

3. Petersilia 2003, 11.

4. Former Massachusetts probation commissioner Ronald Corbett (2015) advocates the elimination of incarceration for technical violations, observing that probation officers still have many tools besides incarceration in the event of a violation, including curfews, community service, residential drug treatment, and more frequent reporting.

5. The Boston rate is similar to national figures: 64 percent of prisoners in the United States were released conditionally in 2015 (Carson and Anderson 2016). In Massachusetts, defendants often serve split sentences involving a period of incarceration followed by a period of probation in the community.

6. At least two-thirds of the young men in the reentry sample were stopped once by police after their release and 30 percent were stopped three times or more.

7. The life course studies by Robert Sampson and John Laub (Sampson and Laub 1993; Laub and Sampson 2003) are the classic works on this subject.

8. The idea of parsimony as a criminal justice principle was proposed by Norval Morris (1974) and adopted by the National Academy of Sciences report on high incarceration rates (Travis, Western, and Redburn 2014, ch. 12).

Chapter 9: Women

1. Lanctôt and Blanc 2002.

2. A number of prison field studies have investigated the distinctive contours of incarceration in women's prisons. Classic studies emphasize the large differences between women's incarceration and men's (Giallombardo 1966; Ward and Kassebaum 1965; Heffernan

1972). This research describes the adaptation of women to prison routines—what Barbara Owen (1998) calls a "program"—and emphasizes the intimate relationships that emerge in the contexts of incarceration. Family-like and sexual relationships among incarcerated women are much more central to the cultural life of the institution (and to scholarship) than is the case for men (see also the review essay by Richie 2004). Throughout their reentry process in Boston, we observed among the women in our sample the projects of adaptation and coping and the intimate relationships among women described in the prison studies.

3. See Snell and Morton 1994; Kruttschnitt and Gartner 2003.

4. See Tripodi and Pettus-Davis 2013; Browne, Miller, and Maguin 1999. Rates of PTSD have been found to be twice as high for incarcerated women as for the general population (Teplin et al. 1996; Kessler, Sonnega, and Bromet 1995). Trauma and abuse in childhood among this population have also been reported at very high rates (Jordan, Schlenger, and Fairbank 1996; Singer et al. 1995). Studies with samples of men and women find that rates of serious mental illness are about twice as high for women (Steadman et al. 2009).

5. Bourgois and Schonberg 2009.

Chapter 10: Race and Racism

1. This institutional history is described by Wacquant (2001). Michelle Alexander's book *The New Jim Crow* (2010) brought the problem of mass incarceration to a national audience and was widely debated and reviewed. Critics questioned the book's claims for the central role of the "War on Drugs" and the marginal role of violence as a social problem in motivating punitive crime policy (Forman 2012; Fortner 2015). While incarceration for drugs, drug enforcement, and the expansion of police powers for drug interdiction have been important facets of the increase in incarceration rates, harsher sentencing for violence and for defendants with serious criminal records has also played a significant role (Travis, Western, and Redburn 2014, chs. 2 and 3).

2. Quoted in Muhammad 2011, 51.

3. Travis and Western 2017, 298.

4. Although researchers have debated the contributions of liberals and conservatives to tough-on-crime politics (Flamm 2005; Murakawa 2014), few doubt that crime politics conjured fears of black criminality in the 1960s and 1970s. Khalil Muhammad (2011) has written about the deep historical roots of black criminality in policy and social science. Studies of the racialized character of crime politics include Edsall and Edsall (1992), Beckett (1997), Mendelberg (2001), Weaver (2007), and Soss, Fording, and Schram (2011). Elizabeth Hinton (2016) traces federal policy and the roles of Nixon and Reagan in drug and crime policy.

5. Western and Wildeman 2009. The long history of racial disparity in incarceration is analyzed by Christopher Muller (2012). There is a large research literature on racial differences in criminal justice involvement, from arrest through sentencing and incarceration. Recent contributions to research on racial disparities in incarceration include Pettit and Western (2004), Tonry and Melewski (2008), and Neal and Rick (2013).

6. Studies of the racially disparate effects of incarceration on socioeconomic inequality include Western (2006), Pettit and Lyons (2007), Western and Pettit (2010), and Wakefield and Wildeman (2013).

7. Rumbaut et al. 2006.

8. Mauer and King 2007.

9. Jaster 1981.

10. Vrabel 2014, 98. Classic accounts of neighborhood change in American cities are provided by Wilson (1987) and Sugrue (1996). A number of scholars have examined the changing racial composition of Boston neighborhoods; key contributions include Gamm (2001), O'Brien (1985), and Levine and Harmon (1992).

11. For the *Globe's* richly reported retrospective on the Boston busing crisis, see Irons, Murphy, and Russell (2014).

12. Anthony Lukas (1986) provides an epic account of the busing crisis. The criticism leveled by Lukas at Judge W. Arthur Garrity in the Boston busing case is answered by Robert Dentler (1987).

13. Simes 2016.

14. In the general population in 2014, the percentage of children under age eighteen living with two parents was 77 percent for whites, 39 percent for blacks, and 65 percent for Latinos (FIFCFS 2015).

15. National Center on Addiction and Substance Abuse 2010; Maruschak, Berzofsky, and Unangst 2015.

16. Braga, Papachristos, and Hureau 2010; Braga, Hureau, and Winship 2008.

17. The social isolation scale was constructed from time use data in the first week after prison release. For an analysis of the scale, see Western et al. (2015).

18. A quantitative analysis of racial differences in earnings and employment is reported in Western and Sirois (2017). Other studies have also found that whites tend to do better on the job market after incarceration than formerly incarcerated blacks and Latinos (Sullivan 1989; Pager 2007; Lyons and Pettit 2011). The social networks of black job-seekers may be less helpful for finding work (Royster 2003; Smith 2007), and the stigma of a criminal record may be worse for blacks seeking work (Pager 2007; Pager, Western, and Sugie 2009).

19. Sampson 2012, 101; Wilson 1987.

20. See Tonry 1995; Tonry and Melewski 2008.

21. Tommie Shelby (2016, ch. 1) describes "structural racism" as the combined effect of institutional racism in several different domains—say, the labor market and the justice system.

Chapter 11: Criminal Justice as Social Justice

1. America's origin story has been told in many ways by criminal justice scholars. Jonathan Simon (2017) in his excellent essay on human dignity refers to the constitutive flaw.

2. Trends in racial and ethnic disparities in incarceration are discussed in the National Academy of Sciences report on the causes and consequence of high incarceration rates in the United States (Travis, Western, and Redburn 2014, ch. 2). The spatial concentra-

tion of incarceration in poor and minority neighborhoods is analyzed by Robert Sampson (2012) and by Todd Clear (2007). Jessica Simes (2016) has studied the spatial pattern of incarceration in the Boston Reentry Study.

3. DiIulio 1996.

4. The high levels of substance use and poor health among the formerly incarcerated white respondents in the reentry study do not appear to be specific to Boston, as similar patterns are reported in national data (National Center on Addiction and Substance Abuse 2010; Maruschak, Berzofsky, and Unangst 2015).

5. Research on the effects of incarceration on crime is reviewed in the National Academy of Sciences incarceration report (Travis, Western, and Redburn 2014, ch. 6). Steven Durlauf and Daniel Nagin (2011) provide a very good review of the literature on deterrence and imprisonment.

6. Wilson 1975/1985, 260.

7. See Gottschalk 2015.

8. Congressman Raúl Labrador, "Labrador, Scott Introduce Bipartisan Bill to Reform Criminal Sentencing" (press release), February 12, 2015.

9. Obama 2017, 816.

10. Tonry 1995, 2014.

11. Tonry 2014, 152.

12. Debates about a social adversity defense or sentence mitigation date at least from David Bazelon's essay on "The Morality of the Criminal Law" (1976). Opposing the idea, Stephen Morse (1976) argued that conditions of poverty are not truly causal for crime and that in any case there is a disturbing paternalism to denying the moral agency of disadvantaged people. Lawyers argue whether social adversity is a legitimate consideration and whether it might operate as a defense (affecting a verdict) or as mitigation (affecting the sentence). The collection edited by William Heffernan and John Kleinig (2000) takes up the issue. Tonry (2014) provides an excellent review of the arguments.

13. The 1990s were the heyday for such discussion; Ben Wattenberg famously quipped, for example, that "a thug in prison can't shoot your sister." See Clear (2016) for a commentary on Wattenberg's comment in the context of the so-called California realignment, a court-ordered reduction in the state prison population.

14. Barry 2005; Travis, Western, and Redburn 2014, 330–32.

15. Molly Baldwin and Yotam Zeira (2017) discuss Roca; Erin Jacobs and Bruce Western (2007) evaluate ComALERT; and Emily Wang and her colleagues (2017) report evaluation evidence for the Transitions Clinic.

16. Coates 2014, 2015.

17. Minow 1998, 4.

REFERENCES

....

Alexander, Michelle. 2010. *The New Jim Crow: Mass Incarceration in the Age of Colorblindness*. New York: New Press.

American Psychiatric Association. 2013. *Diagnostic and Statistical Manual of Mental Disorders,* 5th ed. Washington, D.C.: American Psychiatric Association.

Auyero, Javier, Agustin Burbano de Lara, and Maria Fernanda Berti. 2014. "Uses and Forms of Violence Among the Urban Poor." *Journal of Latin American Studies* 46(3): 443–69.

Baillargeon, Jacques, Ingrid A. Binswanger, Joseph V. Penn, Brie A. Williams, and Owen J. Murray. 2009. "Psychiatric Disorders and Repeat Incarcerations: The Revolving Prison Door." *American Journal of Psychiatry* 166(1): 103–09.

Baldwin, Molly, and Yotam Zeira. 2017. "From Evidence-Based Practices to a Comprehensive Intervention Model for High-Risk Young Men: The Story of Roca." *New Thinking in Community Corrections Bulletin* 5(September): 1–28.

Barry, Brian. 2005. *Why Social Justice Matters.* Cambridge: Polity.

Bazelon, David L. 1976. "The Morality of the Criminal Law." *Southern California Law Review* 49: 385–405.

Beckett, Katherine. 1997. *Making Crime Pay: Law and Order in Contemporary American Politics.* New York: Oxford University Press.

Bennett, William J., John J. Dilulio Jr., and John P. Walters. 1996. *Body Count: Moral Poverty . . . and How to Win America's War Against Crime and Drugs.* New York: Simon & Schuster.

Ben-Shalom, Yonatan, Robert A. Moffitt, and John Karl Scholz. 2011. "An Assessment of the Effectiveness of Anti-Poverty Programs in the United States." Working Paper 17042. Cambridge, Mass.: National Bureau of Economic Research.

Black, Timothy. 2010. *When a Heart Turns Rock Solid: The Lives of Three Puerto Rican Brothers On and Off the Streets.* New York: Vintage.

Bourgois, Philippe, and Jeffrey Schonberg. 2009. *Righteous Dopefiend.* Berkeley: University of California Press.

Braga, Anthony A., David M. Hureau, and Christopher Winship. 2008. "Losing Faith? Police, Black Churches, and the Resurgence of Youth Violence in Boston." *Ohio State Journal of Criminal Law* 6(1): 141–72.

Braga, Anthony A., Andrew V. Papachristos, and David M. Hureau. 2010. "The Concentration and Stability of Gun Violence at Micro Places in Boston, 1980–2008." *Journal of Quantitative Criminology* 26(1): 33–53.

Braman, Donald. 2004. *Doing Time on the Outside: Incarceration and Family Life in Urban America.* Ann Arbor: University of Michigan Press.

Brooks, Lisa E., Amy Solomon, Sinead Keegan, Rhiana Kohl, and Lori Lahue. 2005. *Prisoner Reentry in Massachusetts.* Washington, D.C.: Urban Institute.

Browne, Angela, Brenda Miller, and Eugene Maguin. 1999. "Prevalence and Severity of Lifetime Physical and Sexual Victimization Among Incarcerated Women." *International Journal of Law and Psychiatry* 22(3–4): 301–22.

Carpenter, Georgia L., and Ann M. Stacks. 2009. "Developmental Effects of Exposure to Intimate Partner Violence in Early Childhood." *Children and Youth Services Review* 31: 831–39.

Carson, E. Ann, and Elizabeth Anderson. 2016. "Prisoners in 2015." NCJ 250229. Washington: U.S. Bureau of Justice Statistics.

Clear, Todd. 2007. *Imprisoning Communities: How Mass Incarceration Makes Disadvantaged Neighborhoods Worse.* New York: Oxford University Press.

———. 2016. "'A Thug in Prison Can't Shoot Your Sister.'" *Criminology and Public Policy* 15(2): 343–47.

Clemmer, Donald. 1940. *The Prison Community.* New York: Holt, Rinehart and Winston.

Coates, Ta-Nehisi. 2014. "The Case for Reparations." *The Atlantic,* June.

———. 2015. "The Black Family in the Age of Mass Incarceration." *The Atlantic,* October.

Comfort, Megan. 2008. *Doing Time Together: Love and Family in the Shadow of the Prison.* Chicago: University of Chicago Press.

Corbett, Ronald P. 2015. "The Burdens of Leniency: The Changing Face of Probation." *Minnesota Law Review* 99(5): 1696–1733.

Côté, Gilles, and Sheilagh Hodgins. 1990. "Co-occurring Mental Disorders Among Criminal Offenders." *Bulletin of the American Academy of Psychiatry and Law* 18(3): 271–81.

Council of Economic Advisers. 2016. *Economic Perspectives on Incarceration and the Criminal Justice System.* Washington: Executive Office of the President of the United States.

Dentler, Robert A. 1987. "Boston School Desegregation: The Fallowness of Common Ground." *Trotter Institute Review* 2(1): 9–16.

Desmond, David P., James F. Maddux, Thomas H. Johnson, and Beth A. Confer. 1995. "Obtaining Follow-up Interviews for Treatment Evaluation." *Journal of Substance Abuse Treatment* 12(2): 95–102.

Diamond, Pamela M., Eugene W. Wang, Charles E. Holzer, Christopher Thomas, and des Anges Cruser. 2001. "The Prevalence of Mental Illness in Prison." *Administration and Policy in Mental Health* 29(1): 21–40.

Dilulio, John. 1995. "The Coming of the Super-Predators." *The Weekly Standard,* November 27, 23–28.

———. 1996. "My Black Crime Problem, and Ours." *City Journal* 6(Spring): 14–28.

Drake, Brett, and Shanta Pandey. 1996. "Understanding the Relationship Between Neighborhood Poverty and Specific Types of Child Maltreatment." *Child Abuse and Neglect* 20(11): 1003–18.

Durlauf, Steven N., and Daniel S. Nagin. 2011. "The Deterrent Effect of Imprisonment." In

Controlling Crime: Strategies and Tradeoffs, edited by Philip J. Cook, Jens Ludwig, and Justin McCrary. Chicago: University of Chicago Press.

Durose, Matthew R., Alexia D. Cooper, and Howard N. Snyder. 2014. "Recidivism of Prisoners Released in 30 States in 2005: Patterns from 2005 to 2010." NCJ 244205. Washington: U.S. Bureau of Justice Statistics.

Eason, John. 2017. *Big House on the Prairie: Rise of the Rural Ghetto and Prison Proliferation.* Chicago: University of Chicago Press.

Eaton, William W., Chuan-Yu Chen, and Evelyn J. Bromet. 2011. "Epidemiology of Schizophrenia." In *Textbook of Psychiatric Epidemiology,* 3rd ed., edited by Ming T. Tsuang, Mauricio Tohen, and Peter B. Jones. New York: Wiley.

Edin, Kathryn, and Maria Kefalas. 2005. *Promises I Can Keep: Why Poor Women Put Motherhood Before Marriage.* Berkeley: University of California Press.

Edin, Kathryn, and Laura Lein. 1997. *Making Ends Meet: How Single Mothers Survive Welfare and Low-Wage Work.* New York: Russell Sage Foundation.

Edsall, Thomas Byrne, and Mary D. Edsall. 1992. *Chain Reaction: The Impact of Race, Rights, and Taxes on American Politics.* Rev. ed. New York: W. W. Norton.

Emery, Robert E., and Lisa Laumann-Billings. 1998. "An Overview of the Nature, Causes, and Consequences of Abusive Family Relationships: Towards Differential Maltreatment and Violence." *American Psychologist* 53(2): 121–35.

Evans, Gary W. 2004. "The Environment of Childhood Poverty." *American Psychologist* 59(2): 77–92.

Evans, Gary W., John Eckenrode, and Lyscha A. Marcynyszyn. 2010. "Chaos and the Macrosetting: The Role of Poverty and Socioeconomic Status." In *Chaos and Its Influence on Children's Development: An Ecological Perspective,* edited by Gary W. Evans and Theodore D. Wachs. Washington, D.C.: American Psychological Association.

Falk, Gene, and Margot L. Crandall-Hollick. 2016. "The Earned Income Tax Credit (EITC): An Overview." Washington: Congressional Research Service (January 19).

Farrington, David P., Bernard Gallagher, Lynda Morley, Raymond J. St. Ledger, and Donald J. West. 1990. "Minimizing Attrition in Longitudinal Research: Methods of Tracing and Securing Cooperation in a 24-Year Follow-up Study." In *Data Quality in Longitudinal Research,* edited by David Magnusson and Lars Bergman. Cambridge: Cambridge University Press.

Federal Interagency Forum on Child and Family Statistics (FIFCFS). 2015. *America's Children: Key National Indicators of Well-being, 2015.* Washington: U.S. Government Printing Office.

Flamm, Michael. 2005. *Law and Order: Street Crime, Civil Unrest, and the Crisis of Liberalism in the 1960s.* New York: Columbia University Press.

Food and Nutrition Service. 2012. *Supplemental Nutrition Assistance Program: State Options Report,* 10th ed. Washington: U.S. Department of Agriculture.

Forman, James. 2012. "Racial Critiques of Mass Incarceration: Beyond the New Jim Crow." *New York University Law Review* 87(1): 101–46.

Fortner, Michael Javen. 2015. *Black Silent Majority: The Rockefeller Drug Laws and the Politics of Punishment.* Cambridge, Mass.: Harvard University Press.

Freeman, Richard B., and Harry J. Holzer. 1986. "The Black Youth Employment Crisis:

Summary of Findings." In *The Black Youth Employment Crisis,* edited by Richard B. Freeman and Harry J. Holzer. Chicago: University of Chicago Press.

Gabarino, James, and Deborah Sherman. 1980. "High-Risk Neighborhoods and High-Risk Families: The Human Ecology of Child Maltreatment." *Child Development* 51(1): 188–98.

Gamm, Gerald. 2001. *Urban Exodus: Why the Jews Left Boston and the Catholics Stayed.* Cambridge, Mass.: Harvard University Press.

Garland, David. 2001. *The Culture of Control: Crime and Social Order in Contemporary Society.* Chicago: University of Chicago Press.

Giallombardo, Rose. 1966. *Society of Women: A Study of a Women's Prison.* New York: Wiley.

Goffman, Alice. 2014. *On the Run: Fugitive Life in an American City.* Chicago: University of Chicago Press.

Gottschalk, Marie. 2015. *Caught: The Prison State and the Lockdown of American Politics.* Princeton, N.J.: Princeton University Press.

Grinstead, Olga, Bonnie Faigeles, Carrie Bancroft, and Barry Zack. 2001. "The Financial Cost of Maintaining Relationships with Incarcerated African American Men: A Survey of Women Prison Visitors." *Journal of African American Men* 6(June): 59–70.

Harding, David J. 2010. *Living the Drama: Community, Conflict, and Culture Among Inner-City Boys.* Chicago: University of Chicago Press.

Harding, David J., Jeffrey D. Morenoff, and Claire Herbert. 2013. "Home Is Hard to Find: Neighborhoods, Institutions, and the Residential Trajectories of Returning Prisoners." *Annals of the American Academy of Political and Social Science* 647(1): 214–36.

Harding, David, Jessica J. B. Wyse, Cheyney Dobson, and Jeffrey D. Morenoff. 2014. "Making Ends Meet After Prison." *Journal of Policy Analysis and Management* 33(2): 440–70.

Harris, Alexes. 2016. *A Pound of Flesh: Monetary Sanctions as Punishment for the Poor.* New York: Russell Sage Foundation.

Heffernan, Esther. 1972. *Making It in Prison: The Square, the Cool, and the Life.* New York: Wiley.

Heffernan, William C., and John Kleinig, eds. 2000. *From Social Justice to Criminal Justice: Poverty and the Administration of Criminal Law.* New York: Oxford University Press.

Hinton, Elizabeth. 2016. *From the War on Poverty to the War on Crime: The Making of Mass Incarceration in America.* Cambridge, Mass.: Harvard University Press.

Holzer, Harry J. 2009. "Collateral Costs: Effect of Incarceration on Employment and Earnings Among Young Workers." In *Do Prisons Make Us Safer?,* edited by Steven Raphael and Michael A. Stoll. New York: Russell Sage Foundation.

Irons, Meghan E., Shelley Murphy, and Jenna Russell. 2014. "History Rolled in on a Yellow School Bus." *Boston Globe,* September 6.

Irwin, John. 1970. *The Felon.* Englewood Cliffs, N.J.: Prentice-Hall.

Irwin, John, and James Austin. 1997. *It's About Time: America's Imprisonment Binge.* 2nd ed. Belmont, Calif.: Wadsworth.

Jacobs, Erin, and Bruce Western. 2007. *Report on the Evaluation of the ComALERT Prisoner Reentry Program.* Brooklyn, N.Y.: Kings County District Attorney.

Jaster, Susan E. 1981. "Race and Hispanic Origin of Boston's Population, 1980 and 1970." Working paper. Boston: Boston Redevelopment Authority.

Jerolmack, Colin, and Alexandra K. Murphy. 2017. "The Ethical Dilemmas and Social Scientific Tradeoffs of Masking in Ethnography." *Sociological Methods and Research* (March 30), doi.org/10.1177/0049124117701483.

Jordan, B. Kathleen, William E. Schlenger, and John A. Fairbank. 1996. "Prevalence of Psychiatric Disorders Among Incarcerated Women: II. Convicted Felons Entering Prison." *Archive of General Psychiatry* 53(6): 513–19.

Kachnowski, Vera. 2005. "Employment and Prisoner Reentry." Technical report. Washington, D.C.: Urban Institute.

Kessler, Ronald C., Katherine A. McGonagle, Shanyang Zhao, Christopher B. Nelson, Michael Hughes, Suzann Eshleman, Hans-Ulrich Wittchen, and Kenneth S. Kendler. 1994. "Lifetime and 12-Month Prevalence of DSM-III-R Psychiatric Disorders in the United States: Results from the National Comorbidity Survey." *Archive of General Psychiatry* 51(1): 8–19.

Kessler, Ronald C., Amanda Sonnega, and Evelyn Bromet. 1995. "Posttraumatic Stress Disorder in the National Comorbidity Survey." *Archive of General Psychiatry* 52(12): 1048–60.

Kling, Jeffrey R. 2006. "Incarceration Length, Employment, and Earnings." *American Economic Review* 96(3): 863–76.

Kohler-Hausmann, Issa. 2013. "Misdemeanor Justice: Control Without Conviction." *American Journal of Sociology* 119(2): 351–93.

Kruttschnitt, Candace, and Rosemary Gartner. 2003. "Women's Imprisonment." *Crime and Justice* 30: 1–81.

Kubrin, Charis E., and Ronald Weitzer. 2003. "Retaliatory Homicide: Concentrated Disadvantage and Neighborhood Culture." *Social Problems* 50(2): 157–80.

Kuperberg, Gina R., and David Caplan. 2003. "Language Dysfunction in Schizophrenia." In *Neuropsychiatry*, 2nd ed., edited by Randolph B. Schiffer, Stephen M. Rao, and Barry S. Fogel. Philadelphia: Lippincott Williams and Wilkins.

Lanctôt, Nadine, and Marc Le Blanc. 2002. "Explaining Deviance by Adolescent Females." *Crime and Justice* 29: 113–202.

Lattimore, Pamela K., and Danielle M. Steffey. 2009. "The Multi-Site Evaluation of SVORI: Methodology and Analytic Approach." Technical report. Research Triangle Park, N.C.: RTI International.

Laub, John H., and Robert J. Sampson. 2003. *Shared Beginnings, Divergent Lives: Delinquent Boys to Age 70*. Chicago: University of Chicago Press.

La Vigne, Nancy G., Tracey L. Shollenberger, and Sara A. Debus. 2009. "One Year Out: Tracking the Experiences of Male Prisoners Returning to Houston, Texas." Technical report. Washington, D.C.: Urban Institute (June).

Lee, Matthew R. 2000. "Concentrated Poverty, Race, and Homicide." *Sociological Quarterly* 41(2): 189–206.

Leverentz, Andrea. 2011. "Being a Good Daughter and Sister: Families of Origin in the Reentry of African American Female Ex-Prisoners." *Feminist Criminology* 6(4): 239–67.

Levine, Hillel, and Lawrence Harmon. 1992. *The Death of an American Jewish Community: A Tragedy of Good Intentions.* New York: Free Press.

Lopoo, Leonard M., and Bruce Western. 2005. "Incarceration and the Formation and Stability of Marital Unions." *Journal of Marriage and the Family* 67(3): 721–34.

Lucas, Peter. 2011. "The Open Door: Five Foundational Films That Seeded the Representation of Human Rights for Persons with Disabilities." *International Journal on Human Rights* 8(14): 181–99.

Lukas, J. Anthony. 1986. *Common Ground: A Turbulent Decade in the Lives of Three American Families.* New York: Vintage.

Lyons, Christopher J., and Becky Pettit. 2011. "Compounded Disadvantage: Race, Incarceration, and Wage Growth." *Social Problems* 58(2): 257–80.

Manza, Jeff, and Christopher Uggen. 2006. *Locked Out: Felon Disenfranchisement and American Democracy.* New York: Oxford University Press.

Margolin, Gayla, and Elana B. Gordis. 2000. "The Effects of Family and Community Violence on Children." *Annual Review of Psychology* 51: 445–79.

Martin, Elizabeth, Denise Abreu, and Franklin Winters. 2001. "Money and Motive: Effects of Incentives on Panel Attrition in the Survey of Income and Program Participation." *Journal of Official Statistics* 17(2): 267–84.

Martinez, Damian J., and Johnna Christian. 2009. "The Familial Relationships of Former Prisoners: Examining the Link Between Residence and Informal Support Mechanisms." *Journal of Contemporary Ethnography* 38(2): 201–24.

Maruna, Shad. 2000. *Making Good: How Ex-Convicts Reform and Rebuild Their Lives.* Washington, D.C.: American Psychological Association.

Maruna, Shadd, and Hans Toch. 2005. "The Impact of Imprisonment on the Desistance Process." In *Prisoner Reentry and Crime in America,* edited by Jeremy Travis and Christy A. Visher. New York: Cambridge University Press.

Maruschak, Laura M., Marcus Berzofsky, and Jennifer Unangst. 2015. *Medical Problems of State and Federal Prisoners and Jail Inmates, 2011–12.* Washington: U.S. Department of Justice, Bureau of Justice Statistics.

Mauer, Marc, and Ryan S. King. 2007. *Uneven Justice: State Rates of Incarceration by Race and Ethnicity.* Washington, D.C.: Sentencing Project.

McLanahan, Sara. 2004. "Diverging Destinies: How Children Are Faring Under the Second Demographic Transition." *Demography* 41(4): 607–27.

McLanahan, Sara, and Gary Sandefur. 1994. *Growing Up with a Single Parent: What Hurts, What Helps.* Cambridge, Mass.: Harvard University Press.

Mendelberg, Tali. 2001. *The Race Card: Campaign Strategy, Implicit Messages, and the Norm of Equality.* Princeton, N.J.: Princeton University Press.

Metraux, Stephen, Caterina G. Roman, and Richard S. Cho. 2008. "Incarceration and Homelessness." In *Toward Understanding Homelessness: The 2007 National Symposium on Homelessness Research,* edited by Deborah Dennis, Gretchen Locke, and Jill Khadduri. Washington: U.S. Department of Housing and Urban Development.

Miller, Reuben Jonathan. 2014. "Devolving the Carceral State: Race, Prisoner Reentry, and the Micro-Politics of Urban Poverty Management." *Punishment and Society* 16(3): 305–35.

Minow, Martha. 1998. *Between Vengeance and Forgiveness: Facing History After Genocide and Mass Violence.* Boston: Beacon Press.

Morris, Norval. 1974. *The Future of Imprisonment.* Chicago: University of Chicago Press.

Morse, Stephen J. 1976. "The Twilight of Welfare Criminology: A Reply to Judge Bazelon." *Southern California Law Review* 49: 1247.

Muhammad, Khalil Gibran. 2011. *The Condemnation of Blackness: Race, Crime, and the Making of Modern Urban America.* Cambridge, Mass.: Harvard University Press.

Muller, Christopher. 2012. "Northward Migration and the Rise of Racial Disparity in American Incarceration, 1880–1950." *American Journal of Sociology* 118(2): 281–326.

Mumola, Christopher J., and Jennifer C. Karberg. 2006. "Drug Use and Dependence, State and Federal Prisoners, 2004." Bureau of Justice Statistics Special Report. NCJ 213530. Washington: U.S. Department of Justice (October).

Murakawa, Naomi. 2014. *The First Civil Right: How Liberals Built Prison America.* New York: Oxford University Press.

National Center on Addiction and Substance Abuse (CASA). 2010. *Behind Bars II: Substance Abuse and America's Prison Population.* New York: Columbia University, CASA.

National Research Council. 2008. *Parole, Desistance from Crime, and Community Integration.* Washington, D.C.: National Academies Press.

Neal, Derek, and Armin Rick. 2013. "The Prison Boom and the Lack of Black Progress After Smith and Welch." Working paper. Chicago: University of Chicago, Department of Economics.

Nelson, Marta, Perry Dees, and Charlotte Allen. 1999. "The First Month Out: Post-Incarceration Experiences in New York City." Working paper. New York: Vera Institute of Justice.

Nikulina, Valentina, Cathy Spatz Widom, and Sally Czaja. 2011. "The Role of Childhood Neglect and Childhood Poverty in Predicting Mental Health, Academic Achievement, and Crime in Adulthood." *American Journal of Community Psychology* 48(3–4): 309–21.

Nurse, Anne M. 2002. *Fatherhood Arrested: Parenting from Within the Juvenile Justice System.* Nashville, Tenn.: Vanderbilt University Press.

Obama, Barack. 2017. "The President's Role in Advancing Criminal Justice Reform." *Harvard Law Review* 130(January 5): 811–66.

O'Brien, Margaret C. 1985. "Diversity and Change in Boston's Neighborhoods: A Comparison of Demographic, Social, and Economic Characteristics of Population and Housing, 1970–1980." Boston: Boston Redevelopment Authority.

Opportunity Agenda, The. 2014. *An Overview of Public Opinion and Discourse on Criminal Justice Issues.* New York: The Opportunity Agenda.

Owen, Barbara. 1998. *In the Mix: Struggle and Survival in a Women's Prison.* Albany: State University of New York Press.

Pager, Devah. 2003. "The Mark of a Criminal Record." *American Journal of Sociology* 108(5): 937–75.

———. 2007. *Marked: Race, Crime, and Finding Work in an Era of Mass Incarceration.* Chicago: University of Chicago Press.

Pager, Devah, Bruce Western, and Naomi Sugie. 2009. "Sequencing Disadvantage: Barriers to Employment Facing Young Black and White Men with Criminal Records." *Annals of the American Academy of Political and Social Science* 623(1): 195–213.

Panel on Research on Child Abuse and Neglect. 1993. *Understanding Child Abuse and Neglect.* Washington, D.C.: National Academies Press.

Papachristos, Andrew V., David M. Hureau, and Anthony A. Braga. 2013. "The Corner and the Crew: The Influence of Geography and Social Networks on Gang Violence." *American Sociological Review* 78(3): 1–31.

Patterson, Evelyn J. 2010. "Incarcerating Death: Mortality in U.S. State Correctional Facilities, 1985–1998." *Demography* 47(3): 587–607.

Pattillo, Mary, and John N. Robinson. 2016. "Poor Neighborhoods in the Metropolis." In *The Oxford Handbook of the Social Science of Poverty,* edited by David Brady and Linda M. Burton. Oxford University Press.

Paulle, Bowen. 2013. *Toxic Schools: High-Poverty Education in New York and Amsterdam.* Chicago: University of Chicago Press.

Petersilia, Joan. 2003. *When Prisoners Come Home: Parole and Prisoner Reentry.* New York: Oxford University Press.

Peterson, Ruth D., and Lauren J. Krivo. 2010. *Divergent Social Worlds: Neighborhood Crime and the Racial-Spatial Divide.* New York: Russell Sage Foundation.

Pettit, Becky. 2012. *Invisible Men: Mass Incarceration and the Myth of Black Progress.* New York: Russell Sage Foundation.

Pettit, Becky, and Christopher Lyons. 2007. "Status and the Stigma of Incarceration: The Labor Market Effects of Incarceration by Race, Class, and Criminal Involvement." In *Barriers to Re-entry: The Impact of Incarceration on Labor Market Outcomes,* edited by David Weiman, Shawn Bushway, and Michael Stoll. New York: Russell Sage Foundation.

Pettit, Becky, and Bruce Western. 2004. "Mass Imprisonment and the Life Course: Race and Class Inequality in U.S. Incarceration." *American Sociological Review* 69(April): 151–69.

Rich, Josiah D., Redonna Chandler, Brie A. Williams, Dora Dumont, Emily A. Wang, Faye S. Taxman, Scott A. Allen, Jennifer G. Clarke, Robert B. Greifinger, Christopher Wildeman, Fred C. Osher, Steven Rosenberg, Craig Haney, Marc Mauer, and Bruce Western. 2014. "How Health Care Reform Can Transform the Health of Criminal Justice–Involved Individuals." *Health Affairs* 33(3): 462–67.

Richie, Beth E. 2004. "Feminist Ethnographies of Women in Prison." *Feminist Studies* 30(2): 438–50.

Rothman, David J. 1980. *Conscience and Convenience: The Asylum and Its Alternatives in Progressive America.* Boston: Little, Brown.

Royster, Dierdre. 2003. *Race and the Invisible Hand: How White Networks Exclude Black Men from Blue-Collar Jobs.* Berkeley: University of California Press.

Rumbaut, Rubén, Roberto G. Gonzales, Golnaz Komaie, Charlie V. Morgan, and Rosaura Tafoya-Estrada. 2006. "Immigration and Incarceration: Patterns and Predictors of Imprisonment Among First- and Second-Generation Young Adults." In *Immigration and Crime: Race, Ethnicity, and Violence,* edited by Ramiro Martinez and Abel Valenzuela Jr. New York: New York University Press.

Rylko-Bauer, Barbara, and Paul Farmer. 2016. "Structural Violence, Poverty, and Social Suffering." In *The Oxford Handbook of the Social Science of Poverty,* edited by David Brady and Linda M. Burton. New York: Oxford University Press.

Sampson, Robert J. 1986. "Crime in Cities: The Effects of Formal and Informal Social Control." *Crime and Justice* 8: 271–311.

———. 1987. "Urban Black Violence: The Effect of Male Joblessness and Family Disruption." *American Journal of Sociology* 93(2): 348–82.

———. 2012. *Great American City: Chicago and the Enduring Neighborhood Effect.* Chicago: University of Chicago Press.

Sampson, Robert J., and John H. Laub. 1993. *Crime in the Making: Pathways and Turning Points Through Life.* Cambridge, Mass.: Harvard University Press.

Sampson, Robert J., Stephen W. Raudenbush, and Felton Earls. 1997. "Neighborhoods and Violent Crime: A Multilevel Study of Collective Efficacy." *Science* 277(5328): 918–24.

Sampson, Robert J., and William Julius Wilson. 1995. "Toward a Theory of Race, Crime, and Urban Inequality." In *Crime and Inequality,* edited by John Hagan and Ruth D. Peterson. Stanford, Calif.: Stanford University Press.

Scheper-Hughes, Nancy. 1992. *Death Without Weeping: The Violence of Everyday Life in Brazil.* Berkeley: University of California Press.

Sharkey, Patrick. 2010. "The Acute Effect of Local Homicides on Children's Cognitive Performance." *Proceedings of the National Academy of Sciences* 107(26): 11733–38.

Sharkey, Patrick, Nicole Tirado-Strayer, Andrew V. Papachristos, and C. Cybele Raver. 2012. "The Effect of Local Violence on Children's Attention and Impulse Control." *American Journal of Public Health* 102(12): 2287–93.

Shelby, Tommie. 2016. *Dark Ghettos: Injustice, Dissent, and Reform.* Cambridge, Mass.: Harvard University Press.

Shonkoff, Jack P., and Deborah A. Phillips, eds. 2000. *From Neurons to Neighborhoods: The Science of Early Child Development.* Washington, D.C.: National Academies Press.

Simes, Jessica Tayloe. 2016. "Essays on Place and Punishment in America." PhD diss., Harvard University, Cambridge, Mass.

Simon, Jonathan. 2017. "The Second Coming of Dignity." In *Mapping the New Criminal Justice Thinking,* edited by Sharon Dolovich and Alexandra Natapoff. New York: New York University Press.

Singer, Mark I., Janet Bussey, Li-Yu Song, and Lisa Lunghofer. 1995. "The Psychosocial Issues of Women Serving Time in Jail." *Social Work* 40(1): 103–13.

Skeem, Jennifer L., Sarah Manchak, and Jillian K. Peterson. 2011. "Correctional Policy for Offenders with Mental Illness: Creating a New Paradigm for Recidivism Reduction." *Law and Human Behavior* 35(2): 110–26.

Smeeding, Timothy M., Irwin Garfinkel, and Ronald B. Mincy. 2011. "Young Disadvantaged Men: Fathers, Families, Poverty, and Policy." *Annals of the American Academy of Political and Social Science* 635(1): 6–21.

Smith, Sandra Susan. 2007. *Lone Pursuit: Distrust and Defensive Individualism Among the Black Poor.* New York: Russell Sage Foundation.

Snell, Tracy L., and Danielle C. Morton. 1994. "Women in Prison." Special Report. Washington: U.S. Department of Justice, Bureau of Justice Statistics.

Soss, Joe, Richard C. Fording, and Sanford F. Schram. 2011. *Disciplining the Poor: Neoliberal Paternalism and the Persistent Power of Race.* Chicago: University of Chicago Press.

Steadman, Henry J., Fred C. Osher, Pamela Clark Robbins, Brian Case, and Steven Samuels. 2009. "Prevalence of Serious Mental Illness Among Jail Inmates." *Psychiatric Services* 60(6): 761–65.

Sugie, Naomi F. 2014. "Finding Work: A Smartphone Study of Job Searching, Social Contacts, and Well-being After Prison." PhD diss., Princeton University.

Sugrue, Thomas. 1996. *The Origins of the Urban Crisis.* Princeton, N.J.: Princeton University Press.

Sullivan, Mercer L. 1989. *"Getting Paid": Youth Crime and Work in the Inner City.* Ithaca, N.Y.: Cornell University Press.

Sykes, Bryan L., and Becky Pettit. 2014. "Mass Incarceration, Family Complexity, and the Reproduction of Childhood Disadvantage." *Annals of the American Academy of Political and Social Science* 654(1): 127–49.

Teitler, Julien O., Nancy E. Reichman, and Susan Sprachman. 2003. "Costs and Benefits of Improving Response Rates for a Hard-to-Reach Population." *Public Opinion Quarterly* 67(1): 126–38.

Teplin, Linda A., Karen M. Abram, and Gary M. McClelland. 1996. "Prevalence of Psychiatric Disorders Among Incarcerated Women: I. Pretrial Jail Detainees." *Archive of General Psychiatry* 53(6): 505–12.

Tonry, Michael. 1995. *Malign Neglect: Race, Crime, and Punishment in America.* New York: Oxford University Press.

———. 2014. "Can Deserts Be Just in an Unjust World." In *Liberal Criminal Theory: Essays for Andreas von Hirsch,* edited by A. P. Simester, Ulfrid Neumann, and Antje du Bois-Pedain. Oxford: Hart.

Tonry, Michael, and Matthew Melewski. 2008. "The Malign Effects of Drug and Crime Control Policies on Black Americans." *Crime and Justice* 37(1): 1–44.

Travis, Jeremy. 2005. *But They All Come Back: Facing the Challenges of Prisoner Reentry.* Washington, D.C.: Urban Institute Press.

Travis, Jeremy, and Bruce Western. 2017. "Poverty, Violence, and Black Incarceration." In *Policing the Black Man: Arrest, Prosecution, and Imprisonment,* edited by Angela J. Davis. New York: Pantheon.

Travis, Jeremy, Bruce Western, and Stephens Redburn, eds. 2014. *The Growth of Incarceration in the United States: Exploring Causes and Consequences.* Washington, DC: National Academy Press.

Tripodi, Stephen J., and Carrie Pettus-Davis. 2013. "Histories of Childhood Victimization and Subsequent Mental Health Problems, Substance Use, and Sexual Victimization for a Sample of Incarcerated Women in the U.S." *International Journal of Law and Psychiatry* 36(1): 30–40.

United States Department of Agriculture (USDA). 2016. "Characteristics of Supplemental Nutrition Assistance Program Households: Fiscal Year 2015." Washington: USDA.

Visher, Christy A., and Shannon M. E. Courtney. 2007. *One Year Out: Experiences of Prisoners Returning to Cleveland.* Washington, D.C.: Urban Institute.

Visher, Christy, Vera Kachnowski, Nancy La Vigne, and Jeremy Travis. 2004. *Baltimore Prisoners' Experiences Returning Home.* Washington, D.C.: Urban Institute.

Visher, Christy A., and Jeremy Travis. 2003. "Transitions from Prison to Community: Understanding Individual Pathways." *Annual Review of Sociology* 29: 89–113.

Vrabel, Jim. 2014. *A People's History of the New Boston.* Amherst: University of Massachusetts Press.

Wachs, Theodore D., and Gary W. Evans. 2010. "Chaos in Context." In *Chaos and Its Influence on Children's Development: An Ecological Perspective,* edited by Gary W. Evans and Theodore D. Wachs. Washington, D.C.: American Psychological Association.

Wacquant, Loïc. 2001. "Deadly Symbiosis: When Ghetto and Prison Meet and Mesh." *Punishment and Society* 3(1): 95–134.

———. 2007. *Urban Outcasts: A Comparative Sociology of Advanced Marginality.* London: Polity.

———. 2009a. *Prisons of Poverty.* Minneapolis: University of Minnesota Press.

———. 2009b. *Punishing the Poor: The Neoliberal Government of Social Insecurity.* Durham, N.C.: Duke University Press.

Wakefield, Sara, and Christopher Wildeman. 2013. *Children of the Prison Boom: Mass Incarceration and the Future of American Inequality.* New York: Oxford University Press.

Waldfogel, Joel. 1994. "The Effect of Criminal Conviction on Income and the 'Trust Reposed in Workmen.'" *Journal of Human Resources* 29(1): 62–81.

Wang, Emily A., Clemens S. Hong, Shira Shavit, Roland Sanders, Eric Kessell, and Margot B. Kushel. 2017. "Engaging Individuals Recently Released from Prison into Primary Care: A Randomized Trial." *American Journal of Public Health* 102(September): e22–e29.

Ward, David A., and Gene G. Kassebaum. 1965. *Women's Prison: Sex and Social Structure.* Chicago: Aldine.

Warner, Barbara D., and Pamela W. Rountree. 1997. "Local Social Ties in a Community and Crime Model: Questioning the Systemic Nature of Informal Social Control." *Social Problems* 44(4): 520–36.

Warr, Mark. 1998. "Life-Course Transitions and Desistance from Crime." *Criminology* 36(2): 183–216.

Warren, John Robert, and Andrew Halpern-Manners. 2012. "Panel Conditioning in Longitudinal Social Science Surveys." *Sociological Methods and Research* 41(4): 491–534.

Weaver, Vesla. 2007. "Frontlash: Civil Rights, the Carceral State, and the Transformation of American Politics." PhD diss., Harvard University, Cambridge, Mass.

Western, Bruce. 2006. *Punishment and Inequality in America.* New York: Russell Sage Foundation.

———. 2015. "Lifetimes of Violence in a Sample of Released Prisoners." *RSF: The Russell Sage Foundation Journal of the Social Sciences* 1(2): 14–30.

———. 2016. "The Rehabilitation Paradox." *The New Yorker,* May 9.

Western, Bruce, Anthony Braga, Jaclyn Davis, and Catherine Sirois. 2015. "Stress and Hardship After Prison." *American Journal of Sociology* 120(5): 1512–47.

Western, Bruce, Anthony Braga, David Hureau, and Catherine Sirois. 2016. "Study Retention as Bias Reduction in a Hard-to-Reach Population." *Proceedings of the National Academy of Sciences* 113(20): 5477–85.

Western, Bruce, Jeffrey R. Kling, and David F. Weiman. 2001. "The Labor Market Consequences of Incarceration." *Crime and Delinquency* 47(3): 410–27.

Western, Bruce, and Becky Pettit. 2010. "Incarceration and Social Inequality." *Daedalus* 139(Summer): 8–19.

Western, Bruce, and Catherine Sirois. 2017. "Racial Inequality in Employment and Earnings After Incarceration." Working paper. Cambridge, Mass.: Harvard University.

Western, Bruce, and Natalie Smith. 2018. "Formerly Incarcerated Parents and Their Children." *Demography* (forthcoming).

Western, Bruce, and Christopher Wildeman. 2009. "The Black Family and Mass Incarceration." *Annals of the American Academy of Social and Political Science* 621(1): 221–42.

Widom, Cathy Spatz. 1989. "The Cycle of Violence." *Science* 244(4901): 160–66.

Widom, Cathy Spatz, and Valentina Nikulina. 2012. "Long-Term Consequences of Child Neglect in Low-Income Families." In *Oxford Handbook of Poverty and Child Development,* edited by Rosalind King and Valerie Maholmes. New York: Oxford University Press.

Wildeman, Christopher, and Christopher Muller. 2012. "Mass Imprisonment and Inequality in Health and Family Life." *Annual Review of Law and Social Science* 8(December): 11–30.

Wilson, James Q. 1985. *Thinking About Crime.* Rev. ed. New York: Vintage Books. (Originally published in 1975.)

Wilson, William Julius. 1987. *The Truly Disadvantaged: The Inner City, the Underclass, and Public Policy.* Chicago: University of Chicago Press.

Wolf, Leslie E., Mayank J. Patel, Brett A. Williams Tarver, Jeffrey L. Austin, Lauren A. Dame, and Laura M. Beskow. 2015. "Certificates of Confidentiality: Protecting Human Subject Research Data in Law and Practice." *Journal of Law, Medicine, and Ethics* 43(3): 594–609.

Wyse, Jessica J. B., David J. Harding, and Jeffrey D. Morenoff. 2014. "Romantic Relationships and Criminal Desistance: Pathways and Processes." *Sociological Forum* 29(2): 365–85.

INDEX

....

Boldface page numbers indicate tables and figures.

research, social science: bias of, 12; on crime and violence, 3; data collection for, 2–3; ethical challenges of, 24–25; on mass incarceration, 1–3; on negative effects of incarceration, 5; prisoner characteristics for, 3; retention and contact insecurity, 11–12, **12**; theories used in, 2–3. *See also* Boston Reentry Study

Roca (antiviolence program), 184

Sampson, Robert, 65
Scheper-Hughes, Nancy, 66
schizophrenia, 48–49, 97
Schonberg, Jeff, 66
school. *See* education
Sentencing Project, 158–159
sexual abuse, 65, 80, 152
Sirois, Cathy, 13
Smarter Sentencing Act (2015), 179
social adversity mitigation, 180–181, 198n12
social controls, 66, 68, 75–77
social integration: employment and, 84; freedom and, 5–6, 26–27; obstacles to, 12; prison preparation for, 27; reentry programs for, 85, 92, 94, 184–185; reincarceration and failure of, 122
social justice, 183–186. *See also* criminal justice
solitary confinement, 27, 57, 77
stigma: of crime, 25, 82; of incarceration, 28, 158, 187, 197n18; of violence, 82
stress. *See* anxiety and stress; post-traumatic stress disorder
surveys, 4–5, 11, 189–190n1. *See also* Boston Reentry Study

Titicut Follies (documentary), 47
Tonry, Michael, 180–181
Transitions Clinic, 184

unemployment: of Boston Reentry Study participants, 5, 83–84; crime and, 65; family support and, 7–8; housing instability and, 98; mass incarceration and, 1–2; poverty and, 97–98; race and racism, 65, 92, 98–99, 163, 167, 170; violent crime and, 65. *See also* welfare
union membership, 84, 87–88, 98, 168
United States, incarceration rate in, 1, 3, 139

veterans, 27, 50, 52–53
Veterans Affairs, 27, 50
violence, 7, 63–82; Boston Reentry Study participants and, 67–69, 72–73, 77, 79–82, 193–194n19; chaos and, 64–65, 69–75; criminal justice and, 177–178, 182–183; culture and, 64–66, 78–79; define, 68; domestic violence, 68–69, 72; drug use and, 52, 66, 73, 165; families and, 66–69, 72, 193–194n19; gender and, 139, 152; guns and, 165, 180; during incarceration, 64, 76–77, 80, 177; mass incarceration and, 64, 178; mental health and, 49; positive value of, 66, 78–79, 193n16; poverty and, 7, 63–67, 80–81; punishment for, 63–64, 81–82; racial, 64, 160–162; research on, 3; social controls and, 66, 68, 75–77; solutions for, 183; stigma of, 82; unemployment and, 65; witnessing, psychological harm of, 80–81

war on drugs, 157, 196n1
welfare: for disabilities, 95; drug use and addiction, 5; for former prisoners, 7; as main source of income, 40, 42, 96–99; management of, 96; prison as alternative to, 61; race and, 169; as source of research information, 2
Wilson, James Q., 179
Wilson, William Julius, 65
women. *See* gender
work-release programs, 88, 90, 99